KU-064-515

Good English

'Clear, lively guide to the principles of current usage, refreshingly different from most books of its kind in not merely admitting but insisting on the fact that language is, and should be, a living, changing thing' PUNCH

'This very good book . . .' *Eric Partridge* SPECTATOR

'Packed with shrewd comment' SUNDAY TIMES

'An important book . . . The exercises alone should commend it to the whole teaching profession' SCHOOLMASTER

R. Mackenzie

Lyplan p. 128

Also by G. H. Vallins in Pan

Better English
The Best English

G. H. VALLINS

Good English

Pan Books London and Sydney

First published 1951 by Pan Books Ltd,
Cavaye Place, London SW10 9PG
17th printing 1976
Copyright George Henry Vallins 1951
ISBN 0 330 13038 2
Printed and bound in Great Britain by
Cox & Wyman Ltd, London, Reading and Fakenham

This book is sold subject to the condition that it
shall not, by way of trade or otherwise, be lent, re-sold,
hired out or otherwise circulated without the publisher's prior
consent in any form of binding or cover other than that in which
it is published and without a similar condition including this
condition being imposed on the subsequent purchaser

Contents

Note to this Edition

I acknowledge with gratitude the kindness of the late Wilson Midgley, when he was Editor of *John o' London's Weekly*, in reading the manuscript with a critical but friendly eye. The encouragement and expert help of Mr George Kamm have been invaluable at every stage in the production of the book.

In this edition a few misprints which have persisted from the original edition have been corrected. I am sincerely grateful to all those who have written to me on this point and that. Their kindly interest has encouraged and their erudition has challenged me.
G. H. V.

As to knowledge connected with books, there is a step to be taken before you can fairly enter upon any path. In the immense field of this kind of knowledge, innumerable are the paths, and GRAMMAR is the gate of entrance to them all.
—WILLIAM COBBETT: *A Grammar of the English Language*

PRELUDE

The antic haverings of a pedantic pedestrianism in quest of
Pure English are rapidly producing a new form of Addison's
Disease—for Addison was the first to complain that 'the
late war had adulterated our tongue with strange words'.
—C. K. OGDEN: *Basic English*.

The Scope and Aims of this Book

Any book that professes to set down rules for 'good
English' or 'plain English' or 'direct English' is based on a
fallacy. This book is no exception. There are good
reasons for this, some of which have been hinted at or
touched upon in the following pages. One lies in the
fundamental fact that the language is living and constantly
changing, so that any formalised record of its accidence and
syntax[1] is bound to be, in some measure, out of date.
For example, Cobbett's famous *Grammar* (about 1820),
which is several times quoted in these pages, is out of date;
so is Fowler's *Modern English Usage*, published in 1926; so is
Sir Alan Herbert's *What a Word!*, published in 1935; and
so, already, is this very book, since there is a time-lag
between its writing and its publication, in which the
language has in certain ways, however small and trivial,
developed and changed. For the same reason, every
Dictionary is out of date as soon as it is published. Language always outpaces its grammarians and lexicographers.

Another lies in the fact that there is no such thing as
'standard English'—an English controlled, that is, by a
central Academy, as French is controlled by L'Académie

---

[1] These two words are used from time to time throughout the
book. *Accidence* simply means the classification of the 'accidents'
that befall individual words—that is, *inflexions*, or changes (usually
in the endings) which indicate different functions. *Syntax* is the
set of rules governing the order and arrangement of words in the
sentence. The word itself is derived from a Greek root meaning
'order'.

française. There is, it is true, an 'accepted' standard—of pronunciation, of syntax, of punctuation, of sentence construction. But that 'accepted' standard is not fixed. Certain variations are allowed even by those who pride themselves upon their standard English. We know that this is true of pronunciation, quite apart from marked differences of dialect. But it is true also, though to a less degree, of matters of syntax and certainly of punctuation. Some people are, as we say, sticklers for grammar; others pride themselves upon a loose colloquial style which throws 'grammar' (in the strict sense) to the winds.

It is a proof of this variation in 'accepted' standards, as well as of the keen interest in problems and points of language to-day, that newspapers and literary magazines are full of letters on questions of usage: Is *none* singular or plural? Is *whom* a dying inflected form? Do we write "try *and*" or "try *to*"? Is it wrong to split an infinitive? These, and many other questions old and new, tease apparently the members of many an office staff and even the company at some family breakfast tables. And it is good that it should be so—a sign that ordinary men and women, not directly or professionally interested in language, should recognise, even unconsciously, that it is a living and changing thing.

It is a queer irony, by the way, that the most nearly standardised element in English is its spelling, for, as is pointed out later in the book (page 228), the standardisation of spelling on an etymological basis in the eighteenth century was singularly unfortunate, and is the cause of many of our present discontents. There is a sense, too, in which idiom—that is, the idiom of the fixed phrase, not of actual (*e.g.*, prepositional) usage—is highly standardised. For an idiomatic phrase, like "to upset the apple cart" or "once in a blue moon", is a natural growth of language. Idioms may drop out of language, and new idioms may, and do continually, come in: but those that are part of *current* usage cannot be tampered with. Thus when a leader-writer in *The Times* uses the expression "Their white adversaries are another glass of tea", he is not writing English. In the eighteenth century they spoke of a *dish* of tea; in modern English we speak of a *cup* of tea, for the simple reason that we drink tea out of a cup and not out of a dish. The colloquial idiom (meaning 'something is quite different from something else') is "That is another cup of tea". To substitute *glass* for *cup* is not only to be foolishly affected but also to offend against modern usage. Such idioms are more sacrosanct than syntax. Indeed, one of the reasons why we have syntactical doubts and questions is that idiom influences and sometimes defies pure 'grammar'.

A third reason for this fundamental fallacy has been touched upon in the chapter on jargon. The 'standard' language, or current usage, has within it or, as it were, around it, all kinds of specialised languages which have their own constructions, modes of expression, syntax, idiom. Legal language (see page 148) is perhaps the best example. They, like the main standardised language, have their natural changes, though these changes are usually very slow, and sometimes (as in legal language) scarcely exist at all. True, they sometimes have a bad influence on current usage, by introducing into it verbosities or technicalities. But they themselves exist in their own right. In an official letter, official English, even what is contemptuously called 'officialese', is not out of place, any more than the highly technical language of physical science is out of place in a scientific treatise. But it is out of place, say, in a private letter or a light essay.

"We are no longer," said a writer in *The Times*,

> to be assured of best attention at all times; the favour of our esteemed command will no more be awaited. A curt, utility *you* is to replace the flattering, respectful warmth with which we have grown accustomed to being greeted as 'your good selves'. Tiny faces, that have looked up at us so often from the typed page that they are old friends, now peer appealingly from a tumbril. The guillotine awaits *re* and 'per pro' and the three busy

little brothers, *ult. inst.* and *prox.* Larger—too large—
victims share this sentence of death. *Acquaint* and *com-
mence, dispatch* and *peruse, proceed* and *purchase* are
doomed. Their places will be taken by less-longwinded
citizens of the dictionary, by *tell* and *begin, send* and *read,
go* and *buy.* The gaff has been blown on business English.

He writes with justifiable regret, followed by an equally
justifiable scepticism in his next paragraph, which begins:
"Or—to join the blowers in their pursuit of the colloquial—
has it?" The answer, in the main, is No. Changes are
not made by decree in the various 'jargons' any more than
they are in the 'standard' language. There is no real reason
(except possibly an economic one) why they should be.
Changes made or advocated deliberately, as by Sir Ernest
Gowers in *Plain Words* or Professor B. Ifor Evans in *The
Use of English,* are apt to give rise to a language or 'jargon'
as artificial in its bluntness and simplicity as the original is
supposed to be in its wordiness and circumlocution.
They produce, if they produce anything at all, a 'phoney'
usage, rather like that by which certain advanced Christian
communities address the Almighty as 'You' instead of
'Thou'; and they are peculiarly apt to ignore the basic
principle of language, that, just as no two words are truly
synonyms, so no two different expressions, or ways of
expression, can mean *exactly* the same thing.

It is true to say, however, that when we treat of 'good',
as distinct from 'plain' or 'direct' English, we are on
firmer ground. Since we are still limited by the change-
ableness of language, we have to admit that our pro-
nouncements are valid for only a brief time; and we are
still, though not equally, prone to what may be called the
'fallacy of synonymity'. But the fact remains that for
'standard' speech and 'standard' writing (between which,
of course, there are points of difference) certain syntactical
principles, idioms and conventions are for a reasonable
period reasonably firm. We have therefore to express our
meaning within a linguistic framework that has been
fashioned by custom in the past and has a certain 'shape' in

the present—a shape which, in more literal terms, we define as 'modern usage'. We write or speak good English when, obeying the conventions or principles of modern usage, and paying due respect to the context, we express *exactly* what we mean.

This book, which has the challenging title *Good English*, emphasises this correspondence (or lack of correspondence) between meaning and its expression in language. It outlines the chief basic principles—the pattern of the sentence, and the important agreements and relationships; it deals with the two main conventions of the written language—the form of words (spelling) and punctuation; and it has something to say on the use of imagery and idiom. In some respects it is, in fact, a utility reference book. The unpractised writer who sucks his pen hopefully over the still virgin paper will, it is hoped, find something of value in its pages.

But it goes further. It tries to make the reader sensitive to good English by giving examples of bad English—bad, that is, in the sense that, for one reason or another, it does not *exactly* express the meaning intended. The gross faults are illustrated here, and so are the subtle ones. Most of the sentences or passages given are quoted—they are not made up for the occasion. Cobbett, a hundred and fifty years ago, went so far as to analyse, with a great deal of forthright criticism, the King's speech to Parliament. Something of the same kind of analysis has been attempted here. The object of it, however, is nothing so august as the King's speech; it consists of extracts from (in the main) some half-dozen famous newspapers and periodicals[1], representing, that is, the lapses in English of the educated and practised writer.

It would be pleasant to record that the sentences so criticised were discovered only after years of patient search and endeavour. But that is not so. Half an hour or so

[1] *The Times, The Observer, The Times Educational Supplement, The Times Literary Supplement, The New Statesman and Nation, Time and Tide, John o' London's Weekly.*

with any one of the papers or periodicals concerned usually (but not always) yielded an abundant harvest of examples. This is not a sweeping criticism of the writers of the sentences subjected to analysis; since most of them are journalists of standing and repute, it is rather a reminder of the almost incredible difficulty of writing good English consistently—without the sudden slip, when you feel safest, into a false construction, a doubtful idiom or a mixed metaphor. Andrew Lang said after reading Fowlers' *The King's English*, the predecessor of *Modern English Usage*, that he was "afraid to put pen to paper". As long as such a fear is not downright paralysing, it is a salutary one. Besides, to the humble and unpractised writer such slips of the great as are illustrated here should bring, a little paradoxically, a feeling of comfort.

But we must come back to our old fallacy. Since there is no such thing as standard English, there can be no deviation from it. We are dealing with usage; and since the very term usage implies 'custom' and 'habit', those very constructions in language which in one generation, or even by one class of people, are considered to be wrong, may by the next generation, or another class of people, be judged to be right. What seems to be a kind of 'looseness' in the sentences quoted and criticised here may, after all, be merely a foretaste of common usage in the years to come.

At certain places in the book, the reader is invited to try his hand. A number of sentences, some from the work of ordinary unpractised writers and some from the journals already mentioned, are (or is) presented for judgment. The 'answers' or comments, with which the critic may like to compare his own findings, are given later (pp. 244–252). After that valuable practice, he may care to turn his attention to the text of this book. I hope his search for errors will be a long and difficult one; but I fear it will not be altogether vain.

CHAPTER I

POINTS OF ORDER: AGREEMENT AND RELATIONSHIP

"A sentence is but a cheveril glove to a good wit: how quickly the wrong side may be turned outward!"

SHAKESPEARE: *Twelfth Night.*

The Bare Bones

If we always spoke or wrote in the simplest way, without gestures and dumb-show in speech, or pictures and diagrams in writing, we should use sentences—that is, groups of words—which fell into two parts, a word or words representing what we are talking about, and a word or words representing what we say about it. These are the parts which we know in formal grammar as Subject and Predicate. The names are, in fact, appropriate. Subject explains itself; and Predicate is derived from the Latin word *predico*, which means 'preach'. So the subject is the text and the predicate is the sermon. That is the pattern of the simplest kind of sentence; indeed, it is the fundamental pattern of every sentence, however complicated and however long.

It is obvious that the subject must be represented, in some way or other, by a name. In the simplest form of sentence it will be a single word—a noun or, for convenience, a substitute word called a pronoun (Latin *pro*, 'for', 'instead of'+*noun*). Similarly, the key-word in the Predicate tells us what the subject does or is. In grammar it is called the verb, from the Latin *verbum*, which means 'the word'—an indication, by the way, of the importance of the verb in the sentence. We call it the key-word of the predicate because, even in the simplest form of the predicate, it may not be the only word. This is another way of saying that verbs themselves do not always completely represent what we want to say about the subject; that is, they do not complete the predicate—or, to put it another way, they preach only half the sermon. Thus it is plain that a verb which expresses '*is*-ness' is not normally in itself a complete predicate; it requires a 'completer' or, as we actually term it, a complement. Unless *is* means 'exists', the sentence "Peter is" is incomplete. We require another word, like [*a*] *boy* or *cold*, to give us the complete predicate.

There are many verbs which require another kind of completion. They represent an action that passes across to something, and the predicate is not complete unless we have both the verb and the name of the something which is struck, as it were, by its action. This name is called the object; and, like the subject, in its simplest form it must be a noun or pronoun. Such verbs, because their action 'goes across', are called 'transitive' (Latin *trans*, 'across'+*itum*, from the verb *eo*, 'go').

There, then, are the bare bones of a sentence. All kinds of things may happen when we clothe the bones with flesh, but all expression, whether in speech or writing, is built upon that skeleton framework. Of course, in practice we do not speak in a series of disconnected sentences of the simplest type, using only nouns and verbs. But on this simple subject-predicate relationship is based all the syntax of the language.

To begin with, here is the only real grammatical agreement we have in English. The verb of the predicate is 'bound up with' or 'limited to' the subject. *Finite* is the term applied to it in grammar books; and *finite* simply means 'limited'. The verb is associated with the subject by grammatical relationship very much as the moon is associated with the earth by gravitational pull. If the subject is one (singular) the verb has its singular form; if the subject is more than one (plural), the verb has its plural form; if the subject is a pronoun representing the person speaking (*I*), the verb has the special form which is appropriate to subjects of that type. In other words the verb cannot escape from the gravitational pull of the subject.

To quote the sober words of the grammar book, "The verb agrees with the subject in number and person".

The Collective Problem

This agreement is quite obvious as long as we are able to determine exactly the nature of the subject—whether, that is, it is singular or plural, first person or third. We are not likely to make the mistake of writing "Dogs *barks*", "Peter *play*", "He *are*" or "I *is*"; for in these sentences there is no doubt at all of the number and person of the subject. But sometimes there is a doubt. The subject may be, for example, a collective noun, like *congregation*, *flock, council*, which represents a collection of persons or things, and hovers between singular and plural. In English usage the decision is left to the writer; only, once having made it, he must stick to it. Those who draft the Bye-laws and Regulations of Railway Companies are often caught in two minds, like this: "with respect to which the Company *has* power to act" (singular) and, on the same page, "The Company *are* not, however, to be deemed . . ." (plural). It is interesting to note that in the Education Act, 1944, *Parliament* and *council* are treated as singular nouns, and *local education authority* as a plural:

> No account shall be taken of any time during which Parliament *is* dissolved.

> If the council of any borough or urban district *has*, before the first day of October nineteen hundred and forty-four, lodged with the Minister a claim . . .

> If the local education authority *inform* the Minister that *they* are aggrieved by an order . . .

The following sentence from a National Coal Board statement illustrates the same arbitrary and indiscriminate usage:

> The Colliery Winders' Federation of Great Britain, to which the Yorkshire Enginemen's Association *is* affiliated, *have* decided against a stoppage.

15

There is no apparent reason why *Federation* should be plural and *Association* singular. But the Government, like all the citizens it governs, is entitled to its fancy.

There may be, however, some kind of reason in our choice. On the whole, if we visualise as individuals the persons or things represented by the collective, we tend to make it plural: "The congregation *are* coming out of church", rather than "*is* coming". But if the collective represents something too vast or too abstract to be resolved into its component parts we use the singular. In most recreation grounds the public *is* (not *are*) requested to keep off the grass. But there is no rule. Usage changes: sometimes the singular is in fashion and sometimes the plural. It is consistent respect for the decision that matters.

There are one or two pronouns that have this collective quality, with its resulting difficulties—for example, *all* and *none*. *All* may be a kind of omnibus word, a synonym for *everything*, and then it is singular: "All is not lost", "All is well"; or it may be, especially when it is personal, a clear and definite plural pronoun: "All are gone, the old familiar faces". *None* is an abbreviated form of 'not one' or 'no-one', and would therefore seem to be singular; but in its context it usually has a plural sense: "At the time of the collision several people were in the tram-car, but none *were* injured". Only the literary purist would write *was*, and he would probably be influenced by Dryden's famous line "None but the brave *deserves* the fair". But in a mistaken devotion to 'grammar' he would be sinning against usage. Nevertheless in English a writer troubled by a finicky conscience is allowed to write "None *is*". Where, however, the *one* element is plain and visible, as in *not one*, *no-one*, *anyone*, *everyone*, the pronoun is unmistakably singular.[1]

[1] Note that there is a difference in English between *anyone*, *everyone* as indefinite pronouns and *any one*, *every one* [of us], where *one* is a numerical pronoun qualified by *any*, *every*: "Every one of them is guilty", "Any one of us may be in the same awkward position".

The Partitive Puzzle

Akin to the collective problem is the partitive puzzle, which arises when a noun or pronoun, as subject, represents one, or a part, of many. The complete subject is made up according to the formula, singular noun or pronoun+*of*+plural noun or pronoun: "a basket of apples", "each of us", "none of the soldiers", "a number of people". Usage varies according to the nature of the noun or pronoun before the *of*. If it is unmistakably singular, like *basket*, the verb will be singular; if, like *none* and *number*, it has a collective sense, the verb may be plural. In the following sentence the purist is at work:

> Shall we ever get it? Only when a sufficient number of people recognises that true progress consists in going steadily and warily forward.

Most people would write *recognise*.

With this partitive subject there is always the danger that the verb will be 'attracted' into the number and person of the noun or pronoun following the *of*, even if the singularity of the true subject is obvious. In a moment of carelessness, for example, we may say—though we should probably not write—"A basket of apples *were* standing on the table". There is a greater temptation to error in "each of us", where *us* (first person plural) tends to attract to itself the appurtenances of *each* (third singular): "Each of us *have* finished *our* work" (for *has* and *his*[1]). This force of attraction, which is always strong in usage, has been active in the following sentence:

> The long catalogue of errors and retreats which have marked our foreign policy *are* enumerated by Mr. Voigt in astringent detail.

Here *catalogue* is subject, and recognisably singular; but "errors and retreats" have attracted the verb into the

---

[1] A sex question, which is discussed frankly on page 77.

plural. Worse still, this attraction has led to a confusion of thought on the reviewer's part. It is the errors and retreats that are enumerated, not the catalogue.

True and False Equations

A difficulty sometimes arises in sentences of the pattern: Subject + verb *to be* + Complement. Since in these we have something rather like an equation in mathematics, it is reasonable to expect that both the 'terms', subject and complement, will be of the same number. But that is not always possible; and then there arises the question of the number of the verb. Here is a simple type of example:

> His mischievous presentments of our sovereigns *are* the measure of his affection.

There is no real doubt; there is only a slight dissatisfaction with a verb that, being itself so obviously plural, acts as an equating sign for plural and singular. By way of contrast, here are two sentences in which the writer has, with less reason, made the verb agree with the complement:

> So a few disconnected questions *was* the most that was forthcoming, and all the work fell on the tutor.

> The social contributions made by many of these schools, especially in recently developed towns and suburbs, *is* a major social phenomenon.

The following sentence is of particular interest since it is to be found in the Preface of the *Concise Oxford Dictionary*:

> A third and a fourth peculiarity are the direct results of the preceding ones.

Here we have a double subject, "third peculiarity and fourth peculiarity" $(ax + bx)$ disguised by bracketing (see page 62) as a singular subject, "a third and a fourth peculiarity"— that is, $(a+b)\ x$. The construction, however, is awkward, even though its perpetrator was none other than Fowler himself. See also page 23.

In the following sentences, where the subject is not a single noun or pronoun but a whole clause, the complement more justifiably wins the battle for the verb:

> What this volume contains besides articles on countries [Noun clause: subject (singular)] *are* explanations of such matters as astronomy, climate, earthquakes, light, minerals, pressure, space and wave-motion.

> What I should most miss in wireless *are* documentaries, talks, and similar forms of analysis and portrayal.

But, on the whole, it is wise to take Cobbett's stern and dogmatic advice, "Avoid, then, the use of the verb *to be* in all such cases". Only when the subject and the complement are of the same number is the construction really safe. When they are not, the writer's decision—which will depend more on his 'ear' than on his sense of grammar—is, like the umpire's and the editor's, final. It is usually better, as Cobbett advises, to change the construction: "Besides articles on countries, this volume contains explanations . . ."; or, by equating subject and complement for number, keep the verb *to be*: "Documentaries, talks, and similar forms of analysis and portrayal are the programmes . . .".

The subject-complement equation raises the question of nouns that have a singular meaning with a plural form—*wages, riches, news, alms, whereabouts* and the like. *Wages* (except in the familiar Biblical sentence "The wages of sin is death"), *alms* and *riches* are plural in modern English usage. *News* is singular, and so is *whereabouts*. We never say "What *are* the news?"; and on the newspaper sentence "Its exact whereabouts *are* a secret" Wilfrid Whitten ("John o' London") has the apt comment "If *whereabouts* is here plural, how can the locality be described as 'exact'?"

Trousers, scissors, shears, and some other nouns representing inseparables are undoubtedly plural; but preceded by "a pair of" they may attain a unity that demands a singular verb. *Physics, classics* and (not quite so certainly) *mathematics* are usually singular, perhaps because each represents a single subject of the educational curriculum. *Series* is singular or plural according to the context. We may speak of "two series" or "a series":

> A series of 200 questions requiring only short answers *adds* to the value of the book for the reader who is in earnest.

Weights and measures behave peculiarly as subject. We usually think of them, as it were, in bulk, and tend to make them singular: "Ten miles *is* a long way to walk", "Three tons of coal *is* enough to fill the cellar", "Twenty pounds *is* a considerable sum". In fact, the plural form is often dropped, especially in country speech: "ten mile", "three ton", "two foot", "ten pound". *Pence,* which is a bulk or collective singular, has a distinguishing plural form, *pennies.* At school, when we dared, we wobbled between "Twice eight *are* sixteen" and "Twice eight *is* sixteen"; and usage keeps us wobbling still. Perhaps, too, in these and other sentences like them, the pull of the complement is strong on the verb.

The title of a book even may set a puzzle in agreement. We should probably say, and almost certainly write, "Lamb's *Tales from Shakespear*[1] is an enjoyable book", but when the influence of the singular complement is taken away, a doubt creeps in: "Lamb's *Tales from Shakespear* is?/are? enjoyable". Probably we now forget the title, and consider the tales separately; so the italics[2] should go, and *are* should remain in undisputed possession: "Lamb's Tales from Shakespeare are enjoyable". If we keep the italics—that is, the title—the verb should be *is.* The writer of the following sentence forgot this subtle distinction:

> But *Rejected Addresses are* as good-natured as the transformation of Cowper in "You are old, Father William".

Perhaps, however, a reviewer who appears to confuse

[1] So spelt by Lamb.　　　[2] See page 124.

Cowper and Southey[1] could scarcely be expected to observe the refinements of the English tongue. Sometimes a quotation will lure the writer into error:

> "The homes of the silent vanquished races" *appear*, too, in the late Sir Algernon Methuen's *An Anthology of Modern Verse*.

The quotation, boxed up inside the quotation marks, is a simple unit, that is, it is grammatically singular; and since it is the subject of the sentence the verb should agree with it (*appears*). Here, of course, the writer was led astray by the plural noun *homes* inside the quotation, which (like the flowers that bloom in the spring) has nothing to do with the case.

Plus Signs

Sometimes the subject consists of more than one unit— that is, two (or more) separate nouns, pronouns, phrases, clauses. In mathematical terminology, it may be represented like this, $(a+b+c\text{---})$. Such a subject is normally plural, even if each of its units is singular:

> The Walrus and the Carpenter
> *Were* walking close at hand.

Bishop, and abbot, and prior *were* there.

You and I and honest Casca, we *have* the falling sickness.

The verb does not inflect for person in the plural; so the problem of agreement in person does not arise. But the last sentence reminds us that where we have a multiple subject of all three persons, the subject is regarded (and in this particular sentence expressed) as first person (*we*). If the subject were made up of second and third person, it would be regarded as second, "You and he, *you* . . ."

But language is a strange and subtle thing. Just as collective nouns and pronouns sometimes have a singular

---

[1] Southey, of course, wrote the original Father William poem, which Lewis Carroll parodied.

sense, so do double and multiple subjects. We wrap up the separate items in a single parcel, and think of them as one, not two (or more). If we say "Pen and ink are necessary commodities", we consider the two parts separately, and the verb is plural. The plural complement, by the way, has also had a say in the matter (see page 19). But we may write "Paper and ink is provided", where we have a 'parcel' subject. So "Bread and water *are* two necessities of life"; but, at our discretion, "Bread and water *makes* an unappetising meal". Even eggs and bacon, though one item is actually plural, may resolve themselves into a singular; and Tom, Dick and Harry are magically made one when we qualify them all with *every*: "Every Tom, Dick and Harry *plays* golf nowadays".

These, however, are examples of pairings and groupings that have become fixed and conventionalised in the language. They are often treated as singulars because the various items paired or grouped together are so familiarly associated in our thought that they become, as it were, one. But any double or multiple subject made up of singular (especially abstract) nouns may find itself coupled with a singular verb. Kipling's line in *Recessional* is an example: "The tumult and the shouting *dies*". Probably, once again, attraction is at the bottom of it: the two singulars cry out for a singular verb. Moreover, Kipling required a rhyme for *sacrifice* two lines on. A few other assorted examples are given for the sake of interest:

> The quality of that work, indeed, and its very quantity, *prompts* the reflection that perhaps mis-managed lives and repressed egos are nothing to do with the case.

> For in Middlesex education, and in particular the organization of secondary schools, *has been* and still *is* a party issue.

In both these sentences the second part of the subject is almost parenthetic, and that, perhaps, helps to explain the singular verbs. The punctuation of the second sentence is bad. There should be a comma after *Middlesex*.

> Much idealism and humanitarian sentiment *is* bestowed on little children.

> Frankness and candour between teachers and parents *is* vital before difficulties begin to occur.

In the first sentence *much* holds *idealism* and *sentiment* together; in the second *frankness* and *candour* are so nearly synonymous as to resolve themselves into one noun.

> The wakening minds and the creative impulse in children, both made difficult by this particular school's hard industrial environment, *was* the aim pursued through many activities of bodies, hands and minds.

The subject-complement equation again. No doubt the singular complement has influenced the verb. But the subject, emphasised by the following *both*, seems to call for the plural, *were*. It is interesting to see the opposite effect in the following sentence:

> The squalor and brutality of Denise's home, the harsh tyranny of the factory, and all the vileness of poverty *are* M. Van Der Meersch's hell-brew.

Here the writer might well have taken Cobbett's advice (see page 19). Why not *make up* instead of *are*, the complement (*hell-brew*) becoming object?

A certain carelessness about number is apt to arise when the sentence is introduced by the adverb *there*, the subject itself following the verb. The tendency is to make the verb singular, whatever the number of the subject, probably in the subconscious but erroneous belief that *there* is subject. Here are two examples, where the subjects are double and multiple respectively. The first sentence will pass muster; the second is scarcely forgivable, even if we make all allowance for attraction:

> Then there *was* a big E.M.G. gramophone and a great library of records.

> There *is* school broadcasting, the arts and sciences in general education, geography, geography teaching and the whole technical problem of international understanding through education.

This adverbial construction (*there*+verb+subject) is to be distinguished from the construction in which an impersonal *it* acts as a 'dummy' subject, the real subject following the verb. Here the verb is always singular, agreeing with *it*, whether the real subject is singular or plural:

> It *is* these who make the teachers of quality whom Mr. Rowse desires.

And Doubtful Signs

Sometimes the parts of the subject are not fully joined. In the sentence "Either the captain or the wicketkeeper is out", there is a conjunction *or*; but we actually associate the two nouns with the predicate in turn, one at a time. It is clear, therefore, in this construction (where the subject is not double, but alternative) that the number and person of the verb must be common to both parts of the subject; or, to put it the other way round, the two parts of the subject must be of the same number and person. If we write "Either he or I *am* wrong", the verb agrees with one part of the subject but not with the other. So it does if we write "Neither the dogs nor the canary *was* seriously affected by the gas". However, English is an obliging language. Very often is happens that, owing to losses of inflexion, the verb form is actually common. We can, for example, write "Either he or I *was* wrong" and "Neither the dogs nor the canary *felt* . . .". But where there is a clash between the verb and one part of the subject the construction is better avoided.

Some speakers and writers admit another possibility—to assume that, even here, one and one do make two, and to use a plural verb in agreement: "Neither the dogs nor the canary were affected . . .", "Either he or I are wrong". The writer of the following sentence evidently believed in this easy and quite effective solution:

> But neither this simplification of types, nor the formalised conversations that occur throughout the novel, *are* in themselves necessarily unsuitable to its quick-moving story.

But he has made the usage more doubtful by inserting the totally unnecessary commas, and more difficult by using the phrase "in themselves". It would have been quite easy, and certainly safer, to write "This simplification and the formalised conversations are not in themselves necessarily unsuitable . . ."

In the following two sentences from *Their Finest Hour* Mr. Churchill characteristically overrides mere academic correctness:

> Neither I nor the Chiefs of Staff *were* aware that the decisive code-word "Cromwell" had been used.

> I must confess that at the time neither I nor any of my colleagues *were* aware of the peril of this particular incident.

But lesser writers are not always justified in following the example of the great in such matters as this. When Bertie Wooster, having bought some soft-fronted shirts for evening wear, protested to Jeeves that the Prince of Wales had been seen wearing such shirts a short time before, Jeeves justly remarked that His Royal Highness was allowed certain liberties that were not permitted to ordinary men. Which things are, for speakers and writers, an allegory.

A problem of agreement arises in sentences of this type:

> Moreover, the exaggeratedly fanciful style, with its Latin tags and its feeble pastiche of *Tristram Shandy*, acts as a severe deterrent to any modern reader.

Here the subject (*style*) is distinctly separated from rather than joined to the qualities associated with it (*tags, pastiche*), and the verb is rightly singular to agree with it. The separation is effected by the use of the preposition (not conjunction) *with*, and the marking of the phrase with commas. In modern usage the agreement is made as illustrated here; that is, *with* is looked upon as a separator, not a joiner. There is, in fact, a distinct but subtle difference in meaning between "The King, with the Queen and the Princess, *has been* at Lords to-day" and "The King and the Queen and the Princess *have been* at Lords to-day". The first sentence emphasises the King's presence, and only casually mentions the Queen and the Princess; the second sentence gives equal importance to them all. In neither function nor meaning are *and* and *with* synonymous.

The following sentence also provides a pretty puzzle:

> Well-being or misery, perhaps also peace or war, *lie*, I believe, somewhere between the poles of Food and Peoples.

The writer has done one, or both, of two things—(i) taken *or* as a full joining word, and therefore considered the subject "well-being or misery" plural, (ii) thought of *also* as a conjunction, which it is not and never is, and so 'joined' the second alternative subject ("peace or war") to the first. He is wrong either way. The verb should be singular, and the sentence should be punctuated like this, with the *also* phrase as a parenthesis:

> Well-being or misery—perhaps also peace or war—lies, I believe, somewhere between the poles of Food and Peoples.

Even then, though outward usage is satisfied, the sentence seems lacking in sense—a sorry example of careless writing which bears no real relation to the thought intended to be expressed.

The use of *as well as* requires care. It is a compound conjunction, and therefore (speaking mathematically) a plus sign. But it has a kind of parenthetic effect, like *with*; so it is not necessarily the sign of a double or multiple subject. The following sentence is typical:

> A great deal of very human hate, as well as a small quantity of genuine devotion, *finds* its way into this picture.

Here the "as well as" phrase is in parenthesis (represented

by the commas), and the first half of the subject, which is singular, determines the number of the verb. If a writer wishes to stress the plurality of his subject he will omit the commas and, of course, bring the verb into agreement.

It is important to recognise the repeated subject that is set against ('in apposition to') but not joined to the real subject, and to remember that it does not affect the agreement of real subject and verb.

In the following examples the subject in apposition is in small capitals:

> The last three batsmen, THE TAIL OF A REASONABLE BATTING SIDE, *were* out for ten runs.
> (Plural subject, singular subject in apposition).

> I, ONE SNUG THE JOINER, *am*
> A lion fell.
> (Subject in first person, subject in apposition in third person).

These are the main errors, problems and difficulties that arise in the agreement of subject and verb in the simple pattern of the sentence. Others arise in more complicated sentences, and are dealt with elsewhere in the book. These do not differ in essence from those already illustrated; for they are all equally due to a doubt in the mind of the writer as to the number and person of the subject.

'Shall' and 'Will'

When once its number and person are determined, there is little difficulty with the verb. We do not, in general, have to think consciously of its tenses—past, present, future—of which we have several various forms in English. The use of these is natural to our expression in both speech and writing. Only one tense gives any real trouble. That is the future, which, like most other tenses, is made up of an auxiliary (or 'helping') verb plus a part of the actual verb; but differs from the others in demanding two separate auxiliaries (*shall* and *will*) for different persons, like this:

"I, we *shall* go"; "He, you, they *will* go". To put it more simply, *shall* is the auxiliary for the first person and *will* for the other persons.

That is, indeed, a safe rule as long as we are thinking of an action that is merely future in time. But when Caesar says, on the Ides of March, "Give me my robe, for I will go", he is using a form that expresses more than future. "The cause," he says, "is in my will." And whenever the meaning intended has something in it, not merely of time to come, but of will and purpose, the auxiliary is *will* throughout. Our concern, therefore, is with the first person only, since in the other persons *will* is used both for the simple future and for what we may call the 'determinative' sense. But we have still to decide exactly at what point simple futurity becomes purpose or desire. That decision, and the choice of the appropriate auxiliary, can only be made by the writer himself, according to the meaning he intends.

Here are one or two examples:

We *shall* start on the sixteenth of April.   [Simple future]

I *shall* not be able to play on Saturday.   [Simple future]

We *will* look into the matter.   [Purpose]

I *will* come with you to the match.   [Purpose]

But the choice is not quite so clear-cut as that. Thus, in the last two sentences, we may use the auxiliary *shall* if we change the form and nature of the tense, like this:

We shall be looking into the matter.

I shall be coming with you to the match.

Simple futurity has outdone purpose; but the resultant meaning is, as near as may be, the same. Sometimes, indeed, *shall* deserts the first person to become the 'determinative' auxiliary for the third:

I *will* not cease from mental fight,
Nor *shall* my sword sleep in my hand . . .

Here, perhaps, we have a hint of the usage familiar in the commandments, "Thou *shalt* not . . .", and still current but rare in English, where *shall* is a synonym for the later and more familiar *must*. To sum up, the rule, as stated, is a useful one; but a speaker or writer sensitive to the niceties of usage will realise that the question of *shall* and *will* is a little beyond the law. In more complex sentences, and especially with the past forms of the two auxiliaries, *should* and *would*, the problem also is more complex. But here, more than ever, any expressed rule can be no more than a guide. Beyond that, the choice depends upon the writer's sense of language and upon what can best be called intuition. This bigger problem, since it involves considerations outside the realm of the simple sentence, is dealt with later (page 69).

Some Confusing Verbs

In certain verbs, chiefly those which retain original Saxon inflexions, the forms of the past tense and the past participle are liable to be confused, or there are other points of interest and importance. The most troublesome of such verbs are set out in the list below, with any necessary comments:

Ordinary Present Form of Verb	Past Simple Tense	Past Participle	Comments
awake	awoke / awaked	awaked / awoke	Alternative forms are given in order of preference in modern usage. It is difficult to sort these verbs out. The speaker or writer may, in fact, take his choice, remembering that *awaken* and *waken* tend to restrict themselves to transitive uses.
wake	woke / waked	awoke / woke	
awaken	awakened	awakened	
waken	wakened	wakened	

Ordinary Present Form of Verb	Past Simple Tense	Past Participle	Comments
bear	bore	borne born }	*Borne* means 'carried' and is now archaic or poetic; but it has had a modern revival in the adjective *airborne*. In the specialised sense of birth, *borne* is the past participle when the verb is used actively. "She has *borne* two sons", and *born* when it is used passively, without a following *by:* "A child is *born*" but "Two sons have been *borne* by her".
begin	began	begun	"He has *began*" is still common in careless speech, and sometimes crops up in even more careless writing.
bereave	bereaved bereft }	bereaved bereft }	*Bereaved* in the special sense 'deprived by death'; *bereft*, now archaic, in the general sense 'deprived'.
dare	dared	dared	These are the normal modern English forms; but *durst* is still used as a past tense, usually with *not* and followed by the infinitive without *to:* "He *durst* not do it". *Dare* also has a peculiar form in the third person singular present: "He *dare* not do it", where the normal form would be *dares*.
drink	drank	drunk drunken }	He has/is *drunk: drunken* is always a pure adjective—"a *drunken* man".

30

Ordinary Present Form of Verb	Past Simple Tense	Past Participle	Comments
cleave ('split')	clove ⎫ cleaved ⎭	cloven ⎫ cleft ⎭	A comparatively rare word, and choice of forms is free: but "*cloven* hoof", "*cloven* tongues" (Acts ii. 3), "*cleft* stick". The other verb *cleave* meaning 'stick (to)' is even rarer, and has past tense and participle *cleaved*. Nevertheless, "Orpah kissed her mother-in-law; but Ruth *clave* unto her" (Authorised Version).
flee flow fly	fled flowed flew	fled flowed flown	There is no real difficulty; but it is useful to bring these three somewhat confusing verbs together, and have a look at them once for all.
get	got	got	*Gotten* is now American; it was standard English as late as Cobbett's time (1820).
hang	hung ⎫ hanged ⎭	hung ⎫ hanged ⎭	A picture is *hung*, but a man is *hanged*.
lay (down) lie (down)	laid lay	laid lain	Perhaps the two most troublesome of all related verbs. The first, *lay*, is transitive; the second, *lie*, is intransitive. "I lay down" is the past tense of the verb *to lie down*; "I lay myself down" is the present tense of the verb *to lay down*. One of the most celebrated 'grammatical' errors in literature is Byron's "There let him lay".

Ordinary Present Form of Verb	Past Simple Tense	Past Participle	Comments
lay lie *(contd.)*			*Lie* (to tell an untruth) has *lied, lied.* *Lay, pay* and *say* are the only three verbs in *-ay* that have a contracted past form (*-aid*). All the others, *e.g. stay* and *play*, have *-ayed.*
load lade	loaded laded	loaded laden	The verb *lade* is restricted to ships, except in a few special, semi-metaphorical, uses of its past participle: "a heavy-*laden* bus", "*laden* with my sin".
overflow	overflowed	overflowed	Like *flow*. But the fact that Cobbett (1820) gives *overflown* as the past participle without alternative and that Fowler says *-owed*, not *-own*, is an interesting sidelight on language changes.
pass	passed	passed	An interesting distinction is made in modern usage between the true verbal past participle (*passed*) and the adjective, adverb or preposition (*past*): "I *passed* by your window", "a *past* age", "I walked *past* your window".
put	put	put	Golf has a variant verb *putt*, with past form *putted*: "He *putted* well at the last hole". There is no differentiation for another athletic exercise: "He *put* (not *putted*) the weight".

Ordinary Present Form of Verb	Past Simple Tense	Past Participle	Comments
rise raise	rose raised	risen raised	Another pair like, but not so confusing as, *lie* and *lay*. *Rise* is intransitive, *raise* transitive: "The sun has *risen*", "Theseus *raised* the stone", "self-*raising* flour" (where *self* is object). *Arise* is generally used with an abstract subject: a question, a quarrel *arises*.
shave	shaved	shaved ⎫ shaven ⎭	Formal army language still has "*unshaven* on parade".
shear	sheared	shorn ⎫ sheared ⎭	Sheep are still *shorn*; but with the slow and imperceptible change of usage they will, like metal, eventually be *sheared*.
sew sow	sewed sowed	sewn ⎫ sewed ⎬ sowed ⎬ sown ⎭	Neither of these verbs can make up its mind about the form of its past participle. Fowler (*Modern English Usage*), on the evidence of the Oxford Dictionary, rather hesitatingly decides in favour of *sewed, sowed*. But surely popular usage is against him and them. Now and then the verbs are confused, as the following sentence quoted from a Cheshire paper by *Punch* will testify: "Gardeners and allotment holders in Denton are looking forward to the advent of spring when they will get down

Ordinary Present Form of Verb	Past Simple Tense	Past Participle	Comments
sew sow *(contd.)*			to their task of preparation and seed-sewing." *Punch*'s very apt comment was "Stitchwort?"
swell	swelled	swollen	But "*swelled* [not *swollen*] head" in the metaphorical phrase implying conceit.

These are the chief verbs whose forms may, in varying degree, cause doubt and difficulty. Cobbett's list (1820), from which one or two items have been quoted above, has a few other surprising entries. The past participle of *snow*, he says, is *snown*; *sting* has past tense *stung* or *stang*, *swing* has *swung* or *swang*; *loaden* is the past participle of *load*, *stridden* of *stride*, and *slidden* of *slide*. But Cobbett hated "those dens of dunces called schools and universities"; and it is probable that the forms he gives were spoken by ploughboys rather than written by statesmen. Perhaps the conflict between speech and writing accounts for the dual and doubtful forms of these verbs, which have survived out of the past to delight as well as to puzzle us.

It is an astonishing fact, which has some bearing on this subject, that eighteenth-century writers often used the past tense form of verbs for the past participle. The original title of Gray's *Elegy* was "Elegy *wrote* in a Country Churchyard"; and we find this sentence in Sterne's *Tristram Shandy* (1759): "Everybody knows of the grand system of Universal Monarchy, *wrote* by order of Mons. Colbert". 'Bespoke tailor' and *stony-broke* survive to remind us of this surprising and comforting usage. Indeed, we have not to read very long in eighteenth-century literature to find that correct usage allowed what are now vulgarisms or solecisms. "You *was*", for example, is quite common, where the *you* represents one person; and the reason is not difficult to understand. It is only in comparatively recent years that writers on language have sought to fix and stabilise usage. Their work—especially Fowler's *Modern English Usage* (1926)—has had a beneficial effect on all types and classes of people who desire, or are compelled, to put pen to paper. But, as has already been explained (page 7), it suffers the fate of all records—whether dictionaries or grammars—of a living language: it rapidly becomes out of date. Even Fowler could not catch, once for all, something that by its very nature cannot be caught.

The forms *built, burnt, dreamt, dwelt, knelt, leant, leapt, smelt, spelt, spilt* have established themselves, instead of the forms in *-ed* (*builded, burned,* etc.) which, although quite common in the literature of the past, are now merely the regular stock-in-trade of minor poets, or are used only in certain set expressions: "I *burned* [*not burnt*] with indignation", "*dreamed* a dream". A few others, *crept, kept, slept, swept, wept,* have shed any troublesome alternative forms they ever had. The rest have, on the whole, settled down to the *-ed* ending—for example, *dipped, kissed, slipped, stripped.* This ending has had its ups-and-downs because pronunciation was doubtful; the *e* could be sounded (as in the modern *blessed* when it is a pure adjective) or mute. In older poetical texts the convention is followed, by the editor if not by the poet himself, of replacing the mute *e* with an apostrophe:

> Some, as she sipp'd, the fuming liquor fann'd,
> Some o'er her lap their careful plumes display'd.

The *-t* ending was favoured by some poets, among them Tennyson, Browning and, later, Robert Bridges, who also indulged in propaganda for spelling reform. In their work we get such forms as *dipt, kisst, tost, crost,* which they used, no doubt, partly as an insurance against false rhythm on the part of an ignorant reader.

But the battle of *-ed* and *-t* and the reign of the once

ubiquitous apostrophe are now over. Nevertheless, a few odd doubts and difficulties remain. *Knit*, which according to Cobbett had *knit* also for its past forms, has developed a new past, *knitted*, which is nowadays always applied to socks and pull-overs, except perhaps in the term 'close-knit', and usually, but not quite always, to brows, which are sometimes *knit*. Similarly, a new past, *shredded*, has outdone the old past *shred*. *Seethed* is now the past (tense and participle) form of *seethe*; but the Authorised Version has "Jacob *sod* pottage", and the adjective *sodden* survives to remind us of an old past participle. *Spoil*, in its usual modern sense *mar* or (intransitive) *decay*, has past forms, *spoilt*; but in its older sense, *despoil*, the old form in -*ed*, familiar in the Authorised Version ("They *spoiled* the Egyptians"), is retained. When it first migrated from the land to the world of wireless, *broadcast* tended to develop a past form *broadcasted* ("The play will be *broadcasted* at 9 p.m."), which now and then appeared, even in B.B.C. journals; but *broadcast* has prevailed, on the model of the simple verb *cast*.

Waif-and-Stray Verbs

There are a few 'waif-and-stray' verbs which have survived only in part—that is, certain of their forms are missing. *Shall*, already discussed on page 27, is among them; others are *may, can, must* and *ought*. *Must* is merely a tense having a kind of 'immediate-future-compulsive' significance, and is often 'toned down' in polite Modern English to *should*; *may* is gently permissive, or vaguely doubtful, in simple sentences; its 'subjunctive' force in complex sentences is dealt with later (page 69); and *can* is, in certain contexts, a slightly more positive variant for *may*. All this may (or can) be illustrated from the advertisement pages in the *Times Educational Supplement*:

> Further particulars and form of application *may* be obtained from the undersigned, to whom completed forms *must* be returned within 14 days of the appearance of this advertisement.

Application forms *can* be obtained on receipt of a stamped addressed foolscap envelope, and, when completed, *should* be returned to the undersigned not later than 30th September.

Ought is an old past tense and participle of the verb to *owe*, and survives now as a single tense verb, devoid of any other parts, in its own right. It gives rise to the vulgarism "didn't ought", where *ought* should, but cannot, be an infinitive following the auxiliary *did*. "You didn't ought to be out on a cold day like this" is admittedly indefensible; but "You ought not to be . . ." and "You oughtn't to be . . ." seem suspiciously like English on stilts. Most of us would take refuge in the versatile and obliging *should*: "You shouldn't be out . . .". It is better, in short, to avoid the use of *ought* in the negative.

A similar, but not quite parallel, problem arises with the expression "did, didn't use". Unlike *ought*, the verb *use*, in the sense of 'be accustomed' ("Were it not better done as others *use*?"—*Lycidas*) has all its faculties; "I am used to it" is a familiar and legitimate modern usage; and, on the evidence of a sentence quoted in the *Shorter Oxford Dictionary*, the use of the auxiliary *do* with *use* in this sense has a respectable ancestry: "Jewels do not use to lie upon the surface of the earth" (1662). The odd thing is that we never say or write "don't use" nowadays. But "did, didn't use" cannot be altogether condemned, if only because we have never really admitted "used he?" and "usedn't he?" as alternatives. Nevertheless, the construction is admitted to speech only: in writing a convenient paraphrase has to be discovered.

Unruly Pronouns

There are no other serious problems with the verb in the simple sentence; questions of the subjunctive mood, or what is left of it in English, are dealt with in the next chapter. It is time, then, to turn to the two other possible elements of the predicate—the object and the complement. At one

37

time, in English, as in Latin, Greek and some other languages, nouns changed their form according as they were subject or object, or indeed as they fulfilled other functions in the sentence. English nouns to-day have no such change; the subject form is the same as the object form. But changes survive in some pronouns; and now and then, though not often, we are tempted to use a subject form for an object form, and *vice versa*.

When it is coupled with *you* in a double object, the first person pronoun, for some peculiar reason, tends to have its subject form *I*, instead of its object form *me*. "He will almost certainly blame you and *I* for the mistake", is a simple, if somewhat crude, example of this usage. The error is so common after the half-imperative *let* ("Let you and *I* go") that it has almost become sanctified by use. But the careful speaker and writer will here follow grammatical correctness rather than common and careless usage, and will say "Blame you and *me*", "Let you and *me* go".

Probably most people who mistakenly prefer *I* to *me* have at the back of their mind the glow of satisfaction they had, especially in school days, when they thought (just in time) to say "It is I" instead of "It's me". Of old, this won the approval of the pedant—indeed, it still does. That in a simple sentence the subject and the complement are grammatically interchangeable is undoubtedly true; "Mr. Attlee is the Prime Minister" may become "The Prime Minister is Mr. Attlee" without any fundamental change of meaning. The sentence is an equation, $x=y$, which may be equally well rendered $y=x$.

It is reasonable, therefore, to infer that subject and complement should both have the same, that is, the subject form.[1] But the fact remains that few people would say or write "It's *I*", "This is *he*", "That's *she*". Usage, a trifle shamefacedly, admits the object form to such expressions, "It's *me*", "This is *him*", "That's *her*",

---

[1] The clash between subject and complement in number is discussed on page 18. It must be remembered that this clash does not affect the basic pattern of the sentence, or equation.

perhaps because it can more easily bear the stress. In any case, these expressions belong almost entirely to the spoken tongue. They are rarely seen in writing, and so pass muster with those who, seeing them, might condemn them.

The interrogative pronoun *who?* (subject), *whom?* (object), is mildly troublesome. Since by its very nature it stands in front of its verb, we sometimes fail to recognise it as an object, and say (or even write) "*Who* did you see?", "*Who* have you invited?". It is, on the whole, a natural, and pardonable usage. Indeed, to use *whom?* in such sentences would make most of us feel rather uncomfortably self-conscious. Rather oddly, we are tempted to the opposite error in such a sentence as "*Who* did you say he was?", where we tend to say *whom*, though *who* is above all grammatical suspicion. But that is another story, and it is both told and commented upon on page 83.

Although sentences of a complex pattern have sometimes been given as illustrations, the problems and questions dealt with in this chapter all belong to the pattern of the simple sentence:

PREDICATE

But the agreement and simple relationships discussed here are fundamental to all types of sentence, however long and complicated. In addition, as the sentence develops, other important relationships come into being. The units of the sentence—word, phrase, clause—and their position; the work of the 'cementing' words, conjunctions and prepositions; the correct relationship of pronouns; the function of the various parts of the verb—all these require thought and study. For it is here, in a right conception of the pattern of the sentence and its relationship to the thought expressed, that the true secret of 'good English' lies.

CHAPTER II

THE PATTERN OF THE SENTENCE

"He then commanded six and thirty of the lads to read the
several lines softly as they appeared upon the frame; and
where they found three or four words together that might
make part of a sentence they dictated to the four remaining
boys who were scribes.   This work was repeated three or
four times, and at every turn the engine was so contrived
that the words shifted into new places, or the square bits
of wood moved upside down."

SWIFT: *Gulliver's Travels.*

The Mechanics of Beauty

It is obvious that in the simple sentence the two fundamental parts of speech are the naming word (noun or pronoun) and the doing or being word (verb).   The verb is a
tense form related, as we have seen, in a very definite way
to the subject; and the noun may be (i) a simple *word*,
(ii) a group of words without a finite verb (*phrase*), or (iii)
a group of words with a subject and predicate (*clause*).
But in speech and writing we often wish to describe the
person or thing represented by the noun or pronoun.
To do this we use an adjective, which may itself be a word,
a phrase, or a clause.   Similarly we may wish to indicate
the manner, place or time of the action represented by the
verb—to 'modify' the verb, in the more precise language
of grammar.   To do this we use an adverb, which may itself
be a word, a phrase or a clause.   Our sentence, then, comes
to have this general pattern:

40

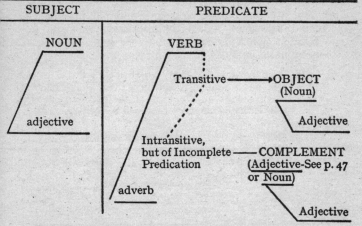

But this, of course, is a mere outline. Each noun, adjective and adverb represented in the sentence pattern may itself be a unit (that is, a phrase or a clause) which itself contains other nouns, adjectives or adverbs. We are reminded a little of Swift's famous quip:

> So naturalists observe, a flea
> Hath smaller fleas that on him prey;
> And these have smaller fleas to bite 'em,
> And so proceed *ad infinitum*.

And the parts of this complicated structure have somehow to be fitted or 'cemented' together. For this we use prepositions, which 'govern' a noun or pronoun, to make up an adjective or adverb phrase, and conjunctions, which join together words, phrases and, more particularly, clauses.

All this is a brief and rather breathless summing up of the complexities of the normal English sentence—complexities which, nevertheless, are more apparent than real, since they arise out of an essentially simple pattern. It is, however, difficult to comprehend this outline without illustration; so here are three perfectly sound and not unduly complicated sentences, taken, appropriately enough, from C. E. Montague's *A Writer's Notes on His Trade*, with a diagrammatic analysis of each into its various parts:

(i) Perhaps they feel that, whether they like it or not, fate has set them to sell in a mart where all other sellers shout at the tops of their voices, so that, unless they shout too, they will never be heard.

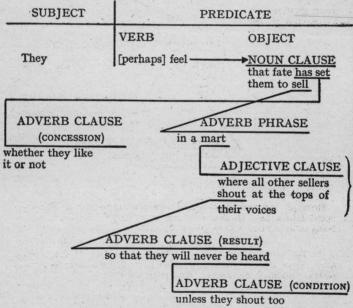

(ii) Many non-commissioned officers have a firm belief that without a due admixture of curses, an order is inaudible to a private, or that it will skid lightly off the private's mind without biting on that unstable surface.

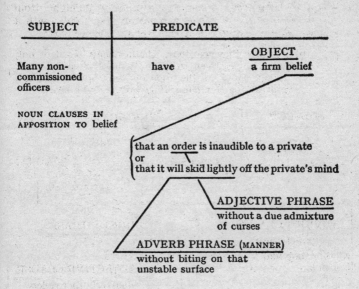

Note: (a) It is possible to regard 'have a firm belief' as a compound verb=*believe;* and in that case the two clauses here described as being in apposition will be simple objects.

(b) The punctuation of this sentence is faulty. If the comma after *curses* stands, there must also be a comma after *that;* but neither comma is necessary. (See page 106.)

(iii) Walking with an elder brother in the streets of Oxford in my youth, I was struck by the looks of a tall oldish man with the shapeliest features, the stoop of a scholarly Jove, and an air of the most distinguished melancholy.

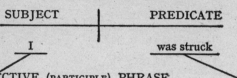

SUBJECT	PREDICATE
I	was struck

ADJECTIVE (PARTICIPLE) PHRASE
walking with an elder brother
in the streets of Oxford in my
youth

ADVERB PHRASE (MANNER)
by the looks of a tall
oldish man

ADJECTIVE PHRASE
with the shapeliest features,
the stoop of a scholarly
Jove,

and an air of the most
distinguished melancholy.

[Note: The sentence could be broken up even further by separating the phrases 'in the streets of Oxford' and 'in my youth', both adverbial modifying *walking*, the first of place, the second of time.]

The very word 'analysis' suggests an arid and forbidding exercise: and, indeed, the familiar "Analyse into clauses" of the examination paper has much to answer for, since it implies that in the pattern of the sentence the clause alone counts; whereas the truth is that the phrase may be, and often is, a far more important part. Such analysis, by obscuring the essential sentence structure, is worse than useless; like Alexander the coppersmith, it has done much evil. The type illustrated here, which attempts to give, in some detail, an over-all picture of the sentences, is at least comprehensive and logical. But it is itself only a means to an end.

No-one, except for a very special purpose, consciously breaks down a sentence into its parts when he is reading, or builds it up part by part when he is speaking or writing. In speaking and more particularly in writing it is the unconscious sense of pattern that really matters; but this uncon-

scious sense must be based on a conscious knowledge.
Words, phrases and clauses—the separate units of expression—do not fall together by accident to make form or
sense. In the very book from which our sentences were
quoted, Montague says: "He who writes to please is apt to
be drawn further and further into the exploration of the
mechanics of beauty, as you may call them." That is why
we have lingered a little on analysis. We have, in fact, been
exploring the "mechanics of beauty", or at least of sense,
since the principles of these mechanics must be known and
recognised by all those who profess to speak and write.

If, then, we have mastered the fundamental relationships, we can more readily appreciate the fascinating and
remarkable detail of the sentence pattern—the behaviour
of individual words, the functions of, for example, verb
parts, the proper position of phrases, the effectiveness of
certain forms of repetition, the function of particular
prepositions and conjunctions, the varied use of pronouns,
especially the relative, and above all, the ways of effecting
what may be called sentence economies. A modern
writer[1] has drawn an interesting and instructive analogy
between sentence analysis and the detection of crime. He
is actually thinking of a Latin sentence; but the analysis
of an English sentence provides as true a parallel.

> If ever, in your salad days—as one of my comic uncles
> calls them—you were compelled to do a Latin unseen,
> you'll know that it presents an accurate parallel with
> criminal detection. You have a long sentence, full of
> inversions; just a jumble of words it looks at first. That
> is what crime looks like at first sight, too. The subject
> is the murdered man: the verb is the *modus operandi*,
> the way the crime was committed; the object is the
> motive. Those are the three essentials of every sentence[2]
> and every crime. First you find the subject, then you
> look for the verb, and the two of them lead you to the
> object. But you have not discovered the criminal—the

[1] Nicholas Blake, *A Question of Proof.*
[2] No; of every crime, perhaps, but not of every sentence.

45

meaning of the whole sentence—yet. There are a number of subordinate clauses, which may be clues or red herrings, and you've got to separate them from each other in your own mind and reconstruct them to fit and amplify the meaning of the whole.

But however much we know of the mechanics, we discover that immediately we set pen to paper—or, rather sit with the pen poised doubtfully above the unwritten page—difficulties and problems arise. Some of them we have already faced in Chapter I. Others belong to this chapter; and when we have become aware of all these, and have learnt the way of solving them, we shall have achieved the critical mind which can appreciate the subtleties of Chapter IV.

Adjectives and Adverbs

The simple adjective and adverb give very little trouble. Luckily for us, adjectives do not change for gender or number in English as they do in French; so there is no question of agreement with the noun or pronoun. Only *this* and *that*, which have the plural *these* and *those* when they qualify plural nouns, are exceptions to this providential accident of language; and they never raise any difficulty.

The numerical adjective *one* can only, by reason of its meaning, qualify a singular noun; but sometimes, owing to the 'telescoping' of two expressions or phrases, it is used to qualify a plural, as in the following sentences, both from the same magazine article:

> Certainly an independent British Television Corporation would develop into a formidable rival of one or more Sound Broadcasting Corporations.

> Britain's allocation for home broadcasting, under the Copenhagen agreement of 1948, consists of only one long and eleven medium wavelengths.

It may be argued that "one or more" is a kind of compound plural numeral like "one or two"; so the first sentence easily passes muster. The second one is open to more objection. But, on the whole, the construction is, if not defensible, at least excusable. The alternative "of only one long wavelength and eleven medium wavelengths" is pedant's, not good, English; so a convenient idiom triumphs, as so often, over 'pure' grammar.

Adjectives are, in fact, unusually well-behaved words. They settle comfortably in front of their nouns ("the *blue* sky") or as a complement in the predicate ("The sky is *blue*"). It is only in verse or for some special emphasis in prose, that an adjective follows its noun, or precedes the verb in the predicate. True, in English we have a way (as they have in some other languages) of unconsciously, or perhaps even deliberately, associating an adjective with the wrong noun. We say, for example, "A nice cup of tea", when we mean "A cup of nice tea". 'Transferred epithet' is the label usually attached to an adjective which has thus gone astray; its aberrations are recognised as part of the custom of language.

There has been, indeed, a new and interesting extension of this usage in recent times. It occurs used at present, mainly in the language of sport: "He throws a pretty dart", "He drives a long ball". Here the modifier of the verb (that is, an adverb or its equivalent) has been replaced by an adjective (*pretty*, *long*) qualifying the object. Jeeves once said of the favourite in the egg-and-spoon race, "They tell me she carries a beautiful egg, sir." This effective twist of syntax is still colloquial, but it may have a future in the standard language. *The Times* is not ashamed of it:

> The fifth wicket fell when Watkins was caught by Griffith, who had kept an admirable wicket in this match.

Adverbs are not quite so straightforward. A few of them, for example, are variable in form. We see in such expressions as "smell *sweet*", "fight *fair*", "walk *straight*", "travel *light*", "wash *clean*", "swing *low*", "run *true*", how the adverb apes the adjective. It is a temptation to use the normal adverb form in *-ly*, *sweetly*, *fairly* and the rest; but it is a temptation to be resisted. The phrases quoted, and others like them, are sanctified by use. In other contexts *sweetly*, *truly*, *lowlily* (not *lowly*, which is itself an adjective) and the other *-ly* forms are appropriate; but not in these. Apparent 'grammar' and normal usage are sometimes, in Shakespeare's phrase, "at equal war".[1]

A special little problem arises in enumerations, where the choice may lie between *first* and *firstly*, *second* and *secondly*, *third* and *thirdly*, and so on. There is no hard-and-fast rule, but it is reasonable to use the simple adjective form when the function seems more adjectival than adverbial; to write, that is, "I have a few more important things to say: *first*, . . . *second*, . . . *third*, . . . etc". We tend sometimes to be inconsistent and mix the two, as in this sentence:

> He had made the incident and the character doubly significant, *first* in their own identity, and *secondly* as symbols of the universal.

The adverbs should be brought into line—either (and perhaps preferably here) *first* . . . *second*, or *firstly* . . . *secondly*.

Sometimes, though rarely, by a confusion of thought an adverb stands where an adjective should be. There is a curious example of this on the introductory page of the Ministry of Education pamphlet *School and Life*, which, like most Ministry pamphlets, is marred by loose and careless English:

> Originally members of the Council were also Sir Charles Darwin K.B.E., M.C., F.R.S. and Miss M. E. Dodds.

This is an extraordinary example of muddle-headed topsy-turveydom. The writer meant to say either

> Sir Charles Darwin K.B.E., M.C., F.R.S. and Miss M. E. Dodds were also original members of the Council.

or

> Originally, Sir Charles Darwin K.B.E., M.C., F.R.S. and Miss M. E. Dodds were also members of the Council.

[1] Fowler has an interesting note on this, called "Cast-iron Idiom".

What he actually wrote is a confusion of the two, and makes little sense, or none at all.[1]

Relatively is an adverb that sometimes gate-crashes in this way, as in the following sentence:

> Relatively to most other professions which are competitive with University teaching for the limited supply of highly qualified graduates, University teachers are for the most part badly paid.

For *relatively* read *relative* (adjective), qualifying the subject of the main sentence, "University teachers". But even then the construction of the sentence is basically unsound. Other professions can be relative only to a profession already named; therefore "University *teachers*" should become "University *teaching*" with the necessary change of verb, *is* for *are*.

The main function of an adverb is to modify a verb; but it can also modify an adjective ("an *exceedingly* fine play") or another adverb ("one that loved *not* wisely but *too* well"). One adverb, *very*, requires a little care; it can modify without question adjectives and other adverbs, and the present participles of verbs. But it will modify past participles only when they have so completely lost their verb force as to become true adjectives: "I was *very* pleased", "He spoke in *very* broken English". Where the participle retains its verbal with its adjectival function, *very* gives way to *much* or *very much*: "And the King was much moved, and went up to the chamber over the gate, and wept". In the following sentence, where the verbal function of the participle is emphasised by the adverb phrase "in social questions", *very* cannot be justified:

> While still at Oxford he became very interested in social questions and for a number of years worked in the East End.

---

[1] Unless, of course, there is a deliberate, but very unnatural, inversion in the sentence.

But the distinction between the participle which is adjective-cum-verb and that which is pure adjective is a nice one; only the very sensitive or the very finicky will therefore discriminate certainly and consistently between *very* and *much*. The others will be thankful that the participle has sometimes a kind of middle state which calls for no choice at all.

One sentence in the last paragraph illustrates an important point that arises, in the main, with the adverb *only*. Just as the adjective must be so placed in the sentence as to be the obvious qualifier of its noun, so must the adverb by its very position clearly modify its intended verb, adjective or adverb. Thus in the sentence referred to, "But it will modify past participles only when they have so completely lost their verb force as to become true adjectives", *only* modifies the adverb clause of time which immediately follows it: "they modify *only* when . . .". This is, in fact, what it is meant to modify. But *only* always tends to slip in as near as possible to the main verb. Without specifically thinking about it, we should probably say or write "But it will *only* modify . . .". Similarly, we should prefer "I *only* saw him once" to "I saw him *only* once". Indeed, in this matter of the position of *only*, logic and 'grammar' usually give up the unequal fight against usage; and what is logically correct often becomes stilted and unnatural English.

The Importance of Position

The position of a word and, more especially, of a phrase or clause is, nevertheless, of the utmost importance, since on it depends the proper relationship of the different parts of the sentence. This fact will be illustrated, indirectly, at various points in this chapter and elsewhere in the book. Meanwhile, it can be illustrated directly by reference to the position of the simplest type (preposition+noun) of the adjective and the adverb phrase, and that of the adjective phrase introduced by a participle. There is, for example, a difference in meaning between the two following sentences because the function of the phrases (preposition+noun) varies according to their position:

> The tall boys *at the end of the line* are asked to stand.

and

> The tall boys are asked to stand *at the end of the line*.

In the first sentence the italicised phrase is adjectival, qualifying *boys*, and in the second it is adverbial, modifying *to stand*. Obviously, since in actual content the sentences are identical, it is the position of the phrase that is significant. It follows, therefore, that the phrase must be so placed in the sentence that it does the work it is intended to do. When the phrase follows the simple preposition+noun formula, we do not often go astray—at any rate, in writing. And if we do, there is always the famous advertisement, harvested by *Punch* long ago, to give us awful warning:

> Wanted armchair for old gentleman *with sliding back and oak legs*.

A more recent example is more excusable but equally ludicrous:

> Leadership in this sense has already been given by France, whose liberal administration under Dr. Queuille, *now a year old*, has pursued free trade and currency policies as far as it can.

And the following sentence seems to throw too heavy a burden upon the poor secretary of the Norfolk Wherry Trust:

> The appeal for the preservation of local sailing craft *by the secretary of the Norfolk Wherry Trust* is timely but too limited.

The phrase "by the secretary . . ." should follow *appeal*. Unfortunately (or perhaps fortunately) errors are not always so obvious as that, or so easily remedied. In the following sentence, for example, both diagnosis and remedy are rather more difficult:

> Ireland[1] has steadily built up a reputation for sensitive craftsmanship and musical sincerity until now, *at seventy years of age*, his music is loved and played in homes all over England.

Whether the phrase is adjectival (qualifying *music*) or adverbial (modifying the verbs *loved* and *played*), the implication is that Ireland's music, not Ireland himself, is seventy years of age. Probably the best way out of the difficulty is to amend the construction thus—"until now, when the musician is seventy years of age, his music is . . ."

The Gerund Phrase

A more subtle form of this error is liable to occur when the noun following the preposition is a verb-noun, usually called the gerund, ending in -*ing*. In the following alluring statement, for example, "*By filling up a coupon, a thousand pounds may be won*", the adverb phrase (italicised) demands a main sentence in which the filler-up of the coupon is mentioned: "By filling up a coupon you may, win . . .". *Punch* rescued this delightful example from the *Melbourne Sun News-Pictorial:*

> With the stolen car travelling at fifty miles an hour, the police again gave chase. Warning shots were fired and, *after travelling several miles at high speed*, a bullet pierced the car's rear tyre.

There is no need for any other comment than *Punch's* own "Nice shooting, officer". To clinch the matter and point the moral, here is a more serious example from *The Times:*

> American supremacy in both the men's and women's games was never more dominant. *After sweeping through all three matches yesterday* the issue was decided by the first tie today.

[1] That is, John Ireland the musician, not Ireland the country.

What exactly swept through all the three matches? Not the issue, surely; and not the supremacy. There is no satisfactory answer. Nothing short of drastic treatment will give the sentence coherence and meaning.

While we are dealing with this verb-noun or gerund, it will be convenient to consider another problem that arises in connection with it. If I say "I had not heard of *your* going", the verb-noun (gerund) *going* is governed by the preposition *of*, and is qualified by a possessive pronoun-adjective *your*. But we are apt to say, and sometimes even write, "I had not heard of you going",[1] where it would seem that the pronoun *you* is governed by the preposition, and the verb-form *going* is a kind of adjective associated with it. If it is a noun (not a pronoun) that comes between the proposition and the gerund, we tend to dispense with the possessive altogether:

> Thus, instead of a *reader* being able to pick up a book containing half a dozen portraits . . .

> The anomaly of the *nation* solemnly punishing itself . . .

A nagging conscience tells us that *reader* should be *reader's* and *nation* should be *nation's*. But nowadays usage covers this as well as several other original sins. In spite of Fowler's ingenious arguments (*Modern English Usage*) under the suggestive heading "Fused Participle", this construction is better avoided; still, however much our conscience troubles us, we cannot very well satisfy it by using a possessive in such a sentence as the following:

> One has sad memories of parties of weary and bored children being endlessly trailed and lectured through one glorious church after another.

Here it is so difficult to find a good alternative that any lingering doubts about the construction are set at rest. But the following sentences make us hesitate:

[1] There are those who argue that there is a difference between 'heard of *your* going' and 'heard of *you* going'. It is, in fact, a question that merits discussion.

American tourists coming home with tales of a five-day week, and short days at that, and of the increasing dependence of all on State-provided services, does not make public opinion more favourable to us.

In a period of moribund craftsmanship and the swift decay of regional self-expression both have been reborn in this one country without either Mr. Porteous or any of us being able to give why and wherefore[1] for this remarkable and enlivening event.

In the first, the omission of the possessive is emphasised by the fact that the gerund (*coming*) is subject of the verb. At first sight, "American tourists" seems to be subject, but the singular verb *does* corrects that impression. Altogether, the 'fused participle' is misleading, and is therefore to be condemned. In the second, the construction "without Mr. Porteous or any of us being able" seems more than usually defiant of logical construction, perhaps because of the *us*.

The Participle Phrase

A very common element in the English sentence is the self-contained adjective phrase, of which the first and key word is a present or past participle:

Seeing him in the distance, I went to meet him.

Warned by the unusual motion of the engine, the driver applied the brakes.

Each phrase by its position qualifies the noun or pronoun (*driver, I*) nearest to it, following the separating comma. But the relationship is not always so simple as that represented here; and the adjective phrase is apt so to get out of position as to qualify the wrong word. In older English usage, there was a certain laxness about the position of this type of phrase. "Sitting within my orchard, a serpent stung me" says the ghost of Hamlet's father to the

[1] See page 165.

astonished Hamlet, suggesting to us (though not presumably to Hamlet himself) that it was a serpent, not Hamlet's father in the flesh, which was taking a quiet siesta in the garden. But Shakespeare, who was often a law to himself, proves little. We have more reliable evidence from Addison, a master of eighteenth-century prose:

> Having notified to my good friend Sir Roger that I should set out for London the next day, his horses were ready at the appointed hour in the evening.

This kind of construction, which according to our modern sense of usage seems at times to give an almost ludicrous meaning, is very common not only in Addison but also in other eighteenth-century writers. And even in modern usage the false or incomplete relationship of name and qualifier, or noun and adjective, is quite usual as long as it does not result in anything so remarkable as a notifying horse or a sitting serpent. To this the following sentences will testify:

> Excitingly acted by Robert Newton, Naunton Wayne and Phil Brown (late of *The Glass Menagerie*), top honours must, however, be awarded to a perfect white poodle named Monty.

Whatever it was that excitingly acted, it was not, we may assume, "top honours". The writer was so taken with his starry list and his allusive parenthesis that he forgot the play or revue which his phrase was intended to qualify.

> Faced by the few poems and *Wuthering Heights*, the language of criticism swells, understandably.

Quite understandably, if in fact language could be so fearsomely confronted, and the critic go scot free.

> He has the true measure of his genius, surely the greatest in the nineteenth century, and having this, the strange legend of his life, far stranger than is yet fully realised, falls into place as the necessary corollary of an unique view of life.

55

Deprived of costume, gesture and visible deployment, its last remaining assets are the verbal paradoxes, and in the intervals between these effervescent lines we become increasingly conscious of the lath-and-plaster plot.

The first phrase should relate to *he*, not to *legend*, and the second (presumably) to a play, not to "its last remaining assets". Both sentences are quoted in full because they exemplify a slipshod carelessness of which the faulty placing of the adjective phrases is only a symptom.

Looking back after the experience of a greater war, it is apparent that by a happy chance few buildings of outstanding merit were damaged during a savage conflict that dragged on for a fortnight and 32 months.

The phrase is left, as it were, hanging in the air, as the only word it can possibly cling to is the impersonal *it* in "it is apparent", which is a mere unsubstantial ghost of a pronoun.

Starting in East Anglia, if you want beauty of place enhanced by richness of performance, there is a Cambridge Festival, lasting a fortnight from July 30.

It is just possible that the writer means what he seems to say: "There is a Cambridge Festival starting in East Anglia". But the odds are against it. More probably he is thinking of a person (? person's) going on a Cook's tour of the festivals, and the word after *performance* should be *you*, with the necessary amendment of the rest of the sentence. This is another, but somewhat different, example of the 'hanging' adjective phrase.

The last example is taken from the introduction to the Hadow Report (Board of Education 1927):

Transplanted to new ground, and set in a new environment, which should be adjusted, as far as possible, to the interests and abilities of each range and variety, we believe that they will thrive to a new height and attain a sturdier fibre.

The writer became so immersed in his phrases and clauses that he transplanted the whole Consultative Committee instead of the children about whom, presumably, he is writing.

It is important to distinguish between the participle adjective phrase, which qualifies the nearest noun (or pronoun) in the main sentence, and that in which a participle qualifies a noun (or pronoun) inside the phrase itself. Because the participle in this type of phrase is not syntactically 'tied' to any word in the main sentence, the phrase is called *absolute* (literally 'untied'). It has the function not of an adjective but of an adverb. In diagram form:

Participle (Adjective) Phrase

Knowing the value of x,   we can find the value of y

Absolute (Adverb) Phrase

The value of x being known,   the value of y can be found.

Note that since the participle is 'untied', the construction of the main clause is free—there is no question of the position of any particular word in it since no word is qualified by the participle phrase.

Three constructions, exemplified in the following sentences, require special comment:

All things considered, it was a good show.

Provided you agree to the conditions, there will be no difficulty.

Granted a mistake was made, even then their refusal was inexplicable.

Each one of the phrases italicised is absolute. The first is obviously so from its construction; the others less obviously, though they may be regarded as variants of the normal pattern ("that you agreed . . . being provided", "that a mistake was made being granted"). The point is that the ordinary participle phrase relationship (page 54) is not necessary here. Oddly enough, the absolute construction with the past participle (in the first sentence) may become the normal adjective phrase construction with the present participle, and yet remain absolute: that is, we can write "Considering everything, it was a good show", where the participle phrase seems to qualify *it*, but in fact, by a dispensation of idiom, is 'untied'. Even more oddly, the past participles in the other two sentences tend in careless writing and speech to become present—"*Providing* you agree", "*Granting* a mistake was made". This usage is to be frowned upon, since the change is unnecessary and obscures the construction.

This is a convenient place to introduce the present participle *owing*, which is normally adjectival in such a construction as "The delay was owing to the bad weather", but becomes part of a kind of compound preposition, 'owing to', in the construction "Owing to the bad weather, we were delayed", where it introduces not an adjective but an adverb phrase. The important point to remember is that in this adverbial use *due* cannot be substituted for *owing*. "The delay was due to the bad weather" conforms, but "Due to the bad weather, we were delayed" does not conform to modern usage. People who write letters to the editor seem peculiarly addicted to using *due* in the wrong place. Here are two examples from the correspondence page:

> *Due* to the greater cross-section of the community to be found in such a school, the Grammar Schoolboy has a considerable advantage.

> After about a month a reply came via various Ministries of Labour (*sic*), stating that, *due* to the cutting down of expense under the National Health Scheme, no jobs could be offered.

Other examples of phrase relationship are dealt with as they occur. The main principles, at least, have been illustrated. Adjective and adverb clauses obey the same general principles—that is to say, in normal usage they are so placed in the sentence as to relate obviously and easily to the words they are intended to qualify or modify. There will be further reference to this later, particularly in connection with relative pronouns (see page 87). Meanwhile, it is necessary to tackle the wider problems of clause relationship, and study those details of sentence construction which arise, directly or indirectly, out of it.

One Clause after Another

The simplest way of linking clauses (that is, sentences) is this:

$$\underset{\times}{S \quad P} \quad \underset{\times}{S \quad P} \quad \underset{\times}{S \quad P} \quad S \quad P$$

Each line represents a clause with its two parts, subject and predicate (S.P.), and each cross a simple linking conjunction, especially *and*. The sentences are not interlocked, but strung out one after the other like a chain, each 'link' or clause having the same standing or importance. It was on this pattern that sentences were commonly constructed in older English. The Authorised Version of the Bible (1611) is full of them:

> And the rain descended, and the floods came, and the winds blew, and beat upon that house; and it fell; and great was the fall of it.

This is an extreme example. In most sentences there is only one change of subject, but one subject is common to at least two predicates (as, in fact, is *winds* in the above sentence):

> And David sat between the two gates; and the watchman went up to the roof over the gate unto the wall, and lifted up his eyes, and looked, and behold a man running alone.

In modern usage we are chary of *and*. We prefer the periodic sentence, in which phrase and clause are interrelated in a more or less complex pattern, and the various parts, as we see from the diagram on page 41, depend upon a main subject and predicate. It is a remarkable fact that when they do venture on the 'linking' construction modern writers often falter in what may be termed their thought sequence, or in their control of conjunctions. Here are two or three sentences, with comments, to illustrate the point:

> This pamphlet is not a tract or a sermon and a disquisition on private morality would be out of place.

A comma after *sermon* might help matters; but even then the second clause is only related to the first by an effort on the part of the reader. The sentence refurbished would run like this: "The pamphlet is not a tract or a sermon; nor is it a disquisition on private morality, which would be out of place."

A similar demand is made upon the reader by both sentences in the following paragraph, where each *and* has a significance that can be properly interpreted only through an alternative construction:

> Any work of this kind must have the weakness that it has little shape, and Goethe did aim at a certain finished conception of form. Further, Professor Weigand has had to leave out the imaginative side and we are faced here with Goethe as a thinker.

The passage is from a review of a book on Goethe; and the discerning reader, having put two and two together, might make something like this of it:

> Any work of this kind must have the weakness that it has little shape—a weakness that is ironical in a book on Goethe, who himself aimed at a certain finished conception of form. Further, Professor Weigand, having been compelled to leave out the imaginative side, has confronted us with Goethe the thinker.

But he would be justified in complaining of both the writer's discourtesy and his slipshod style.

The pamphlet is pleasant and easy to read, happily free from educational verbiage, and it is full of delightful pictures.

By the time he reaches the end of his sentence the writer has forgotten the beginning, and inserts after *and* an unnecessary "it is". Represented algebraically, the construction is "The pamphlet is $(a+b+c)$", where each term represents an adjective phrase; *is* is outside the bracket, and should not creep inside. There is a similar error in the following excerpt:

. . . provided that he felt sure that it would make people happier, cause no suffering to the victim and that it was unlikely to be found out.

The construction is "felt sure that it (1) would make, (2) would cause, (3) was unlikely". Insert *would* before *cause* and delete "that it". The question whether there should be a comma after *victim* is discussed on page 112. In the following sentence from a novel the writer suddenly changes step—or, more literally, changes subject—in the last clause:

The latter occupied a bedroom on the third floor, never took advantage of the more expensive amenities the hotel offered, and her tips were wary and infrequent.

The reader rightly expects "and made wary and infrequent tips".

This sentence from the B.B.C. pamphlet *Broadcasts to Schools 1949–1950* illustrates a common sin of omission:

They contain background notes, book lists, maps and other illustrations, suggestions for preparation for experiments, and for other follow-up activities.

For the punctuation see page 112. The point to be remembered now is that there is an *and* missing before *suggestions*, which introduces the fourth and last unit in the list. The writer has mistakenly imagined that the later *and* (before "for other") will serve the purpose. As the sentence stands, the reader is led to expect a fifth unit in the enumeration.

The result of careless and muddled thought is even more serious in the following sentence, where (as Malvolio might have said) "there is no consonancy in the sequel":

> Regarding a statement by Sir William that the Army recruits lacked appreciation of their responsibilities as citizens, *Education* suggests that this criticism applies to millions of adults and should not be blamed on to the schools.

(Here, of course, *and* is linking not two main clauses but two subordinate noun clauses.) The point is that the subject, *criticism*, cannot be, as the sentence stands, common to the two predicates. We can amend in one of two ways, either ". . . and should not be applied to the schools" or ". . . and this lack of responsibility should not be blamed on to the schools".

A word of warning must be added about substitutes for *and*, especially *also* and *so*. The safest way with *also* is to use it only when it is synonymous with *too* (='as well'): "They also serve who only stand and wait." It is an adverb, not a conjunction; so the following type of sentence, "The carburettor was choked, also the plugs were dirty", does not conform to usage.[1]

Sentences of the type illustrated are written by those who are in too great a hurry or too careless to lay any stress on form and pattern in the sentence. But even the careful writer has to go warily with certain conjunctions, especially the correlatives—those, that is, that consist of two or more co-related words in different parts of the sentence—like *both—and*, *either—or*, *neither—nor*, *whether —or* and (above all) *not only—but also*. The important thing is to place them in the right position, so that they introduce, to use again the language of mathematics, 'like terms'. Thus if I write "I neither saw him nor her",

[1] For more on this see the note on the semi-colon, page 107.

neither is out of position unless *nor* is followed by a like term, that is, a verb: "I neither *saw* him nor *met* her". But the more obvious meaning demands that *neither* should come before *him*: "I saw neither *him* nor *her*". Here are one or two examples to illustrate the point:

> After Alexander had established both *a lack of foresight* and *of policy* in his administration . . .

> . . . revealing, as the best history so often is, both *of the subject* and *the writer*.

> . . . but they urge all winding enginemen to remain at work both *in their country's* and *their own* interests.

The unlike terms are italicised; and here, for each sentence, is one way (out of two) of placing the conjunctions in the correct positions: "a lack both *of foresight* and *of policy*"; "of both *the subject* and *the writer*"; both *in their country's* and *in their own interests*".

In the following sentence, the writer carefully leaves the *by* as it were outside the brackets, and then absentmindedly slips it in again: "*by* (either confirming or *by* supplying)":

> Can some North Country readers help by either confirming this version or by supplying an alternative one?

If he desires to keep the second *by* he must bring the first *by* into the brackets, placing it after *either*: "either *by* confirming or *by* supplying".

There is a curious temptation to repeat the *whether* in the correlative construction *whether—or*. The writers of the following sentences have been tempted and have fallen:

> The question now is whether he and his members will be willing to abide by the Board's ruling, or *whether they* are determined to pursue the aggressive line of the past two years, insisting on their claims, and trying to enforce them by going slow and interrupting the railway services.

> His reference to Hobson, indeed, makes one wonder
> whether he was a good observer of other men or *whether
> he* did not either idealize people or disparage them
> according to the prejudice of the moment.

In the first sentence we have only to take out "whether
they", and in the second to take out "whether he". Even
so, the second sentence is awkwardly cluttered up with
alternatives. The remedy for the following sentence is not
quite so clear:

> But whether this is due to the fact that the Oriental . . .
> feels no need to transgress the rules . . . or *whether he* is
> unimaginative, who am I to say?

By the strict rule of like terms the sentence should run
"But whether this is due to the fact that the Oriental feels
no need to transgress the rules or this is due to the fact that
he is unimaginative . . .". Nevertheless, in practice we
should write "But whether this is due to the fact . . . or to
the fact . . .". In any case, the second *whether* is a shame-
less gate-crasher.

We have lost the full-blooded negative of Chaucer and
Shakespeare, but an unintentional double negative even
now sometimes creeps in. We say, for example, though
we should rarely write, "I shouldn't be surprised if he
didn't come", when we mean we shouldn't be surprised if
he did. But a commoner fault—indeed, a fault so common
that it has almost become a part of modern usage—is the
use of *nor* to introduce a clause or a phrase that is already
negative by reason of a preceding one. In this sentence,
for example, the *not* modifies both verb infinitives *impress*
and *inspire*; the *nor*, therefore, has the effect of doubling the
negative:

> As a nation we do not impress the belligerent nor inspire
> the lovers of peace.

Similarly, in the following sentences two minuses, against
all mathematical rule, are intended to make a minus:

But he is not yet nearly consistent nor accurate enough to hold his own against so eminently sound a player as Cochell.

He does not in the least minimise the many loose ends of Ruskin's many interests, nor the serio-comic aspect of some.

This is not because they hold the views of Mr. Podsnap, nor because they want to retain in their minds, if they ever had it, a picture of Dickens as a knightly and perfect figure.

And the following sentence differs from the other three only because the writer, with an almost Chaucerian gusto, has doubled the negative twice:

It is not his duty to 'write up' a film for the benefit of the salesmen, nor to tell the producer how he ought to have done his job, nor to be tender to its faults for the sake of unfortunate players who have suffered from it just as much as the critic.

It is important to remember that, since they are correlatives, *either—or* and *neither—nor* cannot be added to; that is, we cannot write *either—or—or*, *neither—nor—nor*. Or rather, we should not. The writer of this passage (none other than Jespersen in *The Growth and Structure of the English Language*) has defied the custom of language by doing so:

. . . which, as a matter of fact, are found neither in Shakespeare nor in the Authorised Version of the Bible nor in the poetical works of Milton, Pope, Cowper and Shelley.

The first verb should be made negative with a simple *not*, and the two *nors* made positive: "are not found in Shakespeare or in the Authorised Version or in the poetical works . . .".

Errors with *not only—but also* are commoner and more

serious. Here are excerpts where simple false 'bracketing' is the trouble. The suggested correction is given afterwards:

> This factor should have some weight in nerving resistance to the activities of this body which is engaged *not only* in destroying landscapes *but* their soils.

The words "in destroying" should come outside the bracket: "in destroying (not only *landscapes* but also *their soils*)".

> Unesco seems to me to offer the ordinary man and woman the opportunity to complete that aspect of their wholeness *not only* in terms of faith, *but also* of work; *not only* in terms of hope *but also* of responsibility.

The sentence, as a whole, seems almost innocent of sense; but "in terms", at any rate, should come outside the bracket each time it is used: "in terms (not only of . . . but also of)".

> The theme was . . . handled in such a way as to trace *not only* the history of democratic government, how it has grown, *but also* to show what it has grown into.

The two infinitives *to trace* and *to show* are the like terms; *not only* must therefore take its place immediately before the first: "as not only *to trace* but also *to show*".

The errors in the following sentence are a little more complicated, but fortunately they are easy to correct. Probably the writer altogether forgot his correlatives:

> It is hoped the meeting will show the world that the idea of a United Europe *not only* has a past but that before it lies a great future.

The simple 'bracketing' would be: "has (not only *a past* but also *a great future*)". Obviously the balance of the sentence would be better preserved if *past*, like *future*, were qualified by an adjective (say, *glorious*).

Sometimes a writer completely loses his way after the *not only* half of his expression. In the following sentence, he gets up to *Occupation* with a wonderful flourish, including a satisfying superlative, takes a breath, and then forgets the rest. Perhaps he intended to say "but also one of the truest". Let us hope so. But as it was, his wits went a-wandering and he began a new clause, leaving his *not only* section suspended in mid-air:

> The dossier on Leopold published by the Belgian Socialists before the election, and called *La Question Royale*, is not only one of the most devastating indictments against any European statesman during the Occupation, but not a single fact produced by the Socialists has been effectively contradicted or disproved.

For the other solecism in this sentence, "indictment against", see page 154.

Verbs—Some Doubts and Difficulties

The relationship of the verbs in the various parts (clauses and phrases) of the complex sentence does not raise any very serious problems. Although English is rich in tenses, we use them by instinct, without any conscious regard for 'sequence'. It is only very rarely that a present gets mixed up with a past in an unhallowed union, and we are usually aware of the misdemeanour. In the following sentence, for example, the four simple and uncompromising past tenses *went, kept, had stopped, owed*, demand a past in the final clause:

> The traditional professor who went to bed in his hat or kept his umbrella up after the rain had stopped owed his eccentricity not to pressure of work but to an over-intense absorption in one particular subject, *be* it the theory of relativity or the consequences of the Hundred Years War.

The writer has tried a kind of idiomatic present subjunctive (see below), which has no real counterpart in the past ("were it the theory . . ." is not recognisable modern

English). He should have written "whether it was the theory or the consequences . . .".

This last example, with the comment, is a reminder of the fact that the true subjunctive form is almost dead in English.[1] It survives in a few main sentences of wish or desire like "God *save* the King" and "Britannia *rule* the waves". In dependent clauses (that is those acting as adverbs) it is confined to certain parts of the verb *to be* mainly after the conjunctions *if* and *though*. But "(if) I be" and "(though) he be" seem merely odd now. The following sentence could only occur where in fact it did occur, in a *Times* fourth leader, a journalistic 'feature' which too often ekes out a tenuous humour with some half-hearted period English:

> On the other hand, he will pathetically disapprove if he *be* sentenced to stay at home.

Were as the past singular subjunctive form has held out a little more tenaciously, partly because in the stereotyped phrase "If I were you" the complement *you* has by attraction (see page 17) tended to establish it. It survives, for example, in the parenthetic idiom "as it were", and is indeed quite common in the third person as well as in the first. Even so, it is only a survival. In the following sentence, for example, our modern tendency would be to turn the subjunctive *were* into a blunt indicative:

> It is high time the wide field of Tudor music, both secular and sacred, were explored by many more schools.

Where Shakespeare wrote

> If it were done when 'tis done, then 'twere well
> It were done quickly,

[1] Somerset Maugham remarks in *A Writer's Note-book* that American writers "use the subjunctive much more than we do", and comments: "I surmise that the primness of language which teachers inculcate is forced upon them by the general slovenliness and incorrectness of speech common to their pupils. They are kicking against the pricks: the subjunctive mood is in its death throes, and the best thing to do is to put it out of its misery as soon as possible."

we should write, more prosaically, but less obscurely,
"If it were done (='finished with') when it is done, then it
would be well it should be done quickly". In modern
usage, *should*, *would*, *may* and *might* have dispossessed, in
the main, *be* and *were*. Hamlet, who had some wise words
to say about a number of things, once seemed to touch
lightly on this very subject:

> . . . Or by pronouncing of some doubtful phrase,
> As "Well, well, we know", or "We could, an if we would",
> Or "If we list to speak" or "There be, an if they might",
> Or such ambiguous giving out . . .

The English subjunctive is, indeed, a mood of the mind,
not—or rarely—a technical mood of the verb, reflected in
its form. Its *shoulds* and *woulds* and *mights*, which mercifully have no particular rule[1] to control them, are the
symbols of a "doubtful phrase" and an "ambiguous
giving out". Only occasionally does a *should* get out of
hand, as in the following sentence, where the last clause
should have the indicative "*were* (or better still, *are*)
always to be had", which is, by implication of the *would*
and *should*, doubted by the other two:

> It would be unfortunate that it should come to be con-
> sidered to be the normal practice in the preparation of
> technical films that the services of university teachers and
> others in their position should always be had for nothing.

One other relic of the subjunctive is worth noting—the
had illustrated in the following quotation from Keats's
Endymion:

> O, thou hast won
> A full accomplishment—the thing is done,
> Which undone, these our later days had risen
> On barren souls.

But poetry, and adolescent romantic poetry at that, is the

[1] Except, perhaps, the normal rule of *should* and *would*, which has
been explained on page 29.

last stronghold of this tense, which in plain prose is represented by "would have".

One or two other little problems connected with verbs may be conveniently treated here. The first is illustrated in the two following sentences:

> It would not have helped Sir Stafford Cripps and Mr. Bevin to have had their leader standing in a white sheet at Bridlington.

> I would have liked to have seen Goethe faced with this more tragic age in which we find ourselves.

Here we have a 'double-past' effect, where a perfect infinitive "to have had", "to have seen", follows a tense that is itself perfect in the past, "would have helped", "would have liked". In each sentence the infinitive should be simple present, "*to have* their leader", "*to see* Goethe". The writer of the second sentence has also fallen into the error of using *would* for *should*: "I should (not *would*) have liked to see Goethe . . .".

Some writers have a peculiar propensity to change, in mid-stream, from active to passive or from passive to active,[1] always with a disastrous effect on their sentence construction. Here are two sentences to illustrate the point:

> This fear drives him to strange technical tricks, as another man might be driven to drink or drugs.

[1] The explanation of the terms *active* and *passive* is simple. When the verb represents the action performed by the subject it is said to be in the *active* voice; when it represents an action suffered by the subject, it is said to be in the *passive* voice.

SUBJECT	PREDICATE	
	VERB	
The lion	*beat* (active)———⟶	The unicorn (OBJECT)
The unicorn	*was beaten* (passive)	by the lion (INSTRUMENT or AGENT)

split infinitive

The second half of the equation is inverted; it should run "as it might drive another man to drink or drugs".

> So what he has done with his material is done, perhaps, even better, because instinctively, than he had dared to hope he could do.

Whatever we make of this semi-literate stammering, we can be quite certain that the active verb at the end should be passive, to square up with the passive "is done" at the beginning: "than he had dared to hope it could be done".

A word must be said about the split infinitive, against which the older grammarians were wont to thunder, and the avoidance of which is still almost a superstition with most of us. Fowler, protesting too much, tries to laugh the superstition away, except when the split is of the exaggerated type "*to* always and in every conceivable circumstance whatever and against all odds *do* your duty"; and in his comments himself splits an infinitive *pour encourager les autres*. The truth is that it is sometimes necessary, in the interests of clearness, to put a single adverb between the *to* and the verb form; but the anti-split-infinitive campaign has been so successful that most writers nowadays (in spite of Fowler) will cheerfully commit the sin of ambiguity rather than risk the self-appointed grammarian's frown. Nothing is stranger than the way certain so-called solecisms of speech and writing are subject to a popular condemnation. We hear them or (worse still) see them in writing, and then thank God we are not as other men are.

However, to return. Only very rarely, if ever, should an infinitive be split by more than a single adverb; and not even by a single adverb unless to avoid the split would lead to unnaturalness or ambiguity. Here is an interesting example of self-conscious non-splitting:

> Though I have expressed an absence of warmth towards Goethe or of deep and continuing pleasure in his work, I

71

think this is no less reason for attempting honestly to recognise what he achieved and the value of his conceptions today.

The writer has been at great pains to keep his adverb (*honestly*) out of mischief; but the result is that it seems to modify the verb *attempting* instead of the verb *recognise*. "To honestly recognise" is what he meant, and what he should have written, fearing no man. The following sentence illustrates an even more mistaken finickiness:

> It was a brave thing to do because there have been so many books about Dickens that anyone who has read even a very small fraction of them is apt to wonder if there is really anything more usefully to be said about him.

You can almost hear the writer drawing his breath as he gets near the brink, and feel his self-congratulation when he saves himself (as he thinks) from tumbling in. Yet if he had put the adverb (*usefully*) where it ought to be, between *be* and *said*, he would not have split an infinitive after all.

Jespersen tritely but rightly remarks that the *to* is not essential to the infinitive since after certain verbs—for example, the ordinary auxiliaries—it is left out. *Dare* when it is negative always forgoes the *to*; and when it is positive keeps it only on rare, usually formal or emphatic occasions: "I dare not do it", "I dare say", "He dared to contradict me",

> I dare do all that may become a man,
> Who dares do more is none.

There is still a faint doubt about *help*; but on the whole modern usage has established the omission of the *to* in the following infinitive: "I helped load the van", "I helped him do his homework". The construction is not seriously questioned now (as it might have been twenty years ago) even in normal literary writing:

And therefore, although Unesco is helping other people run two seminars this year, it will not itself hold any till 1950, when we hope there will be two.

Modern usage has also blessed "try *and* do" as well as "try *to* do". Fowler sees a subtle difference between the two constructions, the first being (as an imperative) more persuasive than the second. But this distinction is unnecessary. It is better to take without question what the gods give, and be thankful that "try *and*" is beyond reproach.

Trouble over Pronouns

Pronouns are troublesome words. In the very nature of things, they are apt to become confused, since one pronoun form (like *he* or *it*) may have to relate to more than one noun in the course of a sentence. In one of his lectures Sir Arthur Quiller-Couch, having quoted from North's *Plutarch*, makes the following observation:

> As prose this passage has many merits. Every non-inflected language finds trouble over its pronouns: and our Elizabethans inclined (perhaps wisely) to let that trouble take care of itself. We should be shy nowadays of writing 'whom he had long before caused to swear unto him, that he should kill him when he did command him'; but the meaning is perfectly plain and easy and no more ambiguous (say) than the meaning of St. Matthew xxvii. 43, in the Authorised Version—'He trusted in God; let him deliver him now, if he will have him'.

He might better have quoted this other (and ghostly) example of confused pronouns in the Authorised Version: "and when they arose early in the morning, behold, they were all dead corpses" (2 Kings xix. 35). The explanation is, of course, that the first *they* refers to the Israelites and the second to the unfortunate Assyrians. We are rarely so careless as that in our confusions nowadays; but pronouns can still go badly and sometimes amusingly wrong. Here are one or two examples to point the moral. *Punch* quotes the first sentence from the *News Chronicle*:

> Thousands of pets suffer every year because their owners have been—not intentionally cruel—but careless. A vet gives these warnings. Never throw stones for your dog to chase—he may injure his teeth or swallow them.

Punch's own comment "That's all right—what's the Dental Service for?" is all that is necessary. If, however, we need a 'grammatical' explanation it is this, that *them* is far too near *teeth* to establish its rightful relationship with *stones*. In the following sentence, also quoted by *Punch*, the relationship of *themselves* is faulty or ambiguous: it seems to be object of the verb *assemble*, and to refer to *parts*.

> The refusal by a number of countries to admit completed cars has led to [a firm of] car body makers issuing dismissal notices to 250 of their employees. The countries include South Africa, Eire, and Belgium. They want the parts to assemble themselves.

"Well", says *Punch*, "they're living in a fool's paradise". *Themselves* is, in fact, an emphasising pronoun related to *they*: "They themselves want to assemble the parts", or, by an illogical separation of related words that has become sanctified by usage, "They want to assemble the parts themselves".

But not all examples of pronoun confusion are funny enough to get into *Punch*. *He* and *she* and, above all, *it* require a great deal of careful watching. There is only one rule—to ensure that any pronoun, by its position in the sentence, is naturally and easily associated with its appropriate noun, either directly or indirectly through an intervening pronoun. If potentially ambiguous pronouns begin to pile up, as they are apt to do in indirect speech (see page 121), then it is time to call a halt and introduce a noun here and there to keep the meaning clear. It is a good thing to read over aloud a doubtful sentence, since it is easier to 'hear' than to 'see' a wrong relationship. As Quiller-Couch says, we have to be a little generous in our attitude to pronouns; it is sometimes necessary to ask the reader to co-operate and make for himself a correct noun-pronoun association, even when in the sentence as it is written it may be doubtful or faulty. The last *it* in the preceding sentence is an example. Here the reader will naturally relate it to its appropriate noun (*association*), in spite of the intervening noun *sentence* and its own related *it*. To substitute "this association may be doubtful" for "it may be . . ." is to make assurance doubly sure. The following sentence would be questioned by none but the over fastidious critic; but the *it* logically relates to the subject of the previous clause, "the cultural programme of Unesco", and not, as it should do, to Unesco itself. However, the reader can be relied upon to make the necessary connection; if the writer's conscience had pricked him he would have used the noun—"Unesco must ask itself":

> But in all this work, if the cultural programme of Unesco is to find a balance in importance, in urgency and reality, with the educational and scientific programmes, *it* must ask itself repeatedly what are the needs, in terms of international assistance, of the scholar, the artist, the creative writer.

Cobbett, as so often, has the last word. "Never," he writes, "put an *it* upon paper without thinking well of what you are about. When I see many *its* on a page, I always tremble for the writer." That advice is as good now as when it was given nearly a century and a half ago.

Sometimes related pronouns in a sentence disagree, especially in number. Singular pronouns, like *anyone*, *each*, *everyone* (see page 16) are apt to beget plurals:

> *Everyone* knows where *they* stand, and that is very reassuring for many uneasy people.

> As an example, when the father suggests that when *everyone* has the atomic bomb, *they* will simply blow up the world, the son replies, 'But why should *they*?'

But let *anyone* look at the schools in which infants and still younger children are brought up, in urban and rural areas alike, and *they* will find much to disturb them.

. . . for nearly *everyone* has opinions about modern questions even if *their* knowledge of them is as thin as of Greek science.

The first three sentences need no comment. Unless we are prepared to condone this disagreement as being so common that it has become part of modern usage, we shall condemn them as examples of careless writing. About the fourth there is a slight doubt. The expression "nearly everyone" has, paradoxically, a plurality that does not belong to the simple *everyone*: and it would be difficult to substitute *his* for *their*. But since the construction is suspect, it is better avoided altogether. In a general overhaul of the sentence the last comparison "as thin as of Greek science" should also come in for some serious criticism and treatment.

The following sentence contains a much rarer fault, a disagreement in gender:

Yet if Western Germany is permitted to cover *its* essential import requirements by exports, this export drive would threaten the recovery of *her* neighbours.

This type of error arises only with nouns that are ordinarily 'neutral', but which are formally or affectionately personified (see page 178): the writer, having no very strong views either way about personification or non-personification, is then apt to distribute his pronominal favours equally—to use *its* and *her* without any attempt at discrimination. Perhaps the fault, such as it is, is a faint reminder of the fact that the possessive *its* was not in common use before the mid-seventeenth century; so that either *his* or *her* may stand, for example, in Shakespeare and the Authorised Version (1611), where modern usage would require *its*:

Charity vaunteth not *itself*, is not puffed up, doth not behave *itself* unseemly, seeketh not *her* own.

THE PATTERN OF THE SENTENCE

The sentence quoted on page 17, "Each of us has finished his work", poses a sex (or gender) question that is not capable of any very satisfactory solution in English. *His* or *her*? There is no 'common' pronoun form; so we have either to give the benefit of the doubt to the masculine (*he, him, his*), or to state the alternative awkwardly and frankly, "has finished his or her work". Some people have even gone so far as to invent common forms. A correspondent in *The Times* over twenty years ago suggested *hesh* for 'he and she', *hier* for 'him and her', *hiers* for 'his and her'; and gave a sample passage: "Every youngling is malleable. If hesh has a good nature, you can easily do much with hier, but if hiers nature is evil, the difficulty will be great." Another correspondent suggested *heshe, himmer, hisser*, for the respective combinations, with *hissers* for 'his and hers'. But the introduction of a synthetic formation into the living language is almost as rare an event as the collision of two stars in the universe; so *hesh* and *hiers* and *hissers* are likely to remain dead linguistic curiosities.

However, most writers in order to do a great right do a little wrong, and write the sentence as it is given, on page 17, "Each of us have finished our work". The plural of the personal pronouns knows no difference of sex; and it is wise to use it, if it is at all possible, instead of a more 'grammatically' correct *he* or *she*. In language, as in other ways of life, the letter killeth, but the spirit giveth life. So we have the strange phenomenon, in a book on language, of one maxim cocking a snook at another.

It is important to remember that the pronoun forms associated with the indefinite pronoun *one* are *one* and *one's*, not *he, him, his*. The fact is, *one* is better avoided altogether, and *we* used as a convenient substitute. "One should stand up for one's rights, shouldn't one?" is, at best, Frenchified English; "We should stand up for our rights, shouldn't we?", though perhaps not, in its indefinite sense, altogether satisfactory, will at least pass muster.

We have seen (page 38) that in the simple pattern of the

sentence we are apt sometimes to use a subject form of the pronoun (*e.g. I, he*) where an object form would be 'grammatically' correct. When two pronouns, joined by *and*, are governed by a preposition we are tempted into the same error: "He came with *you* and *I* to see the fireworks." The preposition governs both pronouns—in mathematical language, we have the formula $p\ (a+b)$—and therefore both pronouns should have object forms. One phrase, "between you and I" has become almost standardised in modern usage. Indeed, it goes back to Shakespeare. "All debts," writes Bassanio to Antonio, "are cleared between you and I." Yet this, after all, is a reminder that in Elizabethan English there was little discrimination in the use of pronoun forms. Abbott (*Shakespearian Grammar*) gives many interesting and revealing examples from the plays. Since the modern systematisation of usage we have become more 'case conscious' in our use of pronouns. Such a sentence as "Yes, you have seen Cassio and she together" (*Othello*), which is quoted by Abbott, gives us a mild shock now. But when the construction is a little obscured, a writer may still go astray:

> Drew is the more unexpected of the two, but that is the fault of *we* who have been looking on in not earlier detecting his great, if unobtrusive, merits.

There is a reference to this dubious usage in connection with the relative pronoun (page 83).

The demonstrative pronouns and adjectives (*this, that*) require special care. Their relationship to the appropriate noun must be precise, for the very reason that they are 'demonstratives', pointers-out, the signposts among pronouns. Yet they are often used loosely. It is, for example, interesting to speculate on the precise relationship and significance of *this* in each of the following passages:

> But the promise is in how he says it, and the forceful personality that gives direction and delivery to that substance. *This* makes me believe that there is more to Mr. Thompson's book than mere sexual preoccupation.

Promise, personality, direction and delivery, substance, or the sentence as a whole? The choice belongs to the reader. But certainly the *this* is an inefficient signpost.

> When I came to London at the beginning of the century it was commonly said that 'Shakespeare spelt bankruptcy'. Today, in comparison with *this*, it might be said that he spells fame and fortune. *This* is sure to sharpen the appetite for books about Shakespeare, and to help to win Mr. Brown the multitude of readers he deserves.

Here we have an example of 'woolliness' in the use of *this*. Each *this* is intelligible, without being precise. The result is that the sentence, while reasonably clear in meaning, loses something of its intended effect.

> The author has concentrated on the growth of the British Empire, but *this* has not had the effect of ignoring social and economic aspects of the period.

Presumably the *this* means "this concentration"; but even so, the rest of the sentence is obscure. A reasonable interpretation would be: "but this concentration has not had the effect of causing him to ignore". The purist might object to "this concentration" on the grounds that, like the simple pronoun *this*, it requires a precise antecedent noun, which would, in effect, be the noun *concentration*. But, as Horatio said on a graver occasion, " 'twere to consider too curiously, to consider so".

The following excerpt quoted by *Punch* from a letter in the *Sunday Express* illustrates a very common fault:

> My two sons, five and seven, have never seen a jack-in-the-box. Where have they gone?

There is a jump of the writer's thought from the single—that is, typical—jack-in-the-box to all the jacks-in-the-box (or jack-in-the-boxes)[1] he has ever seen. So his plural

[1] Fowler has an interesting article on the plurals of compound nouns. But the difficulties are not really serious. For the most part, we overcome them by instinct or custom, and where (as here) there may be a doubt, usually both forms (*jacks-in-the-box* and *jack-in-the-boxes*) are admissible.

pronoun, *they*, has a singular antecedent noun *jack-in-the-box*—unless, indeed, it is related (as in *Punch*'s comment "To look for a jack-in-the-box, perhaps") to the noun *sons*.

This disagreement in number relationship is even clearer in the two following passages:

> Over large areas of the world *the gospel* of force is now preached, as it was in Germany before and during the war, with all the weapons and propaganda, all the panoply of a crusade. *These evil gospels*, aimed not only at the overthrow of religion but at the slavery of man, can be met only by a faith as positive and confident as their own.

> Each lecture had its following *seminar*. *These* varied greatly according to the topic.

In the following passages the fault is a little more subtle. The only rightful antecedent of "these interludes" is *interludes*, and of "these orchestrations" is *orchestrations*. But the reader is required to establish and define this relationship by his own interpretation of the clause or sentence preceding the demonstrative. The demonstrative itself, if it is a signpost at all, is a doubtful and misleading one. Both sentences are from the B.B.C. pamphlet *Broadcasts to Schools 1949–1950*:

> This service aims at uniting schools in an act of worship which on each occasion is built up round an episode from the Christian story presented in dramatic form. *These interludes* aim at providing a subject for a simple meditation.

> At the end of each term, a children's choir, accompanied by an orchestra, will sing special arrangements of the songs learned during the term; *these orchestrations* will in part be designed to show the difference in tone between strings, woodwind, and brass.

It is important to remember that such faults as are illustrated in the above sentences cannot always be corrected by a simple manipulation of the pronouns (or adjectives) concerned—the turning, for example, of a singular into a plural. An explanatory word here and there, or, more rarely, a complete reconstruction of the passage, may be necessary. Here, for example, is a suggested amendment of the relevant parts of the two passages last quoted:

> . . . round an episode from the Christian story presented in dramatic form, called an 'interlude'. This interlude aims at providing . . .

> . . . will sing specially orchestrated arrangements of the songs learned during the term. These arrangements (or, eliminating the demonstrative, the orchestrations) will in part be designed . . .

The general moral is—if the demonstrative is used, its relationship must be precise; or, conversely, if the relationship is intentionally loose, the demonstrative should be avoided.

Grammatical Relativity

The relative pronoun has peculiar difficulties of its own, chiefly because it is not only a pronoun but also a conjunction. There are one or two simple facts that are worth memorising about its function and use in the sentence: that it always introduces an adjective clause; that the noun (or pronoun) to which it relates is called its antecedent; that it does not change for number, but has a personal (*who*, *whom*) and an impersonal form (*which*), as well as a common form (*that*); that when it is subject of its own clause it agrees in number and person with its antecedent, the agreement being visible not in the actual pronoun form but in the verb associated with it. Difficulties arise over this agreement only when, for some reason, the antecedent itself is obscured. One special type of sentence leads to error. It is illustrated at its simplest in the following examples:

One of the best textbooks on bidding and play which *has* been written by British experts.

The Y.H.A. is one of the best things that *has* come out of the last twenty years.

A new edition of one of the most scholarly and imaginative anthologies of Elizabethan poetry which *has* ever been produced.

In the first sentence the antecedent is *textbooks*, but the singular verb *has* betrays the fact that the writer thought it was *one*; "textbooks which *have*" is the correct construction. In the second the antecedent is *things*—so the sentence should continue "that *have*", and in the third the correct agreement is anthologies which *have*. Whenever the formula *one of* + a plural noun or pronoun is used, the relative pronoun is liable to attach itself to the *one* instead of to its real antecedent:

He is one of those who *does*

instead of

He is one of those who *do*.

We have again the powerful influence of attraction (see page 17). So common is this fault, especially in speech and less formal writing, that it is profitable to take for illustration an example not of incorrect but of correct usage:

The Natural Sciences programme, like the Educational programme, is one of Unesco's achievements that justify all our hopes and efforts.

'*Who*' and '*Whom*'

Sometimes questions of case arise; and they have an odd way of inspiring letters to the literary and educational press, of which the following is a good example. It was written to the Editor of the *Times Educational Supplement*:

Sir,—I am not myself keen on grammar, but I realize that even a slight knowledge of the subject has one supreme advantage: it enables one to indulge the pleasant human weakness of finding other people wrong. That is what I am doing now; and I am enjoying myself.

Look at this sentence: 'He is the man whom I think wrote the offensive letter.' This is a type of sentence one often sees in modern writings, and sometimes hears on the wireless. And it is a horror. Leaving out the 'I think,' which is, of course, parenthetical, the sentence becomes: 'He is the man whom wrote the offensive letter.' In the original sentence the verb *think* requires no object other than the sentence itself; and the verb *wrote* requires *who* as its subject. To use *whom* instead of *who* in a case like this is not only a grammatical blunder but a piece of linguistic swank; as indeed it is in the question hurled at me the other day: 'Whom do you think I am?' Presumably there are certain people who, knowing little or nothing about grammar, regard *whom* as a more scholarly and more dignified word than *who*.

P. B. BALLARD.

Dr. Ballard, himself—in spite of his opening sentence—a well-known writer on language, has enjoyed himself to some purpose. But his remark about the people who know "little or nothing about grammar" is not altogether justified. After all, the usage is as old as the Authorised Version (Matt. xvi. 15); and the argument that the "I think" or "you think" clause is in parenthesis was demolished by Fowler long ago. But whatever may be the somewhat mysterious syntax of sentences of this type, the simple fact remains, as Fowler rightly says, that in them the relative pronoun is subject of its own clause, and should therefore have the subject form, *who* not *whom*. Here are two other examples of the wrong usage, the first quoted from a letter of Mr. E. M. Forster to the *Spectator*, and the second from a report (in the *Manchester Guardian*) of a speech in the House of Lords:

Perhaps after the storms have swept by and the aeroplanes crashed into one another and wireless jammed wireless, a new creature may appear on this globe, a creature *whom* we pretend is here already.

It was doing justice to two or possibly more people *whom* he felt were unjustly criticised.

The following sentence, in which there is, in fact, no problem of case form, confirms the fallacy of Dr. Ballard's argument concerning parenthesis:

> Napoleon's coach, rolling inexorably across Europe, was not cluttered up with a lot of sea-shells which he did not even know were on board.

It is not possible to put the clause "he did not even know" in brackets; and though *which* is subject of its own clause ("which were on board") in some inexplicable way the pronoun itself, as well as the clause, seems to be governed by *did not know*. Possibly the explanation lies in the double function of the relative pronoun as both pronoun and conjunction; or there is a confusion of this construction with what is familiar in Latin as the accusative (*i.e.* object) and infinitive, that is, a noun phrase made up of an object associated with the infinitive of the verb, like this: "He is a man *whom* I consider *to be* quite unfitted for the job". The parallel clause construction, which has just been outlined and discussed, would be "He is a man who I consider is quite unfitted for the job". Provided we recognise the relative pronoun as a subject in this type of sentence, the syntactical problem does not seriously matter.[1]

There is one construction in which *whom* for *who* has been established by usage. Cobbett, writing nearly a century and a half ago, roundly condemns the use of *whom*

---

[1] A similar problem arises in the following construction, which has dropped out of modern usage:

> We had much work to come by the boat; which when they had taken up, they used helps, undergirding the ship.—Authorised Version.

It is difficult to state exactly the function of the word *which*. To-day we should resolve it into conjunction + pronoun, 'and it': "and when they had taken it up". The word *what* affords an interesting example of this double function in the relative. It is, in fact, a combination of demonstrative and relative (*that which*=the French *ce que*), and the problem of case can be solved by dividing it into its two parts: "I don't know *what* is going on"="I don't know *that* (object) *which* (subject) is going on".

after *than*, pouncing more particularly upon the hapless Doctor Johnson, who wrote "Pope than whom few men had more vanity". The argument is that *than* in this context is not a conjunction but a preposition (see page 90). But time and usage have avenged themselves on Cobbett and justified the Doctor: *than whom* is standard English to-day, admitted and blessed by the Oxford Dictionary. Usage has triumphed over 'grammar' and the ordinary speaker or writer over the pedant.

Defining and Non-Defining

There is a difference in meaning between the two following sentences:

> Old people who are not eligible for a money grant may apply for a food voucher.

> Old people, who are not eligible for a money grant, may apply for a food voucher.

In the first, the clause beginning with the relative pronoun (*who*) is a real adjective: it 'defines' its antecedent (*old people*). Only old people not eligible for a money grant may apply. But in the second sentence the *who* clause is merely in parenthesis. The antecedent is not defined. All old people may apply for a food voucher—they are not eligible for a grant. For an obvious reason the first type of clause is called 'defining' and the second 'non-defining', and they are differentiated by means of the punctuation. The defining clause is not separated from its antecedent by a comma;[1] the non-defining clause is. This useful distinction is a modern one. Eighteenth-century and older writers frequently do not discriminate, and insert or omit the comma as the spirit moves them. Some modern writers inadvertently or ignorantly separate what is obviously intended to be a defining clause from its antecedent:

[1] Unless a phrase, marked off by *two* commas, stands between them.

His father was one of those Francophiles, whose intense love of the landscape, the architecture, the speech and timelessness of an old civilisation was purely aesthetic.

Rarely do we hear of those acts of understanding or goodwill, which surely must exist and without which the foundation of a secure world can barely be laid.

The demonstrative *those* is, in each of these sentences, the signal of the defining relative: "one of those Francophiles whose . . .", "those acts which . . .". There is sometimes, however, an element of doubt. In the following sentence the *of which* clause is possibly intended to be non-defining, as the comma suggests:

But to get that cutting edge requires a care and minuteness of observation, of which there were here no trace.

But it is far more probable that it is really intended to be defining, qualifying the double antecedent "care and minuteness", and the comma is therefore unnecessary. At any rate the writer has allowed his verb *were*, which should agree with the singular *trace*, to be attracted into the plural by the double (that is, plural) antecedent. Still, at all costs he should have avoided ambiguity, and either confirmed the defining nature of the clause by omitting the comma, or written the sentence more effectively like this: "But to get that cutting edge requires a care and minuteness in observation; and of this there was here no trace".

Concerning the following sentence there is no doubt at all; the relative clause "for which it is designed" is defining, and should not therefore be between commas:

It is one of the charms of planning that its effects are felt long after the situation, for which it is designed, has disappeared.

Sometimes the non-defining *which* can have as antecedent not a single noun or pronoun, but a whole clause: "He had not carefully studied every detail, which was a pity". But this use, like the parallel use of the demonstrative (see page 78), is dangerous in that it leads to a looseness of construction that reflects a lack of clearness and preciseness of thought. The relationship of the *which* may become so doubtful that the whole meaning of the sentence is blurred:

> If he has a fault in this book, it is to have oversimplified Constant's character, which sometimes gives him a freakish foreign air.

It is difficult, if not impossible, to specify the antecedent of *which*; and in consequence the following pronoun *him* also becomes ambiguous. Presumably it refers to Constant; it appears to refer to the writer of the book. How utterly homeless a non-defining *which* can be the following sentence will illustrate:

> The blockade exaggerated the inevitable hell of the woman worker with a home, which is the duality of the job, the obligation to do a day's work in the factory and then another day's housework when she gets home.

This sentence is, indeed, past praying for; and the vague use of *which* is only symptomatic of a deeper and more serious syntactical disease.

Now and then—but not often—the omission of a comma turns what should be a non-defining into a defining clause, and makes havoc of the sense. Here are three examples:

> . . . and the conference on the teaching of Western Union in schools which dispersed only a week or two ago.

A comma after *schools* would relate the non-defining *which* to its proper antecedent, *conference*. As the sentence stands, the schools in which the teaching is to be done have already dispersed; or, in the language of grammar, *which* is a defining relative with antecedent *schools*.

> It is to be hoped that this year they may be able to put toys on the market for children of all ages that are neither dull, shoddy, nor expensive.

Again, only a comma after *ages* could relate the non-defining *that* to its true antecedent *toys*; without the comma the antecedent is *ages* or—more doubtfully—*children*.

> A moving and courageous book about hospital life which has been widely praised.

It is, presumably the book, not the hospital life, which has been widely praised. A comma after *life*, making the relative clause non-defining, will put the matter right.

A word must be said about the use of *that* as a relative. This use has had a curious history. *That*, which is primarily a demonstrative, was given relative (that is, pronoun) function quite early in the language, before, that is, the borrowing of the interrogative forms *who* and *which*. During the eighteenth century, however, there was a movement, described and deplored in Addison's paper "The Humble Petition of *Who* and *Which*" (Spectator 78) to establish *that* as the normal relative form. In this, *who* and *which* are made to say: "We are descended of ancient Families, and kept up our Dignity and Honour many years till the Jacksprat *that* supplanted us."

This was, no doubt, true of a passing fashion in usage; but *that* has never, in any sense, generally supplanted *who* and *which*. Cobbett gives a succinct account of its function, which will, on the whole, hold good to-day: ". . . *that*, which is a relative applicable to rational as well as irrational and even inanimate beings". Fowler suggests that, when the antecedent is what Cobbett calls 'irrational' or inanimate, *that* should be used as the defining and *which* as the non-defining relative. But he ruefully admits that English usage scorns logical tidiness of this kind. Moreover, the defining relative often follows the demonstrative *that*, and here, at any rate, in order that an awkward repetition of sound may be avoided, *which* is preferable: "I had never heard of *that* book *which* was recommended by the lecturer", rather than "*that* book *that* . . .". To sum up, in modern usage *that* is a useful variant, for *who, whom, which* (that is, as a subject or object form); and there

are no particular rules defining its use. It has one
peculiarity, that when it is governed by a preposition the
preposition always comes after it, never before: "the room
in which I slept", but "the room that I slept in".

In usual practice the *that* in the last phrase would be
omitted: "the room I slept in". Omission of the defining
relative pronoun is common in modern usage when (as in
this particular example) the relative is governed by a
preposition which follows it, and when it is the direct object
of the verb: "the man [*whom*] I saw", "the book [*which*]
you lent me". In modern usage the defining relative is
never omitted when it is subject of its own clause; but
Shakespeare sometimes omits it:

> I have a mind [*which*] presages me such thrift
> That I should questionless be fortunate.

The non-defining relative is never omitted.[1]

And-whichery

There is a fairly common fault which is sometimes
called by writers on language 'and-whichery'. When two
adjective clauses qualifying the same antecedent are
linked together, it is, of course, legitimate to use a link in
conjunction (*and, or, but*):

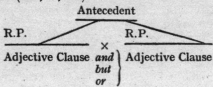

> This is the resolution *which has been passed* and *which
> we must now put into force.*

But when the antecedent is qualified by a simple adjective
or an adjective phrase + an adjective clause, it is not
legitimate to have a linking conjunction preceding the
relative pronoun: "He was a *clever* man and *who was very*

[1] Except by minor poets.

skilful with his hands". The error is usually made in sentences that are rather more complicated than this one. Here are three by way of example:

> Happy today must be the man who has a feeling for two romances, *entirely separate,* but *which can yet be harmoniously blended,* the one of railway travel and the other of beautiful names.

> While Howell was under no great obligation to Swinburne, the man *responsible for their preservation,* and *who actually sold them for hard cash to the collector least likely to have any scruples about them,* was the 'hero of friendship' most loved and trusted by the poet.

> They built magnificent temples and adorned them with sculptures, *founded it is true on the art of India,* but *which have at their best an energy* . . .

In all three sentences an adjective clause is linked to an adjective phrase.

Comparisons and Parallel Constructions

So much for pronouns, for the main principles that govern their use, and for the chief problems connected with them. More particular difficulties or questions are dealt with elsewhere as they arise. It is now time to turn to conjunctions and prepositions, words which effect vital relationships in the sentence, and have peculiar difficulties of their own. Many of these difficulties are connected with idiom, and are dealt with in other parts of this book (chiefly Chapter IV). Meanwhile, some attempt is made here to discuss, with illustrations, the problems connected with the use of these words in expressing the fundamental relationships of comparison and contrast.

The commonest sign of simple comparison is the word *than.* It is a conjunction that can follow only a comparative adjective or adverb and the one word *else.* That rule is well worth remembering; for by it such constructions as "different *than*", "prefer *than*", are condemned. We have also to remember that it does not apply to words which are Latin but not English comparatives (for example, *superior, inferior*, which are followed by *to*, not *than*), and that *other* and *rather* are, by derivation and for the purpose of this rule, true comparatives. The converse also is true—that comparatives, as defined in the previous sentences, can be followed only by *than*. Under the rule, then, and its converse, such familiar constructions as 'no sooner had he gone *when* . . .' and 'hardly/scarcely had he gone *than* . . .' cannot be justified.

The cricket correspondent of a Sunday paper was himself caught out in the following sentence:

> Scarcely had the shrill cheers of youth for Compton died away *than* Robertson, who had begun to look full of runs, also was out, caught behind the wicket.

All that is straightforward enough; but *than* has other problems, which arise mainly from the fact that, except before the relative pronoun in the construction *than whom*, already noted on page 85, it is a conjunction and not a preposition. Certain questions of case therefore crop up, which, in their simplest form, are illustrated in the following sentences:

He is taller than $\begin{cases} \text{I ?} \\ \text{me ?} \end{cases}$

He does more work than $\begin{cases} \text{I ?} \\ \text{me ?} \end{cases}$

The subject form is grammatically correct, since the sentences are elliptical for "He is taller than I am", "He does more work than I do". If the object form (*me*) is to be justified, it must be on the grounds that it is better able than the subject form (*I*) to bear the stress which normally falls on the last syllable of a sentence, and has a kind of 'disjunctive' function, independent of case, like the French *moi* ("Il est plus haut que *moi*", not "que *je*"). We have already considered a parallel usage, the complement after the verb *to be*, on page 38. On the whole, it is better to avoid the elliptical form of the sentence, and express the verb of the *than* clause; but the use of the emphatic form (*me, him, her*) for the subject form is not to be too severely frowned upon unless it leads to ambiguity.

It is important to remember that *than* can, of course, link objects as well as subjects. There is a fundamental difference in meaning between the following sentences:

> He likes you better than *I* [do].
>
> He likes you better than [he likes] *me*.

In the first, the subjects are linked ("*he* than *I*"); in the second, the objects, ("*you* than *me*"). The following sentence illustrates ambiguity with *than*, especially when there is no difference in case forms to provide a clue. Possible interpretations are shown in the brackets:

> The figure of the single pedestrian seems to me a far clearer symbol of a pedestrian crossing than [*it does of*] an orange-coloured globe [*does*]. The two children will suggest a school to most minds rather more certainly than [*they will suggest*] a torch [*will*].

The intended meaning of the first sentence can be expressed, without ambiguity, by a simple re-arrangement of the *than* clauses: "The figure of the single pedestrian seems to me a far clearer symbol than an orange-coloured globe of a pedestrian crossing". But the second sentence requires more drastic treatment: "To most minds a school is suggested rather more certainly by two children than by a torch".

The superlative has none of the problems of the comparative. Two things only have to be guarded against. One is using the superlative when only two things are being compared ("the best of two") and the other the usage illustrated in a familiar journalistic boast: "The highest circulation of any morning newspaper". We have here a fault parallel to that treated in connection with *among* and *like* (page 94); that is to say, we are relating, if not equating, unlike terms. But the expression, for all its false economy, has established itself. To write "The highest circulation of the circulations of all the morning papers" is logical but linguistically ridiculous; and to write "A higher circulation than that of any other morning paper" is so stiltedly correct as to rob the boast of all its fine and generous abandon. All the same, the construction is to be avoided whenever the comparative ("greater, wiser than any other") can be used without sacrificing the superlative effect. For example, the writer of the following sentence might easily have used the simpler comparative construction "that their peasants are more miserable than any I have seen elsewhere":

> I said (and still say) that their peasantry are the most miserable of any peasant populations that I have seen anywhere.

A few sentences are given, with comments, in which a relationship—not necessarily a comparison—of A and B is involved, and in which the syntax, though intelligible, is faulty, or not precise, or illogical.

> The pamphlet on Education for Citizenship published by the Ministry of Education to-day is a much *more suave and gentler* document than the report made on the same subject in 1944 by the Advisory Council on Education in Scotland.

The writer has been trapped into what appears to be a double comparative; *more,* as the sentence stands, modifies both *suave* and *gentler*. He could have said *suaver,* and so got rid of *more* altogether; or, if *more* had to be used, he should have put the simple comparative in -*er* first: "much gentler and more *suave*". It is so easy to avoid this faulty construction that there can be no possible excuse for it.

> One can hardly imagine his doing anything else *except* clamour for a job in a theatre—acting in small parts, doctoring lame plays—anything to get a footing in the charmed circle.

93

There were now other courses open to the would-be engineer *besides* a university degree.

And it is certain that many of them are used in many other civilised countries *as well as* England.

Since the rule for *than* (page 90) is so simple, it seems a pity not to observe it: "doing anything else *than*", "other courses *than*", "other civilised countries *than*". In the first sentence, if *else* is omitted we have the legitimate construction, absolute positive or negative followed by preposition *except* or *but*: "anything *except*", "*nothing* but". The correct comparative construction is, in fact, somewhat stilted in these three sentences; it is better to substitute *several* or *many* for *other* in the second sentence, and omit *other* in the third. In the second sentence there is another error—the two related elements, A and B, are not equated: "other courses" and "university degree" are unlike terms. The sentence should run: "There were now several courses open to the would-be engineer besides those leading to a university degree".

This non-equating of terms is common in certain other constructions:

Among the numerous reprints and estimations of the Henry James revival, there has so far been no opportunity to consider the products of his 'dramatic years'.

Among reprints and estimations (by which, it is reasonable to assume, the reviewer means *estimates*) we should expect to find, not an opportunity, but a reprint or an estimation. So, eliminating the ambiguous *of*, we should recast the sentence like this: "Among the numerous reprints and estimates connected with the Henry James revival, there has so far been no reprint or estimate of the products of his 'dramatic years'." The formula for the construction with *among* is "among *nx* is *x*", where *n* is more than one. In the following sentence, therefore, "abundance of" should be omitted:

Among the abundance of talks which the B.B.C. provides there is seldom the wireless equivalent of the English Essay in the manner of Lamb or Goldsmith or Addison.

Like and *unlike* require careful treatment:

Unlike golf and fishing no expensive equipment is required.

Moreover, like Winston Churchill, Smuts's undoubted claim to greatness does not rest on his peace-time record.

The construction is "Like/unlike *x*, *y* . . .", where *x* and *y* are noun forms representing the names of persons or of the same type of things; for example, in the first sentence, the names of sports, and in the second, the proper names of persons. So the first sentence should run "Unlike golf and fishing, it (e.g. *hiking, running*) requires no expensive equipment"; and the second, "Moreover, like Winston Churchill, Smuts cannot base his undoubted claim to greatness on his peace-time record", or, equating *x* with the existing *y* (*claim*), "Moreover, like Winston Churchill's, Smuts's undoubted claim . . ."

The fourteen colour plates have a quality which seems to me superior to any colour reproductions in any book now on the market.

The writer is comparing unlike terms (*quality* and *colour reproduction*); he should have written "a quality of reproduction superior to that in any other book". The *other* is important; the reviewer intended, but failed, to separate the book he was reviewing from all the others "now on the market".

A readable book, its value is enhanced by a good index, a useful glossary and several maps.

A failure as a playwright, his dramatic efforts added to his academic knowledge.

A methodical and conscientious journalist, his *New Statesman* essays which made a regular weekly appearance over a number of years were of something better than journalistic quality.

Here we have three examples of improperly related nouns in apposition, that is, placed against each other (see page 27). Such nouns should be merely variant names of the same thing: a *book* cannot stand in apposition to its *value*, a *failure* to *dramatic efforts*, a *journalist* to his *essays*. The construction is, at best, an awkward and artificial one; but if it must be used in these sentences, they should run: "A readable book, it has a good index, a useful glossary and several maps, all of which enhance its value", "A failure as a playwright, he increased his academic knowledge through (or *by*) his dramatic efforts", "A methodical and conscientious journalist, he achieved something better than journalistic quality in the *New Statesman* essays which made a regular weekly appearance over a number of years".

The following sentences illustrate the common fault of 'false economy' in certain constructions expressing comparison or contrast. In a laudable effort to be brief, the writer uses one preposition or conjunction where popular prejudice (as Dickens said concerning Mr. Squeers's eyes) runs, or ought to run, in favour of two. If, for example, I say "He is as tall and broader than I am", I make the conjunction *than* serve not only (correctly) for the comparative, *broader*, but also (incorrectly) for the positive "as tall", which should be followed by *as*: "as tall *as* and broader *than*". In each sentence the omitted word is inserted in brackets.

They form a rich mine in which to quarry, full of Dickens at his best, as delightful [*as*] and often more spontaneously delightful *than* he is in his books.

Nevertheless, unless something is done to put the issues fairly and squarely to the country on a much wider scale [*than*] and in rather different terms *from* anything hitherto attempted . . .

A comparison or a contrast implies two elements (A and B)—the names, for example, of persons or things. This necessary duality is sometimes expressed not directly, but at first remove, as in this sentence:

> It was curious to compare the attitude of the invited audience to two new comedies this week, the British film *The Chiltern Hundreds* and the American film *When My Baby Smiles at Me*.

Here the uncompromising singular *attitude* has to gain some reflected plurality from "two new comedies". We cannot compare one attitude; yet only by vague implication are we comparing two. The construction is convenient and common, but it is none the less faulty. Nor does the simple substitution of a plural after *compare* solve the problem; "to compare the attitudes of the audience" suggests a number of attitudes to each film. The examiner who set the question (London, General School) "Compare the positions of Worcester and Great Malvern" avoided the illogicality of *compare*+singular only to fall into the ambiguity occasioned by *compare*+plural. The implication is that both Worcester and Great Malvern have more than one position apiece.[1] It is worth while being exact and precise, even at the expense of a superficial elegance: "It was curious to compare the attitude of the invited audience to the British film . . . with its attitude to the American film . . .", "Compare the position of Worcester with that of Great Malvern".

Most theatre programmes announce that there will be an interval between each scene. The usage is familiar enough to have become accepted, if not quite legitimate. *Between* is obviously a preposition that demands a plural object—either an actual plural ("The goalkeeper stands between the posts") or two nouns linked together by *and* ("between the devil and the deep blue sea"). "Between each scene" may conceivably be justified either because of the plural or 'distributive' quality of words like *each* and

[1] See also page 163 for a difficulty hinted at here.

every (see also page 17), or on the supposition that the phrase is, in fact, elliptical for "between each scene and the next".

Here are two other examples of a similar construction, where *between* governs a singular noun (*imagery*, *writing*) which is associated with a double formula, $a+b$ ("poetic and *prose*", "*for the eye* and *for the ear*"). Ideally, the writer should find another way; but his crime is venial enough to deserve only a word of caution:

> It is also the best example in the book of the difference *between* poetic and prose *imagery*, with which Professor Brooks is mainly concerned.

> The appearance in story form of Miss Jennifer Wayne's famous broadcast series shows clearly the difference *between writing* for the eye and for the ear.

We have a parallel usage with *different*:

> Each school was stamped with the characteristics of the university at which it was held; each was different, all were a success.

Only by 'understanding' the completing phrase "from the other" can we make reasonable sense out of "each was different".

It is important to remember, too, that the formula for *between* when it is not followed by an actual plural is between "x and y"; no conjunction other than *and* is permissible. So *or* should be *and* in the following sentence:

> He must choose between carrying out the duties of that office *or* resigning to make political tours which have entailed prolonged absence from the State.

There is a similar error in this sentence, where the adverb *equally* also demands the formula "x and (*not* or) y".

> It is a welcome newcomer, and makes an equally good fellow-traveller on summer holidays *or* desert islands.

In both these sentences the real trouble is muddled thought on the part of the writers, which is reflected in a confusion of constructions. Each writer (we may reasonably imagine) began with the simple alternative ("must either carry out or resign", "a good fellow-traveller on either a summer holiday or a desert island"), then flirted with the *between*, *equally* idiom, and ended with an unfortunate mixture of them both.

In this chapter an attempt has been made to illustrate with comments, as systematically as may be, the chief principles of sentence construction. Some of the points raised may, at first glance, seem trivial. But they are all symptoms of a fundamental neglect either of those laws which govern the putting together of the various parts of the sentence in order to communicate, without ambiguity, the intended meaning to the reader, or of the custom of language—that individuality of expression which we call idiom—which sometimes seems even to conflict with those laws.

Idiom is the subject of a later section (pages 153 ff.); it has its own special difficulties and points of interest. Meanwhile, there are two or three important things to remember: first, that the primary requirement of a sentence is that it should make sense; second, that the freedom of usage (as distinct from the tyranny of formalised 'grammar') is not mere licence, since it depends upon a real sensitiveness of the speaker or writer to the exact meaning and use of words, to proper and allowed relationships, and to the changes that come, often imperceptibly, in the manner of using language; and third, that a good sentence does something more than 'make sense', for, whether it is spoken or written, in its particular context it has an aptness, a sound, a grace of form and rhythm—qualities which, with others, we sum up in the term *style*.[1]

It is only when we keep all these things in mind—and perhaps a few more—that we can hope to write 'good English'. But just as the expert golfer makes his swing

[1] From the Greek word for 'a pen'.

in obedience to certain laws that he once learnt consciously, by hard and difficult practice, and now obeys without conscious thought, so the true writer, having mastered the fundamental principles, puts them into practice without fussy and pedantic deliberation and care. Stilted 'correct' English in the narrow sense is the work of the learner; natural English is the work of one who by infinite pains has attained to the freedom which is not licence but law.

CHAPTER III

POINTS OF PUNCTUATION

Theseus. This fellow doth not stand upon points.
Lysander. He hath rid his prologue like a rough colt; he knows
    not the stop.
        SHAKESPEARE: *A Midsummer Night's Dream.*

The Period

"Stainless Stephen" long ago, in the early days of wireless, hit upon the simple means of raising a laugh by
peppering his speech with punctuation marks. It is a
device that has worn well. We are still amused. And at
any rate it reminds us that punctuation (that is, 'pointing')
is a matter for writing and not for speech. The inflection
of the voice, its rise and fall, its pauses, its stresses and
cadences make up the punctuation of the spoken word.
When we say "Are we downhearted?" the voice itself asks
the question which, in writing, we indicate by a question
mark. The marks of punctuation, in fact, merely outline
the pattern and nature of the sentence for the reader,[1]
who arrives at the meaning and significance through the
eye, and not through the ear.

[1] Not, however, the reader aloud. Punctuation is 'syntactical'.
It is a guide to the structure of the sentence and the relationship of
its various parts, not an aid to the rhetorical delivery of the sentence by the spoken voice. It has been shown by various scholars
(including Mr. J. Dover Wilson in the Cambridge Shakespeare) that
Shakespeare did, in fact, punctuate for the actor, using a system
entirely independent of normal syntactical punctuation—a system
that is paralleled in the conventional method of marking the 'pointing' in canticles and psalms.

Mr. A. P. Rossiter in an address at the National Conference on
School Broadcasting, 1949 (*B.B.C. Quarterly*, iv. 2), observes: "The
written and spoken languages do differ in vocabulary, though less
importantly than is commonly supposed. Much more in manner
and (not punctuation, but) what punctuation tries (quite ineffi-
ciently) to control: Rhythm, cadence, tone, the pauses, stresses,

Continued overleaf

Punctuation is, then, a convention practised by the writer for the convenience of the reader—that, and no more. Like language itself, it has had its changes through the years; we no longer punctuate like Swift or Johnson or Hazlitt or Dickens. Some of the differences between the punctuation of to-day and that of three hundred (or even two hundred) years ago are fundamental; others are merely matters of fashion or degree.

The basic or fundamental mark of punctuation is the full stop, which marks the end of a complete sentence. In formal grammar the term *period* is applied to both the sentence (especially if it is composed of a number of dependent clauses) and the stop(.) at the end of it. Theoretically, the use of this stop should cause no difficulty at all; and, indeed, it does not to the experienced writer, who can 'see' the pattern of his sentence before he begins to write, and therefore knows exactly where the sentence ends. But the casual or inexperienced writer is not quite so sure. He is apt to let his thoughts form themselves into sentence patterns, to string or fit them together, and to mark the 'periods' only by inserting a few odd commas at the pauses. But even he recognises the general principle that the full stop is the sign of the end; he is only uncertain where the end should be.

The Comma

Between the beginning of a sentence, which is marked by a capital letter, and the full stop indicating the end there will be normally other stops. Chief of these is the comma, which in many ways is the most important as it is the most difficult stop in punctuation. It is often used

---

lifts-and-drops-of-the-voice, the 'rests' which hold a tension for the next note: All those subtle changes of pitch, force, speed, which do so much, which do nearly everything, to determine the intuitive feeling of the hearer, his sense of the speaker's attitude towards his theme; and to his audience, and himself." But this is an over-statement; the ordinary writer punctuates for the silent reader. To mark the rhythmical pattern of the sentence he would have to devise a new system of punctuation.

indiscriminately. Writers sometimes sprinkle commas on the paper like pepper out of a pepper-pot. But used scientifically, with a due regard for its rightful and varied functions, the comma is the writer's friend and ally in his efforts to communicate with the reader. In its simplest use the comma marks the natural pause at the end of a phrase or a clause—as, for example, an adjective (participle) phrase:

> Having discussed the situation, the Committee adjourned for a week.

or an adverb clause:

> When they had discussed the situation, the Committee adjourned for a week.

If the phrase or clause is transferred from the beginning to the middle of the sentence, it is placed between commas: "The Committee, having discussed the situation, adjourned . . ."

But these, as Launcelot Gobbo said, "are simple scapes". A comma out of place in a legal document has been known to cost thousands of pounds; and even in ordinary writing an errant, or superfluous, or omitted comma may work great havoc. A few sentences in which the writer used his commas ignorantly or with careless abandon are given below, with necessary comments:

> It is not that things are bad, nor that there is any noticeable fall below the expected level, but rather that tiredness somewhere has crept in, there is a failure to crack the whip, or else a failure to respond to the crack of it.

> Granted that it was academic and rather priggish, with some off-the-peg and some very unlikely characters, also a good many emotional platitudes; nevertheless, it was neither patronising nor pretentious, in fact it was quite simple.

The first sentence should end at "crept in", and a second sentence begin with "There is a failure"; or, if the writer

meant to include the last clause in the single sentence, this
clause should be properly joined and related to the previous
clause—like this: "but rather that tiredness somewhere has
crept in and that there is a failure either to crack the whip
or to respond to the crack of it". To his other sins this
writer adds the use of *nor* for *or* as the conjunction introducing the second clause (see page 64).

The pattern of the second sentence is "granted *x*, nevertheless *y*". There is certainly, therefore, no call for the
strong semi-colon (see page 107) after *x*. In addition, the
writer, no doubt boggling at the use of another *and*, pre-
tends that *also* is a conjunction, and imagines that a simple
comma after *pretentious* is sufficient, even though the last
clause ("in fact . . .") has no conjunction to join it to the
one before. Both sentences illustrate the deplorable effect
of careless punctuation on the syntactical pattern of the
sentence.

An omitted comma may faintly puzzle, or seriously mis-
lead, the reader:

> After an exciting hour and a half's play at Huddersfield
> yesterday Yorkshire gained their fifth win in a row and
> their thirteenth championship victory with three wickets
> to spare.

A comma is expedient after *yesterday*, and necessary after
victory. Yorkshire won this particular game with three
wickets to spare; the sentence (as it is punctuated) says it
was their fifth win in a row, and thirteenth victory, and
that in each of them they had three wickets to spare. The
comma after *victory* has the effect of making the final
phrase (correctly) adverbial, not (incorrectly) adjectival.

> If Glover lost the other Ulster boy, Drew, did nobly in
> beating Young at the 20th.

A puzzle at first sight; but a comma after *lost* gives the
solution, and the Ulster boy whom Glover apparently lost
becomes the conqueror of the hapless Young.

In the following sentence a comma is expedient, if not necessary, after *week*:

> Holloway being in the news this week I turned first to the page about the Prison. . . .

Here we have an absolute phrase (see page 57), which should, like other phrases and clauses, be separated by a comma from the main sentence. But this sentence is really introduced for the sake of the next one:

> The Critics, having mauled *Ann Veronica,* and provoked much anguish thereby, the B.B.C. has made handsome amends by a full-dress production of this play.

Again the construction is absolute. The reader should go on without stopping to *thereby*, until, after the comma, he reaches the subject of the sentence ("the B.B.C."). But the comma after *Critics* is a real gate-crasher. It suggests to the reader that "The Critics" is itself the subject ("The Critics, having mauled and provoked, said? did? discussed? . . ."); but no predicate materialises, and the real subject pops up just in time to give a clue to the intended construction. The comma before *and* is also unnecessary. This point is discussed more fully later, in the note (page 112) on some niceties and subtleties of punctuation. But meanwhile, to point the moral, here is, on the other hand, a sentence that cries out for a comma before *and*. The reader's eye travels on without let or hindrance to the word *laughter*, as if that was the object of *does not grip* as well as of *won*:

> This is a bold experiment, but it does not grip and unhappily won the laughter of a large number of schoolboys who were there on the night of my visit.

In sentences whose structure is elaborate or unusual, a single comma[1] is apt to intrude at vital syntactical points, thus:

[1] Apart, that is, from those marking off *e.g.* single words inside the main structure.

PREDICATE

(a) <u>Subject (Adjective Phrase)</u> $\downarrow$ <u>Verb</u>
                   ,

(b) <u>Subject</u>   <u>Verb</u> $\downarrow$ <u>Object</u>

Such a comma has the effect of (a) separating the subject
from its verb, or (b) the verb from its object. Two commas
may be necessary or desirable, or none at all—but never
one. The following sentences illustrate the point:

> . . . while light conversation, punctuated by squeals of
> pain is to be expected.

Comma also after *pain*, or no commas at all.

> There is something wrong with him which, with careful
> handling may be put right.

Comma also after *handling*, or no commas at all.

> Why he should regard this as a criticism, I cannot make
> out.

The comma has intruded between verb and object because
the normal order of the sentence parts is inverted, and the
object, coming first, is so long that the writer pauses for
breath.

> The new scheme instils a fresh interest in education and at
> the same time, engenders the beginnings of a sense of
> social responsibility.

The subject, *scheme*, has two verbs, but is divorced by the
intrusive comma from the second of them. The phrase
"at the same time" should either be put between commas
or be left without any commas at all.

    The comma has other uses, one of which has already been
dealt with in connection with non-defining relative clauses
(page 85), and another of which is illustrated in the note on
parenthesis (page 109). But it must be remembered that,
outside the few particularised constructions mentioned and

illustrated here, the question to comma or not to comma has to be answered (to adapt a phrase of Sam Weller) "according to the taste and fancy of the writer". Yet perhaps not altogether in these modern days, when punctuation, like syntax itself, has tended to become more formal and scientific. The writer can no longer scatter his commas with easy abandon as he tended to do in other days; for by his commas he may be, and sometimes is, judged.

The Semi-colon and Colon

In general, the comma neither joins nor separates; it may be called, in relation to the full stop, a 'quarter stop'. For the longer syntactical pause or break in the sentence there is the semi-colon, the 'three-quarter stop'. It is particularly useful before a 'conjunctive adverb' like *therefore, however, so* (=*therefore*), *on the other hand*, which does not (like a real conjunction) join, and at the same time implies that its clause is not separate from what has gone before:

> The question was not discussed; so there is nothing to be done in the matter.

> He was not involved in the crime; on the other hand, he did nothing to prevent it.

The use of the comma before *so*=(*therefore*) is a laxity to be frowned upon. It is, however, common among writers who are either merely careless or (as in the following examples) indifferent to the 'pattern' of the sentences:

> I had nothing in the world to do, so I got into one of the bullock-carts that were waiting at the landing-stage and was driven to the club.

> Fitzroy Maclean began to wonder whether he was growing smug in his pleasant assignment, so he applied for a transfer to Moscow, and the first phase opened.

A semi-colon is desirable, if not necessary, before the *so* in each sentence. See also page 62.

And here, in a sentence from C. E. Montague's *A Writer's Notes on His Trade*, is the semi-colon in its more general use. It is rather like a rest in music:

> His work, in the rough, is a kind of hulking 'prentice figure of himself; and then he divests this lumbering hobbledehoy of his graceless superfluities of verbiage, his trumpeting, booming, grimacing and facetiousness; he trains the creature down; he files and bevels it into concision, proportion, modulation and wit.

In that sentence there are four distinct clauses neither joined by conjunctions nor separated by full stops; so the semi-colon comes into its own. But, like the comma, the semi-colon has to be used wisely, and with definite purpose. We have already noticed (page 104) the use of a semi-colon for a comma. The writer of the following sentence also, and even more obviously, threw a semi-colon in merely for luck:

> The social scientist, at least in the programme Unesco has devised for him, is dealing with unmeasurables, with human attitudes of aggressiveness and conflict, with misconceptions and prejudices; with those very international tensions which are at the core of our present situation.

Having begun with commas (after *unmeasurables* and *conflict*) he should have stuck to them, or used a dash (see page 109).

Printers make a conventional, and rather subtle, distinction between the semi-colon and the colon(:). But in actual practice it is better to use the colon only as an 'introducer', of, for example, a quotation, a passage of direct speech ("Mr. X said:"), or a list of items. There are plenty of examples in the text of this book, wherever an illustrative sentence is introduced. Here is a somewhat unusual example, taken from *The Times*:

> One thing is certain, whatever the outcome: every citizen will do well to take very much to heart the Prime Minister's simple plea for harder work.

If the colon is used at all in the body of the sentence (that is, not as an introducer) it should usually divide two parallel or antithetical clauses: "Law is the essence of freedom: licence only leads to tyranny". But even here, as in similar constructions, the semi-colon is sufficient. Certainly in the following sentence the colon is only worse by a tail than a semi-colon, which would itself be unnecessary and, indeed, out of place:

> I turned first to the page about the Prison and found that the Public Library provides it with a trained librarian plus a library orderly two evenings every week for the prisoners to come and choose their books: about 250 being issued each time.

Marks of Parenthesis

The comma, as we have seen in the note on the non-defining clause (page 85), is sometimes a mark of parenthesis. There is an illustration of it in the previous sentence, where the words between commas are parenthetic and, indeed, contain another parenthesis which is indicated by brackets. But the parenthesis marked by commas is not a true 'aside', since it is still a syntactical part of the sentence. Extreme parenthesis, that is, a phrase or clause independent of the general construction of the sentence, is marked by brackets, particularly in formal and explanatory notes, as used throughout this book for page cross-references. Here is a simple example of a non-formal use: "The second man (the first left without scoring) played well for twenty-three". The best stop for the normal parenthesis, which, though it is an 'aside' or digression, still fits in to the general sentence pattern, is the dash. This is the stop beloved, naturally, of the great digressive writers, like Sterne in *Tristram Shandy* and Lamb in *Elia*:

> I speak not of your grown porkers—things between pig and pork—those hobbydehoys—but a young and tender suckling—under a moon old—guiltless as yet of the sty—with no original speck of the *amor immunditiae*, the

hereditary failing of the first parent, yet manifest—his voice as yet not broken, but something between a childish treble and a grumble—the mild forerunner, or *praeludium* of a grunt.

This inspired stammering is the quintessence of writing, and its punctuation is no casual accident but an integral part of the style. Nevertheless, ordinary men are well advised to use the dash sparingly, though by no means to eschew it altogether. Here, by way of simple example, are two workaday sentences from Board, or Ministry, of Education pamphlets:

Of the names which we have suggested—Grammar School, Modern School and Senior Classes—the first is intended to be applied to schools of the existing 'secondary' type.

Of the other main matter in Section 5—the school's relationship with parents—it is possible to say a little more.

It is a peculiar thing that some writers, when they use dashes, forget to mark the end of the parenthesis:

With living costs more than doubled, with the impoverishment of everybody except the manual worker, the artist's case would only have to be stated—with the irrefutable data of studio-rent, cost of materials and frames, food, heating and lighting, dealers' 33 per cent commission, and it would immediately be recognised that, unless subsidised or protected, *that* particular 'cultural' activity is at an end.

This sentence is, at best, a mere conglomeration of words; but it makes no sense at all unless the comma after *commission* is replaced by a dash.

And here are two notable examples of a bracket-and-dash madness that seems to have no method in it:

The artist's reaction—and it is not only *mine* but that of all artists not in some manner privately protected (and the latter are usually not those with most vitality, since vitality offends) this reaction will probably seem not only impolite but unjust.

The writer is in obvious trouble. He begins one parenthesis
with a dash, ventures on a secondary parenthesis inside
the main one, has to catch his breath by repeating "this
reaction", and forgets entirely to close with a dash his main
parenthesis. Neither, by the way, does he know how to
use the term *latter*, which should have the same 'tight'
relationship as a demonstrative pronoun to its associated
word or antecedent (see page 78).

> Housing and building are to give a future saving—
> provided spending here (as, indeed, elsewhere) does not
> continue to edge upwards—of £70m., but the tangled and
> costly network of housing and allied subsidies will remain
> uncombed.

There is no reason at all for the use of either dashes or
brackets: "Housing and building are to give a future
saving of £70m., provided spending here, as indeed elsewhere . . .". The metaphor at the end might be added
to the little collection on page 205; combing a network is a
queer trade.

Brackets always go in pairs. But a dash can exist in
single blessedness, and then it usually introduces not so
much an 'aside' as a climactic afterthought. It is the sign
of the dramatic pause, and is therefore a particularly
expressive stop, designed to represent a deliberate accent of
the voice or gesture of the body. If the dramatic pause is
not intended, then the normal stop is the comma. We
can, for example, punctuate a famous couplet of Pope in
three different ways, which may be labelled 'neutral',
'expressive', and 'dramatic':

> *Neutral*
> Here thou, great Anna! whom three realms obey,
> Dost sometimes counsel take and sometimes tea.

> *Expressive*
> Here thou, great Anna! whom three realms obey,
> Dost sometimes counsel take, and sometimes tea.

Here, the comma after *take* has ensured just long enough

a pause to check the reader and keep him a little in suspense.

Dramatic
Here thou, great Anna! whom three realms obey,
Dost sometimes counsel take—and sometimes tea.

This is Pope's own punctuation. The dash symbolises a laughing gesture; it is a sign pointing to the joke, the amusing apposition, with its effect of anti-climax, of *counsel* and *tea*.

This suggested classification of pauses answers the familiar question, "Do you put a comma before *and, but, or* when they link two co-ordinating clauses together?" It all depends upon your meaning or intention. "Naaman was a mighty man in valour but he was a leper" is a plain undramatic statement; "Naaman was a mighty man in valour, but he was a leper" is a trifle more dramatic; "Naaman was a mighty man in valour—but he was a leper" deliberately points the dramatic antithesis. Good punctuation should always reflect the writer's mind. Under-punctuation (which is fashionable to-day) throws a great deal of the burden of interpretation on the reader, and sometimes leaves him with obscurities and ambiguities. Over-punctuation has the same effect as unnatural variations of the voice and exaggerated gestures in speaking.

Question and Exclamation

The question mark (?) stands at the end of a direct question:

Had Zimri peace, who slew his master?

If winter comes, can Spring be far behind?

Except when, for effect, it is placed at the end of a series of closely related questions, the question mark has the effect of a full stop—it is followed, that is, by a capital letter.

The exclamation mark (!) should be very sparingly used at the end of complete sentences. Here it often has the effect of forced or facetious emphasis; it is the writer's way of calling the reader's attention to his own clever points or intended jokes. Sentences expressing wonder or surprise, of the pattern

How jocund did they drive their team afield!

How bow'd the woods beneath their sturdy stroke!

are rightly followed by an exclamation mark. But those of the pattern "He actually stopped and spoke to me", "It was indeed a fine day", "I ventured everything—and lost" require nothing more than a full stop; the words *actually* and *indeed*, and the expressive dash in the last sentence supply all the necessary element of surprise or wonder.

The exclamation mark usually follows an isolated and self-contained interjection like *Hurrah!*, *Alas!*, *Oh!*, *Ah!*, *Behold!*; and here it has not the effect of a full stop—that is, it may be, and often is, followed by a small letter. Sometimes even these words are incorporated in the remainder of the sentence, and the exclamation mark is delayed, as in these examples given in the *Rules for Compositors and Readers at the Oxford Press*:[1] "Alas for his poor family!", "Alas, my noble boy!" When *Oh!* thus becomes part of a complete exclamation it is usually spelt *O*, and is not followed by any stop at all: "O for a draught of vintage!"

In general, the exclamation mark is a stop for poetry and rhetorical prose. Except after simple interjections it has little part in ordinary writing. In modern English usage emphasis is effected, not by stops or artifices (like, for example, italics—see page 124), but by the careful and deliberate arrangement of the words, sometimes out of their normal position.

A Counterblast to Quotes

Quotation marks ('quotes') or inverted commas are the most troublesome marks in punctuation; and the irony

[1] Referred to hereafter as *R.C.R.*

of things is that we could easily do without them. In fact, we did until the end of the eighteenth century. There are no quotation marks in the Authorised Version (1611),[1] or Boswell's *Johnson*, or Goldsmith's *The Vicar of Wakefield*. By a simple convention of capital letters (see later, page 130), the following sentence, which contains direct speech inside direct speech, is immediately intelligible:

> And when he came to himself, he said, How many hired servants of my father's have bread enough and to spare, and I perish with hunger! I will arise and go to my father, and will say unto him, Father, I have sinned against heaven and before thee, and am no more worthy to be called thy son.

But written or printed according to our modern convention this sentence breaks out, as it were, into 'punctuatory' measles:

> And when he came to himself he said, "How many hired servants of my father's have bread enough and to spare, and I perish with hunger! I will arise and go to my father, and will say unto him, 'Father, I have sinned against heaven, and before thee, and am no more worthy to be called thy son'."

We have only to glance at this example to realise what a nuisance quotation marks are. One of the simplest and most beneficial reforms in English usage would be their total abolition. They are a nuisance to the writer, who (as we shall see later) is often puzzled to determine their correct relationship with other stops; an irritation to the reader, who does not need them, although he may imagine he does; and both a nuisance and an expense to the compositor. There is not a word to be said for them. "Thou whoreson zed! thou unnecessary letter!" cried the exasperated Kent. "Thou whoreson quote! thou unnecessary

---

[1] It is interesting to note that they are not used in the Revised Version of the Bible (1884), though that appeared long after their introduction.

stop!" might be an appropriate adjuration of the exasperated writer to-day.

However, since they are established in modern usage, it is important that we should conform to the conventions of their use—conventions which have been fixed, in the main, by the great printing and publishing houses. In general, then, quotation marks are exactly what their name proclaims them to be—marks to indicate quotations. In writing and typewriting they are represented by two short strokes ("), and in print by inverted commas (") at the beginning, and normal commas (") at the end of the quotation, the strokes and commas being set on a level with the tops of the letters. Quotations may be from the written language (that is, in the widest sense, literature), as, for example, the numerous sentences quoted in this book from periodicals and pamphlets; or they may be from the spoken language—when we write down, in what is known as direct speech, the actual words of a speaker.

The basic rule for the use of quotation marks in *direct* speech is a very simple one: they are placed immediately before and after the actual words quoted. In sentences where the quotation is single and straightforward only two questions arise: Where are other stops placed in relation to the quotation marks? What are the stops that succeed and precede interpolated explanatory phrases like "he said" and "he asked"? The answer to the first is inside the closing quotation marks;[1] and the answer to the

---

[1] Printing Houses differ on the position of other stops in relation to quotations, from writing or from speech, which are casually introduced into a sentence. Some follow the convention for printing reported speech—that is, place them *inside* the closing quotes. But syntactically and logically, such stops are independent of the quotations; they are guides to the main sentence structure, and should not, therefore, be placed *inside* the closing quotes marking an incorporated word, phrase or clause. In this book, accordingly, they are printed *outside* the closing quotes, as in the following examples:

(Page 8). For an idiomatic phrase, like " to upset the apple cart" or " once in a blue moon", is a natural growth of language.
(Page 12). Andrew Lang said after reading Fowler's *The*

  Continued on next page

second depends upon the syntactical construction of the passage or speech quoted—whether, for example, it is made up of one or of more than one sentence. Here is a short extract from a modern novel (*Summer Lightning* by P. G. Wodehouse) which will illustrate most of the points in the punctuation of direct speech:

> Lady Constance looked over her shoulder.
> "The sky still looks very threatening," she said, "but you might be able to get out for a few minutes. Mr. Baxter," she explained, "is going to show Miss Schoonmaker the rose-garden."
> "No, he isn't," said the Hon. Sir Galahad, who had been scrutinising Sue through his monocle with growing appreciation. "I am. Old Johnny Schoonmaker's little girl—why, there are a hundred things I want to discuss."
> The last thing Sue desired was to be left alone with the intimidating Baxter. She rose quickly.
> "I should love to come," she said.

The main points to be noted are: (i) in the writing of direct speech each speaker has a separate paragraph; (ii) the first piece of direct speech in the above extract illustrates the broken single sentence. There are actually two sentences in this paragraph, spoken by the same speaker, and each broken by an explanatory phrase ("she said", "she explained"). The 'break' is enclosed in commas, like a parenthesis. In older writing it would often be

---

King's English, the predecessor of *Modern English Usage*, that he was "afraid to put pen to paper".

The following sentence (page 34) causes a little difficulty:

Punch's very apt comment was "Stitchwort?"

According to *R.C.R.* no punctuation mark is placed after an enclosed question or exclamation mark at the end of a sentence; that is, here the full stop for the main sentence is omitted. Similarly, if both the quotation at the end of the sentence and the main sentence itself require a question mark or an exclamation mark, one stop is made to do for both, and is placed *inside* the closing quotes:

Did you hear him say "Are we downhearted?"

Logically, there should be another ? *outside* the closing quotes.

actually enclosed in brackets. Diagrammatically, the construction is:

If there were a three-quarter break, there would merely be a semi-colon in place of the second comma. It is important to notice that the quotation marks are closed not at the end of the first sentence, but at the second break, which is in the middle of the next sentence (after *Baxter*); (iii) in the next paragraph the first sentence is finished before the break. Here a comma ends the actual quoted words, a full stop follows the break, and the next sentence begins, with a capital letter, of course, after the full stop—like this:

"——————,"   . "C——————."

(iv) the last piece of direct speech illustrates the completed quotation before the break. This ends with a comma, and the whole sentence (of which the quotation is a part) ends in the usual way with a full stop.

The only ordinary stops illustrated in the above annotated extract are the comma and full stop; but the principle is the same for all other stops used in straightforward direct speech.[1] When a quotation (either from speech or from literature) appears inside a quotation it is usually included in single quotation marks.[2] There is a simple example in the passage quoted from the Authorised Version on page 114. When such a quotation within a quotation

---

[1] The position of the semi-colon and the colon in relation to quotation marks rarely, if ever, arises. If a sentence of direct speech containing a semi-colon or a colon is broken by an explanatory phrase ("he said" etc.) the stop is placed after the phrase:

"It was raining all the afternoon," he said; "so we sat indoors by the fire."

[2] Some printers (and especially the Oxford University Press) use single 'quotes' (' ') for the main speech and double quotes (" ") for any quotation inside it. So the sentence given later would be punctuated like this: 'Do you know the origin of the phrase " the simple annals of the poor"?'

occurs at the end of a sentence the position of the ordinary stops requires some care:

> "Do you know the origin of the phrase 'the simple annals of the poor'?"

Here, the question mark belongs to the whole sentence, and comes outside the single 'quotes' of the interpolated quotation, but inside the main sentence closing 'quotes'. A curious thing happens if the inside quotation happens itself to be a question:

> "Do you know the origin of the phrase 'Who goes home?'"

The question mark of the quotation has to do duty also for the whole sentence. If it did not, we should have the following punctuation: "... home?'?" Compare the rule for casual quotations in the sentence, given in a footnote on page 115. And here, to sum up, is a passage of dialogue from a modern novel (A. G. Macdonell's *England, Their England*):

> Donald hid his perspiring face in his hands. He simply could not bear to watch the public humiliation of a friend. He cursed himself for having come to the meeting, for having come to Eldonborough at all. Now it was beginning—the chairman was asking for questions—the humiliation was about to start—yes, there was the first one—a snorter too.
>
> "Mr. Chairman, when the candidate says he is in favour of work for all, how does he propose to provide it?"
>
> Donald groaned. The very first man had put his finger on one of the vital weaknesses. Sir Henry rose.
>
> "I am very glad indeed that the question has been asked," he said, "and I should like to take this opportunity of thanking the gentleman who asked it, and of congratulating him. Our policy, roughly speaking, is to see that jobs, and adequately paid jobs, are provided at once for everyone." He sat down again amid applause.
>
> Donald gasped. "Good God!" he thought, "they'll start throwing things."
>
> The man who had asked the question rose again.

"Thank you very much," he said, and sat down. Again Donald gasped.

There was only one other question. A fierce-looking young man, wearing a red-and-white handkerchief round his neck, asked aggressively:

"Mr. Chairman, I should like to know what the candidate's policy is about housing."

Sir Henry rose, thanked the gentleman who had asked the question, and congratulated him, and stated that his policy was to get the maximum number of houses built at the minimum cost in the shortest possible time.

The fierce-looking young man thanked the candidate, and the meeting diffused itself into votes of thanks, resolutions of confidence, and the National Anthem.

The dashes in the third sentence represent the pauses in a broken speech of what might be called running commentary. Note that the first passage of actual direct speech is introduced without any explanatory clause ("he said", "he asked"). This is common practice, especially in novels, where the speaker can be identified without difficulty or doubt. The last piece of dialogue follows a colon at the end of an introductory paragraph.

Indirect Speech

In the last sentence of the foregoing extract the writer has slipped from direct speech into indirect speech—that is, instead of quoting the actual words of the speaker he reports them in words of his own. This sentence in direct speech would read:

> Sir Henry rose. "I thank the gentleman who asked the question," he said, "and congratulate him. My policy is to get the maximum number of houses built at the minimum cost in the shortest possible time."

The process of turning direct into indirect speech is very familiar in both speaking and writing. There is no fundamental difficulty about it. We do it every day, without any conscious effort, in ordinary conversation. A says to B: "Will you be going to the dance to-night?" B reports this to C like this: "A asked me if I was going to the dance to-night." C reports it to D like this: "A asked B if he was going to the dance to-night."

This simple example illustrates all the main points in the process. First, the person of the pronoun changes, according to the identity of the reporter. If the reporter is the person spoken to, the pronoun changes from second to first; if he is a third person, the person changes from second to third. Second, the direct question (indicated by the question mark) becomes indirect, object of the verb *asked*, and there is no question mark. Third, the verb goes backwards in time (that is, tense), because naturally speech can be reported only after it was originally spoken. Last, the reported words are not enclosed in quotation marks, since they are not, in fact, actual words quoted. This point cannot be clearly brought out in the three sentences given as illustrations above; but it is quite clear in the punctuation of the last sentence (already noted) of the passage on page 119.

One or two minor points arise. We have already seen what happens when a direct question becomes indirect, after a verb of asking. Similarly, a direct statement may become indirect, after a verb like *said, stated*:

"I shall not be living here much longer," he said.
He said that he would not be living there much longer.

And the direct imperative becomes an infinitive in indirect speech after a verb like *told, commanded*:

"Stand over there!" said the teacher.
The teacher told him to stand over there.

Some adverbs of place, especially *here*, and adverbs of time, especially *now*, change according to the meaning and context. There is an example in which *here* becomes *there* in the sentences illustrating the indirect statement above. Similarly, the direct "I now decided to look for another post" becomes indirect "He then decided to look for another post". There is no rule about this change.

The speaker or writer will make it, without any undue anxious thought, where it is necessary.

The major problem is the inevitable confusion of pronouns when those which are first and second person in direct all become third in indirect speech. We are apt to get an abundance of differently related *he*'s and *him*'s. Little can be done about it. Sometimes it is possible to repeat the original noun at intervals; and now and then it is necessary to resort to the ugly device of elucidating a pronoun by appending it to its noun in brackets: "He (the speaker) said that he (the listener) owed him a shilling". But on the whole the writer of indirect speech has to rely on the sense of the reader. The speaker can clarify the pronouns by intonations of voice and by gestures; the writer has to give such explanatory aid as is possible.

Here, for example, is a piece of direct speech. It is the retort of the King of Brobdingnag to Gulliver ('Grildrig') after Gulliver, in a series of interviews, had been singing the praises of his "own dear England". The punctuation is modernised. As explained on page 114, there are no quotation marks in the original text; and in certain other details the original punctuation differs from that of modern English:

> His majesty, in another audience, was at the pains to recapitulate the sum of all I had spoken; compared the questions he made with the answers I had given; then, taking me into his hands, and stroking me gently, delivered himself in these words, which I shall never forget, nor the manner he spoke them in: "My little friend Grildrig, you have made a most admirable panegyric upon your country; you have clearly proved that ignorance, idleness, and vice are the proper ingredients for qualifying a legislator; that laws are best explained, interpreted, and applied by those whose interest and abilities lie in perverting, confounding, and eluding them. I observe among you some lines of an institution which, in its original, might have been tolerable, but these half-erased, and the rest wholly blurred and blotted by corruptions. It doth not appear, from all you have said, how any one virtue is required towards the

procurement of any one station among you; much less, that men are ennobled on account of their virtue; that priests are advanced for their piety or learning; soldiers for their conduct or valour; judges for their integrity; senators for the love of their country; or counsellors for their wisdom. As for yourself," continued the king, "who have spent the greatest part of your life in travelling, I am well disposed to hope you may hitherto have escaped many vices of your country. But, by what I have gathered from your own relation, and the answers I have with much pains wringed and extorted from you, I cannot but conclude the bulk of your natives to be the most pernicious race of little odious vermin that nature ever suffered to crawl upon the surface of the earth."

And here is the same passage written in indirect speech:

He told Grildrig that he had made a most admirable panegyric upon his country. He had clearly proved that ignorance, idleness, and vice were the proper ingredients for qualifying a legislator; that laws were best explained, interpreted, and applied by those whose interests and abilities lie (or lay) in perverting, confounding, and eluding them. The king observed among them some lines of an institution which in its original might have been tolerable, but those half-erased, and the rest wholly blurred and blotted by corruptions. It did not appear from all Grildrig had said how any one perfection was required towards the procurement of any one station among them; much less that men were ennobled on account of their virtue, that priests were advanced for their piety or learning, soldiers for their conduct or valour, judges for their integrity, senators for the love of their country, or counsellors for their wisdom. As for Grildrig himself, who had spent the greatest part of his life in travelling, the King was well disposed to hope he might hitherto have escaped many vices of his country. But by what he had gathered from Grildrig's own relation, and the answers he had with much pain wringed and extorted from him, he could not but conclude the bulk of their natives to be the most pernicious race of little odious vermin that Nature ever suffered to crawl upon the face of the earth.

The nouns *Grildrig* and *King* are used at intervals in order to clarify the pronouns. It is important to note that expressions like "he went on to say" are not necessary as long as the report consists of indirect statement; for example, the parenthesis "continued the King" of the direct speech is ignored in the indirect. But when indirect statement turns into indirect question or indirect command expressions like "he asked", "he told" must be introduced to indicate the change:

> *Direct*
> "I am so glad to see you," she said. "When will you be coming again?"

> *Indirect*
> She said she was very glad to see him, and asked him when he would be coming again.

Punctuation of Quotations and Titles

Quotations from literature are enclosed in quotation marks and are incorporated into the normal structure of the sentence.[1] When the quotation consists of more than one line of verse it should be written in verse form; and since it is obviously a quotation the quotation marks may be omitted. Sometimes the punctuation of the quoted passage, especially at the end, has to give way to the punctuation of the sentence itself:

> In the much quoted lines,
>
> > "Brightness falls from the air,
> > Queens have died young and fair,
> > Dust hath closed Helen's eye",
>
> all that is said, on the surface, is an old truism; you might excusably say that Nashe was putting a commonplace badly.[2]

[1] See footnote on page 115.

[2] In the book from which this is taken (C. E. Montague's *A Writer's Notes on his Trade*) quotation marks are not used for the quoted passage. They are inserted here for the sake of illustration.

After the word *eye* there is a full-stop in the poem. This is omitted in the quotation, and the comma *after* the closing quotation marks belongs to the sentence structure.

Words or phrases which are used in an unusual or particular sense are often enclosed in quotation marks. In this book single marks are used. There are examples on pages 62, 79, 107.

Quotation marks, either single or double, are sometimes used to indicate book titles, names of ships, etc.: T. S. Eliot's "Murder in the Cathedral", Herrick's "To Daffodils", the return of the "Amethyst". But it is better to relieve them of this duty, and italicise[1] the titles or names instead: T. S. Eliot's *Murder in the Cathedral*, Herrick's *To Daffodils*, the return of the *Amethyst*. Articles (*a, an, the*) are usually in practice, incorporated into the body of the sentence, and not included in the title. We write "Have you seen the *Daily Telegraph* to-day?" rather than ". . . seen *The Daily Telegraph* . . .".[2]

In the following sentence from the *Times Educational Supplement* the writer has fallen between two stools:

[1] Underlining in writing is the equivalent of italics in print. The use of underlining (that is, italicising) should normally be restricted to the indication of titles, etc., as explained in this paragraph, and to the indicating of particular words for the reader's benefit, as is the practice throughout this book. Underlining (that is, italicising) to indicate emphasis should be used very sparingly, and with very definite purpose. There is an example of it in the text of this book (page 11), where the word *exactly* is deliberately italicised for emphasis.

[2] It is a convention that *The Times* should always be given its article (not 'the *Times*' or *Times*), and it is a pity that this convention is not followed for other titles beginning with *The*. But this matter of articles in titles has complications, since the articles are often used elliptically. Thus, "Have you a *Daily Telegraph*?" means "Have you a copy of *The Daily Telegraph*?" "A. E. Housman wrote the *Shropshire Lad*" means "A. E. Housman wrote the poem called *A Shropshire Lad*". No one would advocate writing or saying "Have you a *The Daily Telegraph*?" or "A. E. Housman wrote the *A Shropshire Lad*". Indeed, in this elliptical usage even the august *The Times* has to lose its article: "Have you a *Times* to spare this morning?"

Mr. Robert Gathorne-Hardy's *Recollections* of Logan Pearsall Smith cover a period of 18 years, the last and least lovely of his friend's life.

The title of the book is *Recollections of Logan Pearsall Smith*; it should be written so, and the verb agreeing with it should be singular, *covers* (see page 20). But he really intended *Recollections* to be an ordinary common noun, not part of a title. He should therefore have written it without italics, and preferably with a small initial letter. His verb would then be correctly plural: "Mr. Gathorne-Hardy's recollections of Logan Pearsall Smith cover . . ."

The Apostrophe s

There are two marks in writing which do not belong to punctuation proper—the apostrophe (') and the hyphen (-). The apostrophe always indicates the omission of a letter, or letters, in a word. It is most familiar with s ('s, s') in the possessive of nouns and of certain pronouns. Here it represents, in the singular, the *e* in the old original possessive suffix *-es*; the plural is not derived from the Old English form, but is merely an artificial variant of the singular.

The rule for what is commonly, if loosely, called 'the apostrophe *s*' is surprisingly simple. In the singular, 's is added to the singular form of the noun: *dog—dog's*; *lady—lady's*; *hero—hero's*. When a noun ends in s in the plural (as 99.8 per cent of English nouns do) an apostrophe is added after that s: *dogs'*; *ladies'*; *heroes'*. When a noun does not end in s in the plural, 's is added to the plural form: *men's*; *children's*; *sheep's*. It is important to remember that if a singular noun ends in s, the apostrophe s is nevertheless added to it, following the normal rule: *Dickens's*, not *Dickens'* (which looks like a plural) and certainly not *Dicken's*, which would mean 'of Dicken'. Similarly, *Keats's*, not *Keats'*, and certainly not *Keat's*. Only classical names ending in s (*Brutus, Perseus, Thucydides*) tend to break this rule; but it is better, in practice, to keep the rule intact and write 'of Brutus', 'of Thucydides', rather than *Brutus'*, *Thucydides'*. In fact, whenever the apostrophe *s* would lead to awkward cacophony the '*of* + noun' construction is preferable.

There is a laudable tendency in modern usage to omit the apostrophe, especially in plural nouns, where the nouns are adjectival without any real possessive sense: 'Womens Institute' 'Boys School', 'Students Union', 'Miners Federation'.

Certain pronoun possessive forms ending in *s* have no apostrophe: *hers, ours, yours, its, theirs*. Nobody knows why; but the fact remains that it is so. Others that make the possessive with the *s* suffix behave like nouns; and as they are all singular, the apostrophe always comes before the *s*: *one's, everybody's, anybody's* (but, for example, 'of all', 'of each').

In words where there is elision the apostrophe takes the place of the letter or letters actually omitted: *doesn't* (for 'does not'), *it's* (for 'it is'), *o'er* (for *over*). *Won't* is the contraction for 'will not' and *shan't* for 'shall not'. There are many words in England that are, in fact, beheaded or curtailed forms of longer words, but have no apostrophe to indicate the omission of letters; they have established themselves as complete words. A good modern example of these is *bus* (for *omnibus*) which up to a few years ago was normally written and printed *'bus*. But in current English usage *omnibus* is an archaic word, *'bus* is a misspelling, and *bus* is correct in its own right.

The apostrophe is almost as big a nuisance as quotation marks. But it has established itself in English, and there seems to be no way of our getting rid of it now. Bernard Shaw has tried by precept and example; but as yet in vain. The conventions of printers, which for some odd reason always tend to make difficult what could be perfectly simple, are too strong for him and for all of us.

Technical, as distinct from colloquial, curtailments ("good huntin' and shootin'") are indicated by what printers call a full point, and ordinary people a full stop. Some representative examples, suggested by the list in *R.C.R.*, are given:

Exod. (for Exodus)	*lb.*	*St.*
Sept.	*oz.*	*Bt.* or *Bart.*
Yorks.[1]	(both sing. and	*Co.*
	plur. — never	*Ltd.*
	lbs. and *ozs.*)	*Esq.*
	Mr./Mrs.	

Contractions represented by initial letters have always had a place in the language, and many new ones have developed in recent years largely owing to the influence of the two wars and the development of the committee-ridden Welfare State. The conventional way of 'punctuating' such contractions is to put a full stop or period after each initial letter concerned, the letters themselves being capitals: *B.B.C.* (British Broadcasting Corporation), *L.M.S.R.* (London Midland and Scottish Railway), *N.F.S.* (National Fire Service). But the habit of making, where possible, 'words' out of the initials, like *DORA* or *Dora* (Defence of the Realm Act) and *CEMA* or *Cema* (Council for Education in Music and the Arts), has encouraged a tendency to get rid of the stops even in initial contractions that do not make 'words'—to write *BBC*, *LMSR*, and *NFS*. It is likely and desirable that in the end the unpunctuated form will prevail; already *BBC* (not *B.B.C.*) has established itself in the *Radio Times*. But the process is likely to be a slow one, since in this as in other points of language an established convention is strong.

Contractions of (chiefly Latin) phrases, where the initials are sometimes written in small letters, are always punctuated—*A.D.* ('Anno Domini'), *P.S.* ('Post Scriptum'), *i.e.* ('id est'), *e.g.* ('exempli gratia'), *s.v.* ('sub verbo'), *p.m.* ('post meridiem'). Note, however, *MS.* (with one

[1] *R.C.R.* says that *Hants* should have no full stop since it is an old contraction.

full stop only), where the contraction is made up of two letters in a single compound word (*manuscript*). The plural is *MSS*.

Fowler, in *Modern English Usage* (s.v. Period), tried to establish a custom by which the full point (or stop) was not used when the last letter of the complete word survived in the contraction: thus he advocated *Mr* for *Mister*, *Thos* for *Thomas*, *bot.* for *botany* and *bot* for *bought*. But he had no better luck than Bernard Shaw.

The Hyphen Puzzle

Hyphens are puzzling things. Indeed, there are few rules, or even customs, to guide us. Fowler says: "The chaos prevailing among writers and printers or both regarding the use of hyphens is discreditable to English education"; but the article of which this is the opening sentence is so learned that only those erudite in the *minutiae* of language could be expected to master it. Do we write *headmaster, head master* or *head-master*? Fowler says categorically *headmaster*, "the accent being on the second element". *R.C.R.* says the same. But, oddly enough, the *Shorter Oxford Dictionary* gives only, in this order, *head master* and *head-master;* it does not recognise Fowler's or *R.C.R.*'s *headmaster* at all. Neither does *Chambers*'s (1943), which gives only *head-master*. The printers and some dictionaries say *to-day, to-morrow*: but, as Fowler says, "few people ever dream of inserting the hyphen". It only remains, "a very singular piece of conservatism", because its "omission is corrected every time by those who profess the mystery of printing".

On the occurrence or non-occurrence of hyphens in normal compound words, therefore, this book has nothing to say—for the reason that the writer, as distinct from the printer (who must follow his own mysterious rules) can do very much as he likes about it. The following examples taken from one issue of the *Observer*, most of them from one article, are given for the curious reader to adjudicate upon: "to commit a *revenge-murder*", "a book for *study-reading*", "the best *star-part*", *star-players*, *title-role*, *guest-house*, "a *last-war* interlude", *double-crossed*, "a *tucked-away* Civil Servant", "a *once-dashing* youth", "wild *winter-weather*", "the *street-corner* blast", *deer-forests*, "myriads in *holiday-camps*". One thing, however, must be said. Associated words which are otherwise unhyphened gain a hyphen (or hyphens) when they are used as attributive adjectives. *R.C.R.* gives the example "out-of-date (or up-to-date) records"; but "the records are out of date". Here are three examples of a forgotten hyphen:

> The ingredients of comedy, of romance, and of first rate theatre. (*first-rate*)

> The first night audience. (*first-night*)

> Mrs. Bradford gives common sense and understanding advice to young mothers. (*common-sense*—unless the reviewer means that she was giving (i) common sense and (ii) advice.)

This fourth example is separated from the others only because the associated words are not obviously, although they are in fact, attributive:

> It is probably the most sought after of the colleges. (*most-sought-after*)

That care has to be taken with the more complicated hyphenated expressions the following examples (the first three from Fowler) will show: "fellow-Free Churchmen", "the mid-nineteenth century politicians", "ex-Chief Whip", "unself-conscious", "a well-looked after ruin", "Grammar Schoolboy". The distribution of the hyphens should be as follows: "fellow Free Churchmen", "the mid-nineteenth-century politicians", "ex-Chief-Whip", "unselfconscious", "a well-looked-after ruin", "Grammar-School boy". *R.C.R.* gravely advises printers that, to avoid ambiguity, the phrase "bad printers' errors" should be given a hyphen in the appropriate place: "bad printers-errors".

Hyphens are used for convenience to show the broken vowel in such words as *re-enter, co-ordinate, co-operate*, where *ree-, coo-* would be misleading. They also point an artificial *ad hoc* distinction: *recover* (from illness) but *re-cover*[1] an umbrella, *recreation* (that is, 'leisure pastime') but *re-creation* of an atmosphere. *Punch* recently quoted a sentence in which an omitted hyphen has made havoc of the sense:

> Members of the Lancashire County Cricket Club committee debated far beyond their usual time in Manchester this afternoon, but the only official information coming from the secretary, Mr. Geoffrey Howard, at the conclusion of the meeting was the fact that young Johnny Kelly, the club's young batsman from Bacup, has been freed to negotiate terms with Somerset. All the other professionals have resigned.

Luckily for Lancashire the professionals have *re-signed*; and "the mood of restrained optimism . . . said to be reigning in Yorkshire" (*Punch*) is unjustified.

Capitals

Closely bound up with punctuation is the use of capital letters. Here again we are in a somewhat vague, indeterminate world. The capital which marks the beginning of a sentence, or of a sentence within a sentence, has already been considered. In older writing most nouns were written with an initial capital. But capitals are now reserved for proper nouns—in general, the names of persons and places and, usually, the adjectives derived from them: *Clement, Churchill, England* (*English*), *Westminster, America* (*American*). In English (though not in French) the names of the months and of the days of the week are written with capitals: *January, September, Tuesday*—but

---

[1] Shakespeare has the distinction without the hyphens in a typical play on words: "I am, indeed, sir, a surgeon to old shoes; when they are in great danger, I *recover* them."—*Julius Caesar*, i. I.

not usually the names of the seasons: *summer, winter.*
Nouns representing personified abstractions usually have a
capital, especially in verse:

> Or pining *Love* shall waste their youth,
> Or *Jealousy* with rankling tooth
>   That inly gnaws the secret heart,
> And *Envy* wan, and faded *Care,*
> Grim-visaged comfortless *Despair,*
>   And *Sorrow's* piercing dart.

But outside these fairly well-defined limits, the writer
has to walk warily in a kind of no-man's-land. Certain
adjectives derived from proper nouns have become so
'common' and familiar that they are spelt with small
letters: *Jove—jovial, Saturn—saturnine, Lilliput—lilliputian.*
Titles, when they are used formally, have a capital: *Mr.*
Churchill, the *Duke* of Edinburgh, C. Lamb, *Esq., Lady*
Clare; but when they do not relate to any particular
person the nouns *duke, squire, lady* and the rest may be,
and often are, written without the capital. Common nouns
often take on proper status when they have a particular,
as distinct from a general, significance, and also when
they are associated, in a phrase with proper nouns; and
adjectives that qualify such nouns usually follow suit: the
Earth (as a planet), *Ash Wednesday, Lancashire County
Cricket Club, Daily Telegraph, War Office, Blood Transfusion
Service.* In titles the first word always has a capital; but
after that, conjunctions, prepositions and articles are
written with small letters: *A Tale of Two Cities, The
Cloister and the Hearth, The Lord of the Isles, Far from the
Madding Crowd.*

These are, of course, mere guiding rules. The good writer
will observe the main conventions; but beyond these he has
the privilege and responsibility of deciding between what
printers call "upper and lower case"—capitals and small
letters. His use of capitals, like his punctuation generally,
should exactly correspond with his meaning.

FIRST INTERLUDE FOR ENTERTAINMENT

The following collection of sentences and passages is made for the curious reader who appreciates and enjoys the subtleties as well as the more obvious points of construction, expression and syntax; and the comments are designed not only to explain (where necessary) the errors, but also to elaborate (where possible) the principles referred to in the preceding pages.

First, here are four quite simple sentences in which the writer has forgotten towards the end of the sentence the basic construction of the beginning. They are all of the cumulative, rather than the complex type; that is, of the general pattern:

$$\underline{S \quad P} + \underline{S \quad P} + \underline{S \quad P} + \underline{S \quad P}$$

In no one of them is the fault syntactically serious. They merely illustrate, in even the simplest patterns, the effect of a loose connection between thought and expression:

1. This Mr. Gathorne-Hardy has done here with grace, skill and (if we except the last third where he tells us either too much or too little) with a nice sense of design.

The long parenthesis makes the writer forget that his original *with* was outside the bracket—*with* $(a+b+c)$—and he wrongly puts it inside before the last term: "*with* a nice sense".

2. The ugliness, the lack of manners, style, dignity and courtesy, these are the aspects of democracy that he sees.

Theoretically a sound sentence, but it promises more than it performs. The very phrase "these are the aspects" implies that several aspects have been enumerated; but in fact there are only two—the *ugliness* and the *lack*. The writer deceives himself and tries to deceive the reader into believing that *manners, style, dignity* and *courtesy* are all 'aspects', which, of course, they are not. In mathematical terms, his intended construction was "$a+b+c+d+e+f$ ... these are ...". His actual construction, however, is "$a+b\ (e+d+e+f)$ ... these are ...", and it leaves the reader a trifle disappointed after the fine flourish of the opening.

> 3. Archaeologists go and dig, modern linguists go abroad and listen, entomologists catch insects, and even for the classicist Italy and Greece are sources comparable with the Ashmolean and Fitzwilliam Museums.

The fourth clause obviously breaks the pattern fixed by the first three. But it would have been quite easy, and certainly more effective, for the writer to end as he began: "and even classicists find Italy and Greece to be sources comparable with the Ashmolean and Fitzwilliam Museums".

> 4. The very phrasing of them suggests that Shakespeare was a man acquainted with every height and depth, every sunlit meadow and every foul morass, every greenwood and every slum in the globe of human experience and in his greatest work he used this mingled material to noble and lovely purposes.

Here is a more subtle point. If the last clause ("and in his ...") is intended to be the second object of *suggests*, either the *he* should be omitted or, if it is retained, the conjunction *that* should be repeated: that is, the clause should run "and in his greatest work used" or "and that in his greatest work he used". As it stands, the clause may be (and probably is intended to be) taken as a comment of the writer's, independent of what is suggested by the "very phrasing". A mere trifle—but the pattern of the sentence is upset a little, and there is a suspicion of ambiguity.

Such looseness and inconsistency is emphasised in sentences of a more elaborate construction:

5. Group I was to consider the opportunities and
status of the teacher as they are or might be, and the
qualities he should possess. Group II was concerned with the teacher's freedom, with the nature
and limits of his office; the third with his relations to
other groups, such as the trade union movement;
while the fourth group was to consider the most
effective preparation for a teacher.

This writer has given no attention to the economies of
language. The result is he has not only wasted words but
also failed to achieve any pattern in his sentence, which,
properly constructed, would run:

Group I was to consider the opportunities and status
of the teacher, as they are or might be, and the qualities
he should possess, Group II the teacher's freedom, with
the nature and limits of his office, Group III his relations
to other groups, such as the Trades Union movement,
and Group IV the most effective preparation possible for
him.

The unnecessary repetition of the verb ("was concerned
with", "was to consider"), the foolish variation "Group
I—Group II—the third—the fourth group" (a sure sign of a
careless or muddled writer), and the redundant *while*
introducing the last clause are all eliminated. Now the
sentence has the 'shape' which the writer seems at the
beginning to intend, and afterwards almost wantonly
destroys.

6. There seem to be three main motives for this reform;
it is thought that knowledge of this kind is valuable
in itself and enables one to live a "fuller life"; it is
thought that it would produce better citizens, more
deliberate and responsible democrats; and, thirdly,
some industrialists believe it would produce better
employees and that production would go up; that
the good engineer or salesman must be more than a
master of his job.

This passage is almost past praying for. No *motives* are, in fact, stated or defined; and since the writer himself gives no real clue to them, it is better to replace *motives* by the less specific word *reasons*. Then substitute a colon for a semi-colon after *reform*, and make the three reasons subordinate to the general statement "it is thought". Deleting the second "it is thought", we accept the sentence as it stands down to *democrats*. After that, the original is so confused that we can only reconstruct it like this: "and, third, that it would produce better employees, who must be more than master of their job, and that production would go up". To make the expression even more precise insert *first, second, third* in the appropriate places: "it is thought, first, that . . .", "second, that . . .", "third, that . . .".

7. It is noticeable that proper celebration of the feast has coincided with a musical awakening of the nation, though to assign a causal connexion one way or the other would imply a view about the efficacy of saintly patronage.

   The chronicled events of St. Cecilia's life make little or no mention of music. A Roman maiden, her story seems to have been told in glorification of the virginal life. But though her taste for earthly music may not have developed until she had practiced the celestial mode, which, no doubt, suggested to her

   That we on earth with undiscording voice
   May rightly answer that melodious noise

   she has proved a most worthy patroness and successor to the Muse.

This is merely careless, indifferent writing. It is impossible to understand what is meant by "a causal connexion *one way or the other*"; and the stated implication is equally obscure. Probably *view* should be qualified by an epithet like *favourable*; at any rate, it should be followed by the preposition *of* not *about*. The next sentence is basically unsound. Its subject should be *chronicle* not *events* ("The

135

chronicle of the events . . . makes"). In the following sentence there is an interesting example of the 'hanging' phrase in apposition (see page 27). "A Roman maiden" can only be in apposition to *she* or *Saint Cecilia*, certainly not to "her story". It is hardly to be wondered at that after all this the writer cannot distinguish between *practice* and *practise* (see page 184).

> 8. Even to pick up Coleridge's collected poetical works is to have proof that his life was not one of indolence and his poetical works mark only a small part of his achievement and the one to which he himself paid least concern. Livingston Lowes in *The Road to Xanadu* showed what a wealth of reading lay behind that miniature miracle of a poem *The Ancient Mariner*, and the picture of Coleridge that we should have is one who whatever might have been the state of his ill-health or however much he might have been indulging in opium, continued to read and to contemplate and to believe that men of goodwill could ultimately put a better face upon the world.

There are three chief comments to be made on this passage;

(a) In the first sentence the three *ands* are the trouble. The sentence should be reconstructed in some such way as this: ". . . is to have proof that his life was not one of indolence and that his poetical works mark only a small part of his achievement—the part to which he himself paid least concern".

(b) "the picture of Coleridge . . . is one who . . .". It is possible there is a misprint here, as *one* (=picture) can hardly be the antecedent of *who*; but it is more likely that the writer did not check the balance of his equation, and so allowed himself to write nonsense. The insertion of *of* before *one* will put the matter right, except that a comma is necessary after *who*.

(c) There are two examples of mixed idiom:

(i) "to which he himself paid least concern": the idiom is "pay *heed/attention* to", never "pay *concern*". Amend—"with which he least concerned himself" or "to which he paid least attention".

(ii) "could ultimately put a better face upon the world": "to put a *good/brave/better* face upon things" is an idiom meaning in general "to face things with courage and hope". But that is not what the writer means here: he means "could ultimately reform the world".

There is also a curious confusion in the expression "whatever might have been the state of his ill-health". Why not simply "the state of his health", or "however ill he might have been"?

The following sentence from the same article shows again the strange inability of the writer to correlate thought and expression:

9. It is interesting to contrast the difficulty of making one's way through the entangled thicket of Coleridge's contemplations in this volume with the comparative ease of the witty and lucid narrative of Bertrand Russell in the *History of Western Philosophy*.

He is contrasting unlike terms—the *reader's* difficulty with the *writer's* ease; so his sentence, though apparently sound, actually makes nonsense. Amend: "with the comparative ease of reading (or "of making one's way through") the narrative of Bertrand Russell".

10. The audience is encouraged to shout and sing as loudly as it likes. I believe it is this identification of the audience that makes one come home from Benjamin Britten's *Let's Make an Opera* at the Lyric so much more satisfied than one ever is after the merely passive enjoyment of any show. Watching, I realised how passionately the audience enjoyed being made to sing quite difficult music. They really

felt that they both understood a bit more how an opera was being made, and had taken part in its creation. I think if I were a musician or a producer today, I would start with the assumption that the audience have become much more educated about music, and that the certain road to success is to make them feel that they are, to some degree, performers.

This is loose and sloppy English. To begin with, the *audience* in the first sentence is almost ostentatiously singular ("as loudly as it likes"), but the writer forgets that by the time the audience crops up again, and then he replaces *it* with *they* and *them*, giving it (or rather, them), of course, a plural verb. "Identification of the audience" is difficult: identification with what? The word used absolutely like this can only mean the identifying of the audience by, say, a policeman or a detective; but it is clear the writer does not mean that. Towards the end of the same sentence *ever* should be *usually* and *any* should be *a*. In the last sentence there are four minor faults:

(i) superfluous comma after *today* (see page 106).

(ii) "educated *about*" for "educated *in*".

(iii) *would* for *should* ("I think I *should* start"—see page 29).

(iv) "*to* some degree" for "*in* some degree".

11. Their task has perhaps been easy in Berks and Bucks, neither of which have, for instance, a great cathedral city, but give the opportunity, grasped eagerly, of presenting the little-known attractively.

There are two faults here, one obvious and one more subtle. The obvious one is the disagreement between subject and verb—*neither* (singular) and *have* (plural). The more subtle one arises because the writer has forgotten, or never realised, that the verb *give* requires a different subject: "*neither . . . had*", "*both . . . give*".

12. Plain living and high thinking is an explanation of superior stature that fits in with the present Minister of Food having been nourished at Magdalen, but, looking back into the past, it is seen to leave some awkward gaps.

The writer has made a brave, but vain, effort to correlate three ideas in as brief and concise a sentence as possible:

(a) Plain living and high thinking make people tall.

(b) The Minister of Food is tall and was nourished at Magdalen, a college famous for plain living and high thinking.

(c) Nevertheless, our past experience is that plain living and high thinking leave awkward gaps (in diet?).

Unfortunately, the writer has achieved

(i) a disagreement of verb and subject.[1]

(ii) a false equation ("plain living and high thinking" =an explanation).

(iii) a doubtful gerund or fused participle (page 53), and

(iv) a false relationship of the participle phrase.

Only drastic treatment will avail:

The statement that plain living and high thinking make people tall fits in with the fact that the present Minister of Food was nourished at Magdalen, but our own past experience teaches us that they leave some awkward gaps.

13. It is a thousand pities that the public is not encouraged to read essays and impressions and short portraits. The painter is permitted to choose his own frame; the writer has a huge one forced on him. Thus, instead of the reader being able to pick up a book containing half a dozen portraits he is com-

[1] Unless, of course, we argue that "plain living and high thinking" is the expression of a single idea, and therefore may be singular.

pelled to read a whole volume devoted to one person alone, irrespective of whether the sitter would not be far better off exhibited in short space. This is one of the most maddening aspects of modern publishing.

First, the writer embarrasses himself with the mild 'portrait' metaphor. We are never quite sure whether the portrait is an actual picture or a short biography. The other troubles are:

(i) fused participle (see page 53): "instead of the reader being able".

(ii) the 'irrespective' construction. If this is used at all, the formula "irrespective of" must be followed by the statement of a fact, not of an implied supposition; or, to put it another way, "irrespective of whether . . ." is not English. Amend—"irrespective of the fact that the sitter would be better off . . .".

(iii) The *this* of the last sentence is a singularly vague demonstrative (page 78).

14. One could not possibly find a better example of the opposite style than in the collected works of Roy Campbell, both in his lyrics and his satires. Here is a poet whose immense stride of language, and whose power, derives from the vitality of his verbs. They are transitive, masculine verbs which drive his verses hard, yet control and knit them together, like a cowboy and his herd.

Here is a writer who having designed a particular type of sentence deliberately (as it seems) spoils his own design. Thus the construction of the first sentence is wrecked by a couple of intrusive *in*'s: the example actually *is* (not, is *in*) the "collected works, both his lyrics and his satires". The second sentence contains a false agreement (double subject, $a+b$, singular verb), and a well-meant repetition of *whose*, which, together with the commas, could have been avoided by a trifling revision:—"whose power and immense stride of language derive".[1]   Finally, in the last sentence there is a simile so loosely related that far from interpreting it obscures the meaning.   Yet the correction is simple: "as a cowboy drives his herd".

What special virtue is there, by the way, in a *transitive* verb? The writer probably means *active*, if indeed he means anything at all.

[1] Admittedly there is a trifling ambiguity—but for once it has to be condoned in the interests of neatness.

CHAPTER IV

JARGON, CLICHÉ AND FIGURE

> "I can conceive that after what occurred in New York it might
> be distressing for you to encounter Miss Stoker, sir. But I
> fancy the contingency need scarcely arise."
> I weighed this.
> "When you start talking about contingencies arising,
> Jeeves, the brain seems to flicker and I rather miss the gist.
> Do you mean that I ought to be able to keep out of
> her way?"
> "Yes, sir."
> P. G. WODEHOUSE: *Thank You, Jeeves.*

Case and its Understudies

Sir Arthur Quiller-Couch, lecturing to his Cambridge
students about thirty years ago, said this: "Whenever
in your reading you come across one of these words, *case,
instance, character, nature, condition, persuasion, degree*—
whenever in writing your pen betrays you to one or other
of them—pull yourself up and take thought." It is, in
some ways, a rather exaggerated and even foolish recommendation—not worthy of the lecturer at his best. But
any writer or lecturer on Jargon, as he was, is (as we say)
batting on a sticky wicket; and Sir Arthur in this particular
lecture does not, to sustain the figure, bat as well as usual.
The fault, however, is in the subject, which is apt to lead
writers on language into all kinds of unguarded statements
and downright errors, and, worse still, into a series of
fundamental heresies, which we shall touch upon later in
this chapter.

But to return to Sir Arthur's solemn warning. The
words he quotes, like every other word that is not a mere
relic or archaism, have their proper uses. They also have
their dangers; that is to say, they can be used in contexts
where they are superfluous and indeterminate, or even

false, in meaning. Quiller-Couch singles out the word *case* for special dishonourable mention; and Fowler gives three columns to a recital of the iniquities of a word which, he says, more than any other word is "resorted to as a trouble-saver, and is consequently responsible for so much flabby writing". Still, Fowler admits and illustrates its legiti-mate uses—*a law case, put a case, in any case, meet the case, in case of . . . , hospital case, a case of measles*—in which there is present the etymological meaning of the word, 'a thing that befalls or happens' (Latin *casus*, from *cadere*, 'to fall'). But in all the following sentences, except the first, the word *case* is open either to condemnation or to suspicion. Neces-sary notes are added to each sentence.

> The suggestion that with a longer term there should be fewer tutorials does not meet the case.

> In suitable cases Germans are to be allowed to pay short visits to relatives or friends in this country.

Punch quotes the second of the above sentences from an evening paper and comments: "This Side Up". The writer means, "Germans who satisfy the authorities", and this (or something like it) is what he should have written.

> More than twice as many boys of 18 today have passed the Higher School Certificate examination than was the case ten years ago.

You can see the poor writer trying to finish the sum, wondering exactly what should follow *than*, and falling back weakly and lazily on *case*. He could have gone on, quite simply, ". . . as passed it ten years ago", and only the last-ditcher among pedants would raise an eyebrow.

> I have suggested that there is one zone where we have not seen the specific work that we would have liked—and that is in the case of the ordinary normal child, the primary and secondary school pupil.

The writer was afraid to go on in what was, in fact, the only way open to him: "and that is the zone of the ordinary normal child . . .". Certainly, the expression is queer; but if he begins with *zone* he must end with *zone*. To fly to "in the case of . . ." is rank cowardice.

> It is clear that, except in a very small number of cases, candidates who could not pass school certificate would not qualify at the end of their two-year course and ought not to become teachers.

Here, *cases* is an intruder. The writer could easily have kept it out: "It is clear that, except for a very few, . . .'

> Had he been more observant, he would have noticed that in almost every case there is a light in these cottages.

In the context, they were not actual cottages but pictures. That is no reason, however, why the writer should not have written ". . . that there was a light in almost every one of these cottages".

The other words mentioned by Quiller-Couch are not in such bad case. *Instance*, as Fowler says, is merely *case's* understudy. In the last sentence quoted, for example, the substitution of *instance* for *case* is a mere superficial change: the sentence undergoes no real change of heart.

Character and *nature* have the bad habit of appearing in verbose adjective phrases on the pattern "of a (adjective) character/nature", when the simple adjective would do. "The wound was of a serious nature" is a roundabout way of saying the wound was serious; and "Propaganda of an abusive character" simply means "abusive propaganda". Similarly, the phrases in "a man *in a dying condition*" and "a politician *of the Liberal persuasion*" can be stripped down to the simple adjective, "a *dying* man", "a *Liberal* politician". For *degree*, Quiller-Couch gives the example "A singular degree of rarity prevails in the earlier editions of this romance"; but this belongs more properly to what is called a little later in this chapter "reviewers' English". The ordinary writer, if he counts ten before committing himself to *case*, need only count, say, two before he ventures on *degree*.

Regard and *respect* are two other words that tempt writers into woolly periphrasis, or roundabout language. "With regard to" and "with respect to" both have their uses; but usually they can be replaced by simple conjunctions like *about* or *concerning*. "As regards" is more, and "in respect of" (which has a certain formal appropriateness) is less, to be avoided.

On Familiar Style

But these are no more than symptoms of a malady that attacks most of us when we put pen to paper. It is a remarkable thing that our spoken language, even if halting and 'ungrammatical', is at least direct and forceful. We call a spade a spade. But immediately we begin to write, or prepare a speech or lecture, the language seems to formalise, to become abstract, to fall into set patterns. And, indeed, this is in some measure both natural and right. There is, after all, a difference between the language of conversational (as distinct from rhetorical) speech and the language of writing. It is not so much that one is, or may be, composed of slang and colloquialism, and the other chastened into a serious dignity; the difference between them is subtler than that. Most of us, when we write, have a fear of dropping into colloquialism, and so go to almost any lengths of stilted periphrasis to avoid it. Hazlitt recognised the problem, and pronounced upon it in his Essay *On Familiar Style*:

> It is not easy to write a familiar style. Many people mistake a familiar for a vulgar style, and suppose that to write without affectation is to write at random. On the contrary, there is nothing that requires more precision, and if I may say so, purity of expression, than the style I am speaking of. It utterly rejects not only all unmeaning pomp, but all low, cant phrases, and loose unconnected, slipshod allusions. It is not to take the first word that offers, but the best word in common use; it is not to throw words together in any combinations we please, but to follow and avail ourselves of the true idiom of the language.

> To write a genuine familiar or truly English style, is to write as any one would speak in common conversation, who had a thorough command and choice of words, or who could discourse with ease, force and perspicuity, setting aside all pedantic and oratorical flourishes.

But admirable as that is in spirit and intention, it gives little practical help to the unpractised writer. Modern experts on usage have sometimes given more definite advice: "Use the active verb and the concrete noun"— "Avoid a phrase when a single word (for example, an adjective) will do"—"Repeat a word rather than indulge in what Fowler calls *elegant variation*" (that is, calling Shakespeare Shakespeare at the beginning of a sentence and the Swan of Avon towards the end)—"Be brief and concise"—"Prune and subtract rather than elaborate and add". And to all this has been added, in recent years, a plea for the short, simple (if possible, Saxon) word, in preference to the polysyllable which had its origin in Latin or Greek. That has been the song of many advisers on how to write English; even Mr. Churchill joined in the chorus recently, remembering, perhaps, his brief flirtation with Basic English during the war.

There is, no doubt, something in it—a valuable hint, not to those who rarely get as far as ink and paper, whose stock of words and expressions is pretty limited, anyhow, but to those who rather fancy themselves at a phrase, and are apt to measure the effect, and even the meaning, of a sentence by the length of its words or the rotundity of its phrases. It is, normally, better to write "The women went into the next room" than to write "The female contingent proceeded to the adjoining chamber". And yet—. There is a fallacy somewhere. Our 'rule' can be only a mere rule-of-thumb, a useful warning for the writer who is too sorely tempted into doubtful ways.

And for this reason. Any maxim which lays it down, more or less dogmatically, that one type of word, or one type of construction is better than another violates a fundamental principle of language—the principle that just as no two words, so no two modes of expression, can mean precisely the same thing. For example, a passive construction cannot have exactly the same significance as its corresponding active construction: it is negative, whereas the other is positive. "The lion beat the unicorn" is not identical with "The unicorn was beaten by the lion". It is conceivable that a writer would deliberately intend "The unicorn was beaten . . ."; and not "The lion beat . . ."; and to say to him "Use the active rather than the passive verb" is mere impertinence.

Plain English

The cult of "plain English" has been very much to the fore of late. Sir Ernest Gowers's book *Plain Words*, written for Civil servants, "to help officials in their use of written English," is a recent manifestation of it. There is doubtless much of value in it, but also much to dismay the reader who has a regard for the principles of the living language. For he guides the officials into a welcome simplicity and directness only by a dogmatic assertion that a 'synonymous' phrase or clause would accurately express their meaning, and that what is right in one context is necessarily right in another. "No one",[1] he says, "listening to the news broadcasts in March, 1947, could fail to note that the unfortunate people whose homes were flooded were never taken to other houses; they were all evacuated to alternative accommodation." The implication is, of course, that "were taken to other houses" is plain English for "were evacuated to alternative accommodation". But this implication is unjustified because it ignores real *nuances* of meaning ("alternative accommodation" was, as many people know, by no means the same as "other houses") and the natural development of the language (*evacuated* has now established itself, and has a significance beyond *taken*).

[1] For *no-one*. See pages 16*n*., and 130.

True, Sir Ernest Gowers uses his blue pencil to good effect. Out goes that offending word, that woolly superfluous clause, that otiose adverb, that periphrastic phrase. Thus:

> *Example:* Authorities should be definitely discouraged from committing themselves to purchase in advance of approval. If they do so commit themselves they should be asked in every case to explain why they have done so. Where it is decided to accept the explanation it should none the less be made clear to the Authorities that we shall not be prepared to recommend a loan for more than the figure acceptable to us.

This, says Sir Ernest, contains the following padding, all of which can be struck out without harming the sense: *Definitely, so commit themselves, in every case, they have done so, none the less, to the Authority* (sic), and *be prepared to.* He may be right; but it is at least conceivable that the writer, following a legal tradition, desired to 'cover' himself at every point. After all, 'official', like 'legal', language, with its apparent circumlocutions and repetitions, is designed to provide for every possible contingency and guard against every 'twist' of interpretation. The writer of the following notice in a railway time-table is forced to use a language that will satisfy the law and protect the Executive in any legal action:

> The London Transport Executive does not undertake nor shall it be deemed to undertake that the trains will start at the times specified or at all, or will arrive at the times specified. It will not be liable or accountable for any loss, damage, or inconvenience arising from any inaccuracy in this time-table or from the failure of the train to start or arrive at any specified time or by reason of withdrawal, delay, deviation or breakdown arising from any cause. By issuing it the London Transport Executive makes no warranty as to the running of any train.
>
> —*Metropolitan Line Time-table.*

That is, in the true sense, jargon. The jargon of official and commercial language is not always so defensible, but it does not deserve the foolish and indiscriminating attacks that are sometimes made upon it. Sir Ernest Gowers's kind of blue-pencilling is, in fact, as dangerously facile as it may be unjust and misleading. It could be applied, not without reason, to the opening sentences of his own book:

> The purpose of this book is to help officials in their use of written English. To some of them this may seem a work of supererogation,[1] calculated only to place an unnecessary burden on a body of people already overburdened.

This is not written in "plain words". Sir Ernest's blue pencil would probably alter and reduce it to something like this:

> This book is written to help officials to write good English. Some of them may think it a superfluous book, designed only to burden unnecessarily a body of people already overburdened.

And if Sir Ernest protests that this does not exactly represent his intended meaning, then the argument of much of his book falls to the ground.

The truth is that the language is far too big and living a thing for any dogmatism about "plain English" to have validity. What is plain English—or, at any rate, good English—in one context is not plain (or good) English in another. Do what we will, the language changes, words come and go, fashions in speech and writing, like other fashions, are variable, and never, in the words of the collect, "continue in one stay". Every period has its own crop of new words that arise, for the most part, to fulfil an immediate need; and every period has its reactionary souls, who vainly and sometimes bad-temperedly resist the inevitable change. But language is the most democratic

[1] An expression which Fowler includes in his list of Hackneyed Phrases.

of all institutions; it obeys the will of the people who speak
and write it, not the prejudice of self-appointed dictators.

Sir Ernest Gowers, who himself has a tilt at some selected
words and usages (*bottleneck*), "become a casualty", *emergency, global, implement, liquidate, recondition* and *rehabilitate* are among them) quotes Mr. Ivor Brown as defending
the verb *contact* (a person) and Sir Alan Herbert as exclaiming with rather puerile facetiousness: "My brothers,
let this verb be sabotaged by every possible avenue".
But Mr. Brown's blessing and Sir Alan's curse are equally
irrelevant; the word *contact*, if (as seems probable) it
remains in the language, will remain by the usage of us all;
just as *chiropodist* remains, though Fowler in his most
perverse and fatuous mood would have us say *corn-cutter*.

Jargon

We are here on the boundaries of, if not actually in, the
realm of true jargon. For new words, and subsequently
new usages, often come into language through the speech
or writing of special sections of the community. Some of
it, like for example, thieves' cant or jargon remains individual, a thing apart. But other types of jargon, though
they remain individual, often influence, or contribute to,
the general language—the jargon, for example, of school,
of trade, of profession, of sport, of politics. All these have
added to our vocabulary many words and phrases that
were current or fashionable for a short time, and a few that
remain permanent. Men and women carried into civilian
life the idioms they had picked up while on service; and
some of these idioms, like "had it", "in the clear", "haven't
a clue", are already showing signs of establishing themselves. Recently I heard the chairman of a meeting
(himself an ex-R.A.F. officer) address a hall full of other
ex-R.A.F. men like this:

> The erk who was D I-ing the kite didn't have a clue, and
> his oppo told him he'd better get weaving or Chieffy would
> tear a large strip off him. Then Corp came up in a flat

spin with the gen that Groupy wanted the kite in an hour.
The erk muttered that he wasn't carrying the can for anybody, that he wasn't Joe, that he couldn't care less about
scrambled eggs, and that anyway he was browned off.

That was jargon. They understood it, and those of
us who were not in the R.A.F. could at least grasp its
general meaning. Some of it, probably, will remain as
part of the language; but whether that is so or not, it will
have had a positive, and probably beneficial, influence on
our vocabulary and manner of speech.

All true jargon has a dual aspect: it is a *private* language,
parts of which (words, phrases, expressions, idioms) become incorporated in the *public* or *general* language.
Many of our familiar words and expressions have in fact
graduated in this way. Again, the process has always been
a democratic one. There is no point in the attempt of
writers in language to boycott certain words and expressions
while they are, as it were, suspended between the private
and the public or general vocabulary.[1] These abide not
their question, but the question of us all.

Such writers do, in fact, protest—and not without reason
—against the too familiar use of 'jargon' when it is newly in
fashion. Shakespeare himself did. "You are now", says
Feste in *Twelfth Night*, "out of your welkin. I would say
'element', but the word is overworn." Each decade (at
least) is as clearly marked by its fashionable 'jargon' as
each year by, say, its popular songs.

A recent editorial note on Jargon in the *Times Educational
Supplement* is apposite:

> It surprises us to read of the ancient mariner listening to
> the birds' "sweet jargoning." But this abused and
> abusive word was once properly applied to the chatter of
> birds. Men, as they increased in presumption, supposed,
> as they had not sufficient wit to follow what the birds were
> saying, that they were not saying anything but merely
> babbling. So "jargon" came to mean gibberish. Now

---

[1] Between? See page 98.

by another insulting twist it is used of the technical language of scholars, scientists or professional men. "A piece of jargon" is the dyslogistic synonym for "technical term." It is only when one is impatient with an expert that one is tempted to use the word, and impatience usually arises from the suspicion that he is describing in a grand manner something quite obvious which one probably knows more about than he does. Thus scientists who confine themselves to theatres which the ordinary person makes no pretence of having explored usually escape this charge: bio-chemists, electronicians and experts in cuneiform writing have their technical vocabularies but are seldom abused for using them. Psychologists, grammarians and educationists, on the other hand, trespass on ground to which "common sense" already stakes a claim. They must justify their neologisms by showing that it is convenient to have a term for what they wish to denote, that a suitable one does not already exist and that the one they coin is appropriate.

That is true: technical language, which, after all, is true jargon, is dangerous only when it impinges, by indiscriminate or unintelligent use, on the general or popular language. The jargon of modern education provides, as it happens, an excellent example. It is not too much to say that a great deal of teaching in the schools to-day is rendered vague and sometimes futile by the indirect influence of a jargon which, drifting down from Ministry of Education pamphlets and the educational Press, has infected not only the language but also the thought and method of the teachers themselves, and of all (including, of course, parents) who are interested in education. "Fluid time-tables", "free activities", "individual expression", "social studies", "basic skills", "learning by doing", "centres of interest", "projects"—the phrases are bandied about and given a kind of mysterious, if not mystic, significance of their own: but no one knows precisely what they mean. It is in such language that a film projector, or an epidiascope or even a blackboard is called a "visual aid", and "aural aid" is just another name for a wireless set.

But to return for a moment to that padded and pulpy language which Quiller-Couch rather loosely called jargon. It is one aspect of what used to be, somewhat unjustly, termed *journalese*. At one time it was fashionable to laugh at the sports journalist who wrote that "in a local derby" Liverpool beat Everton "by the odd goal in three", or that an opening batsman "wielded the willow to good effect". Such phrases have now, to quote Shakespeare again, become "overworn", and we laugh at them with the kindly indulgence of memory. Indeed, the popular journalist has fled to another kind of idiom—an imitation of clipped, American slickness, which is itself beginning to have its influence, a good influence in the main, on the language. The conjunctionless, elliptical style of the *Daily Express* is—however much we may dislike it— more in keeping with the modern trend of language than the ponderous and literary style of the *Manchester Guardian* and *The Times*, or the critics' and reviewers' English of the literary magazines.

Some peculiar characteristics of what may be called 'literary' journalism are apparent in the illustrations throughout this book, but especially in those brought together in the Interludes.

Idiom

The word *idiom* has been used several times in the preceding pages. It is ultimately derived from a Greek word meaning 'own', 'peculiar', and is thus defined in the Oxford dictionary: "form of expression, construction, phrase, etc. peculiar to a language; a peculiarity of phraseology approved by usage, and often having a meaning other than its grammatical or logical one". Idiom of construction is illustrated, as it occurs, in many sections of this book; but there are certain manifestations of it that give rise to special doubts and difficulties. Most troublesome of all is the idiom of prepositions. We can clear out of the way without ceremony the hoary question whether a preposition is a good, or correct, word to end a sentence with. The answer is Yes. Though by its very name a preposition is 'placed before' a noun, modern English idiom allows, and has always allowed, it to be placed after, and often as the last word in the sentence. We have met it in connection with the relative pronoun (page 89); Fowler gives examples in writers from Chaucer onwards; and here, to give an up-to-date example, is a sentence from a review I was reading in the *Observer* immediately before I began to write this page:

> No nation had had to look Kipling's two impostors so often in the face; triumph and disaster alternate in a fashion more interesting to read *about* than tolerable to live *through*.

Normal or familiar prepositional idiom does not bother us over-much. We say without thinking that we live *in* Manchester but live *at* 16 Liverpool Road, that we get *in* (or *into*) a train but live *in* fear, faith, anticipation but *at* peace, odds, variance. These are part of the texture of everyday language. But when we get a little away from the perfectly familiar, doubts begin to arise. In a sentence quoted on page 67, there is this expression: "is not only one of the most devastating indictments against any European statesman". Most of us would have to look at it at least twice before we realised that the writer had confused the two constructions "indictment *of*" and "case *against*", and that therefore "indictment *against*" transgressed prepositional idiom.

Certain prepositional constructions in everyday use cause most of us a little uneasy hesitation. A few representative constructions are given, with the warning that they belong to *current* usage. Other constructions may be familiar in the language of the past (that is, in literature) and may therefore be recognised by the dictionary, which merely records, without pronouncing upon the question of right and wrong:

admit	Normally transitive: "admit a fault"; but the special idiom "It admits *of* no other explanation" should be noted.
agree	*With* a person, *with* a statement already made or an action already performed, *to* a proposition.
averse	*From* rather than *to*, often followed by a gerund.
compare	Compare A *with* B. This is the safe construction. Fowler admits compare *to* in certain circumstances: but his argument is too subtle for ordinary writers.
compose	A is composed *of* B and C.
comprise	A comprises B and C, not *is comprised of*.
connive	Connive *at* e.g. a crime, a misdemeanour.
consist	in the 'physical' sense (='is made up of') consist is followed by *of*: "The equipment necessary for cricket consists of stumps, bats and a ball". Compare *compose* and *comprise* above. *Consist* is followed by *in* when the idea of material composition is not present. Usually, but not always, the gerund follows *in*: "The game of golf consists in a ball being played from the 'teeing ground' into the 'hole' by successive strokes".
dependent/ independent	Dependent *on*; but independent *of*.
differ/different	A differs/is different *from* B: but indifferent *to*.
initiate	Initiate a person *in* or *into* e.g. a society or ritual.
instil	Instil a thing *into* a person; but inspire, imbue a person *with* a thing.
prefer	Prefer A *to* B or prefer A *rather than* B, but not prefer A *than* B (see page 90).
prevent	Prevent *his going* (see page 53) or prevent *him from going*.
replace	Replace A *with* B: substitute B *for* A.

Meanwhile, since this matter of idiom is all important, here is a short anthology of muddles and errors in idiom, with such notes as are necessary:

> For the larger part of an uncommonly stirring tussle under a kindly sun among five or six counties, many dared to hope that Worcestershire might renew old glories.

"Tussle *among*"? The writer was perhaps afraid of *between*, believing that it should introduce only two contestants, not five or six. But *among* eliminates or at any rate minimises the idea of a tussle; *between* is better, but if it is (superstitiously) barred, *by* or even *of* might fill the bill.

His 'field survey' *into* the behaviour of typical working and middle-class families confirms the novelist's opinion that the popular attitude to furnishing the home is primarily emotional.

"Inquiry *into*" but "survey *of*": the writer has confused two constructions. Note also that if *middle-class* has a hyphen *working* should be *working-*.

In the first place, we are given a wholly new aspect *on* his Italian sojourn.

"Light *on*" but "aspect *of*".

The student can, with the index, get a good plain statement of what is known and what has been written on the point.

The one preposition *on* will not do for both *known* and *written*. "Known *of*" is the construction; even then, "what is known of the point" can scarcely pass muster. For *point* read *subject*.

In England, for example, the State insists that children should be given some religious instruction, but is indifferent, within broad limits, as to the kind which is given.

"Indifferent *to*" not *as to*. How can one be indifferent "within broad limits"?

It is better for Britain to conform with the dollar trade-system . . .

"Agree *with*" but "conform *to*".

This, taken in conjunction of the earlier examples I gave, might be a clue worth following.

"In conjunction *with*", not *of*.

This is part of Professor Strich's argument as he shows Goethe stretching out to one literature after another and interpreting them all into a conception of a world culture.

This is a confusion not so much of two idioms as of two distinct ideas: "combining them all (i.e. various literatures) into a world culture" and "interpreting them as a conception of a world culture". The writer has fallen disastrously between the two.

> The impetus given to Serbian nationalism by the triumph of the two Balkan wars convinced Austria that there was no alternative between the elimination of Serbia and the disintegration of the Habsburg Empire.

Unfortunately, the idiom is "alternative *to*"; but since this is impossible here, if the intended meaning is to be kept, the use of *alternative* must be wrong. The writer means "There is no middle way between the elimination and the disintegration". But instead of playing about with the dangerous word *alternative* he could have expressed himself in a real and simple alternative: "convinced Austria that either Serbia must be eliminated or the Habsburg Empire would disintegrate". But even this is not altogether satisfactory. A conditional construction would be safer: "that unless Serbia was eliminated the Habsburg Empire would disintegrate".

> Let me register an unfavourable comparison between Alistair Cooke's invigorating American Letters and Yvette Guyot's (Third Programme) heavy-handed and ill-delivered Letters from Paris.

Third Programme indeed! The idiom—see page 155—is "comparison of A *with* B". But why *unfavourable?* The sense is topsy-turvy, if, as would seem reasonable, *unfavourable* applies to the first half of the comparison. But if the writer had rid himself of his pompous journalese he would have begun "Let me compare favourably . . .", and the correct "A *with* B" would, it is hoped, have followed naturally.

> Mr. Grigson finds a landscape as haunted as that of Kubla Khan and makes out a good case that Coleridge may have had it in mind.

The idiom is "make out a good case *for*"; but the writer either did not know it or forgot it, and went over to another construction altogether. He could have written either "argues convincingly that Coleridge . . ." or "makes out a good case for Coleridge's having had it in mind". He violated idiom by combining the two.

> An exchange of letters . . . raises afresh the perennial question *of* how best to render a foreign text into English.

A clause which expresses the actual (indirect) question should be placed in apposition to the word *question*, without any intermediate preposition: "the perennial question how best to render . . .". Sometimes *of* is the intruder, and sometimes *as to*:

> It was subdivided into the practical question *as to* whether a young man was more likely to contract venereal disease abroad than at home.

Here *as to* should be omitted. But in another construction *of* and *as to* are not merely legitimate but necessary: "The question *of* expenses now arises", "Any question *as to* his sanity must be reserved until later". It is important to remember that *as to* should never follow "*the* question".

> They should be considered *as* no more than the result of a conscientious endeavour to extract from the mass of evidence sent as accurate a general picture as possible.

Here the conjunction *as* is the intruder. The construction is elliptical for "*consider* [noun] *to be* [noun]", known in Latin as the accusative and infinitive. Normally, as here, the verb *to be* is omitted; but that is no reason why *as* should pretend to take its place. *Regard*, however, welcomes the *as* that *consider* rejects: "*regard* [noun] *as* [noun]": "I regard him *as* a friend", "I consider him a friend".

> Mr. Maurice Samuel aims to give us full value for our money.

There were also questions aimed *to find* out how far the material of the broadcast was already known.

Aim, unlike *purpose* or *propose*, is not transitive, and therefore cannot have an infinitive as object: that is, while we can say "*purpose/propose* to give" we cannot say "aim to give". The idiom is "aim *at*"; but because of its own *to* the infinitive cannot be governed by a preposition. We have, therefore, to use the other noun form of the verb, the gerund: "aim at *giving/finding*."[1] The following sentence illustrates a similar error in idiom with the adjective *intent*:

> . . . two of them ardent Communists intent *to use* every occasion and every human contact for party purposes . . .

The idiom is "intent *on*+gerund": "ardent Communists intent *on using*".

> It will be a test not so much of big hitting *but* of delicate pitching and accurate putting.

> These sharply contemporary novels have the same effect on me *that* those books by American scientific journalists and technocrats used to have.

For *but* and *that* substitute *as* "so much of A *as* of B", "the same effect on me *as*". Similarly after *such*: "It was such a storm *as* you would rarely see in England." In this construction *such* is not followed by the normal relative pronoun (*who, which, that*). If *so much* is omitted from the first sentence we have the simple negative *but* construction (see page 94), which the writer probably intended to use before the temptation to add *so much* overcame him.

The sentences already quoted illustrate, for the most

---

[1] The American idiom is, nevertheless, *aim* + infinitive, "aim to give", and this is gaining ground in English. Similarly, the American preference for *like* as a conjunction, where we use *as* ("I think as —not *like*—you do") is becoming more familiar in English usage. It is significant that Mr. Churchill used it in *Their Finest Hour*: "I should deprecate setting up a special committee. We are overrun by them, like the Australians were by rabbits".

part, problems and difficulties of constructional idiom with
certain single prepositions or conjunctions; though in one
or two of them other syntactical principles are involved.
The sentences that follow exemplify faulty control of
idiomatic phrases and expressions. They are all symptomatic of woolly and muddled thought or (now and then) of
a vain attempt to be clever.

> We must be ready now to work harder and live less well,
> or presently we shall be hard put to live at all.

The idiom is "hard put to it"; but the writer, mistaking
the *to* of the infinitive for the *to* of the idiom, forgot "to it"
altogether. Probably his mind was confused with the
similar expression "find it hard to live".

> To my taste, M. Marais is about as wrong in the part of a
> nervous, vacillating poet, as anyone could be.

> All I protest is that modern uniforms have so many
> special meanings for us that they are dangerous in this
> particular play.

These are peculiar and interesting examples of a mental
muddle which results—as so often—in confused idiom.
A book, a picture, or, for that matter, M. Marais may
not be to my taste. I can protest that such and such a
thing is so, or protest against such and such a thing.
But I cannot use "To my taste" and "All I protest" as
introductory phrases: the idioms are: "In my opinion" or
"To my way of thinking" and "All I can say". It is
remarkable that responsible journalists who never would
commit malapropisms with single words (see pages 192ff),
quite frequently commit them with idioms, and do not,
apparently, realise their error.

> A book of this kind, so powerful it is, makes us once again
> call down anathema upon these ideologies, of the right or
> the left, which set up these monstrous abstractions.

You can "call down fire upon" (Luke ix. 54), or even
"curses upon"; you can *anathematise* a person or thing;

but you cannot "call down anathema upon". *Anathema* means 'an accursed thing' or, simply, *accursed* (Rom. ix. 3). So, if *anathema* must be used, the expression should be "makes us once again call all these ideologies anathema".

> One reason, I dare say, why Christopher Morley was so enjoyable to British ears springs from the fact that he likes us and our ways and our country.

The construction with *reason* (noun) is "The reason is *that*" (introducing a noun clause as complement): "One reason why he was enjoyable is *that he likes us*". It is important to remember this, because many writers, and more speakers, are tempted into "The reason is *because*". But to return to the sentence under discussion. It is not the reason but the enjoyment of Christopher Morley by British ears (whatever that may mean) that "springs from the fact that he likes us".

There is a similar confusion in the following sentence:

> The first volume to appear, however, is rather disappointing. Several reasons account for this.

The reasons do not account, but certain qualities or characteristics of the book. If *reasons* is to be used the second sentence should run: "There are several reasons for this".

> For the Kaufman-Moss-Hart play concerns this plot of buying a decaying shack, without benefit of plumbing, and there camping for insanitary week-ends.

This is an example of reviewers' cleverness gone wrong. "Without benefit of clergy" is a recognised ancient legal term meaning "the privilege allowed to clergymen of exemption from trial by a secular court" (*S.O.E.D.*). But "without benefit of plumbing" is not a parallel imitation. There might possibly be a benefit of plumbers; there certainly could not, in the idiomatic sense, be "benefit of plumbing." "Without the benefit of (having) plumbing" might pass muster; but the simple "without plumbing" would be better. It is an interesting fact that this false idiom was used by three different writers in the same periodical in the space of three weeks or so.

> To treat a long series of autobiographical episodes satirically is one thing; but to write a narrative drama in verse form, without any real feeling for the stage or any interest in the mechanics of character, is to court disaster.

By the time he reached the end, the writer forgot the beginning of his sentence. The formula is: "A is one thing: B is another", and from that there can be no deviation. If, moreover, B "is to court disaster", A must be at least tolerably successful, in order that the antithesis may be maintained. Probably this is what the writer meant; but alas! no-one will ever know. Here is a similar lapse:

> At the moment we are trying to teach children to fly before they are physically capable of learning to walk.

The writer falls between the two stools of idiom and literal language. He could scarcely intend to use *fly* literally in this context; so we must assume he is using the idiom, which is "to run before (you) can walk". Probably by the use of *fly* he was trying to modernise the idiom; but language will suffer no such liberties. And to finish with his own verbose pomposities instead of sticking to the original formula was, as the writer of the previous sentence would say, to court disaster.

And here, to end with, are a few mixed or imperfect idioms for the reader to sharpen his wits on, with brief notes to give him a little initial help, or to suggest kindred idioms and parallel problems.

> But it is easier to be wise after the event than in the thick of it.

"Easier *after* than *during* the event" or "than in the thick of *things*".

> It is nearly thirty years ago since *Encounters* was first published.

"Nearly thirty years *since*" or "nearly thirty years ago *when* or *that*", but not "thirty years *ago since*", which is saying the same thing twice over.

> There are still those who think that the day schools are trespassing outside their proper sphere in organising meals and social activities.

"Trespass *on* e.g. forbidden territory", "go/act/travel *outside* their proper sphere".

> The school is naturally anxious to complete its work in peace and shelter before its pupils are thrown into the scramble of life.

"In peace (or rest) and quietness"; "peace and shelter" in this context is a queer phrase. If the idea of shelter is to be brought in, the formula should be abandoned and the sentence recast.

> Any such proposal must be examined from the points of view of both undergraduates and teachers.

> National Service and Short Service commission officers wishing to make the army their careers.

"From the point of view", "make the army their career" (sing.) would be the normal idiom here. But the very real difficulty remains in English. Do we say "The men and women shook their head", as if they had one head between them, or "The men and women shook their heads", as if they had half-a-dozen heads each? There is no rule: the reader has to use his own discretion.

> There are, for example, in English literature, many different children's tastes to be catered for.

"Many different tastes among the children" is presumably what is meant. The adjective before *possessive noun+noun* is apt to qualify the wrong noun: "soft men's hats" would have an unfortunate connotation in writing, though the voice might, by stress, link the *soft* to *hats*.

To assign a causal connection one way or the other would imply a view about the efficacy of saintly patronage.

See page 135.

The fear has substance; there are many and varied openings to tempt away the able man or woman.

"Openings *for*", "attractions *to tempt away*" or, better still, simply *tempt*.

About foreign novelties, which used then to be published in reckless abundance, there had needs to be greater selectivity than about British.

"There had *need* to be", "there *needs* must be".

English children nowadays, I understand, do not read Frances Hodgson Burnett, so *The Secret Garden* (Empire) will have to stand on its own recognizances.

"*Stand* on its own *feet*", "*enter* into *recognizances*", though what this could mean in this context is a puzzle. For the comma after *Burnett*, see page 107.

One does not, however, see Jane herself pivoting a novel around anything so indecorous.

"Pivot *on*", not *around*; so "centre *on*", not *round*, though this idiom is becoming common, and threatens to pass into usage.

Of the English writers it may be said that most are excellently qualified to command the confidence of their countrymen.

"*Command* respect", "*win* confidence". So in this sentence, "One can see Rossetti as never before in the fascination he commanded", *commanded* should be replaced by *exercised* or simply *had*; "command fascination" is not English.

. . . though the age of the audience seems to vary at different times between four and twelve.

Here we have an odd confusion of three idioms or expressions: (a) to vary from four to twelve; (b) to be between four and twelve; (c) to be, at different times, anything between four and twelve. Only in (c) can the phrase "at different times" appropriately occur; so that is the construction the writer should have used.

> Not one of those of my acquaintance has been guilty of any such fall from grace.

"Has *had* or *sustained* any such fall from grace", "has *been guilty of* any such misdemeanour or crime"—a simple confusion of two idioms. Better still, "has so fallen from grace".

> . . . to give why and wherefore for this remarkable and enlivening event.

"The reason *for*", "the why and wherefore *of*".

The fact that the following examples are taken from one number of a certain periodical, most of them from a single article, is at once a reminder that it is difficult even for practised writers to avoid mixing idioms, and a justification for the somewhat detailed treatment of the subject here:

> (i) Perhaps it is that Christmas goods are in better supply and of finer quality than since 1939.

It is arguable that the modern phrase "in short supply", though it is often condemned by purists, is in fact a necessary addition to the language. But it is a fixed idiom, and so it should remain; "in short supply" is (or may be) good English but "in shorter/better supply" is not. In his last three words the writer has made a reckless economy; "than since 1939" may have a meaning, but it is hard to get at. He means, and should write, "than they have been at any time since 1939".

> (ii) For reasons that have been sufficiently well thumbed over recently, the choice appears to lie between January and February and mid-May and June.

A reason may, perhaps, be aired; it certainly can be stated; but it cannot be well thumbed over. Where exactly the choice appears to lie remains a mystery. Possibly the writer means between January and February *or* between mid-May and June. That at any rate seems to be the only reasonable interpretation.

> (iii) It can hold on to office to the last ditch while at the same time side-stepping the two charges that it shirks a Budget or that it intends to bring in a vote-catching Budget.

One can die in the last ditch, but cannot perform there the peculiarly athletic feat of holding on to office and at the same time side-stepping a couple of charges. There are two other faults in this remarkable sentence: *while* is superfluous, and, since there are two charges to be side-stepped, *or* should be *and*.

> (iv) . . . and before you know Mr. Strachey is off to East Africa again.

"Before you know", may be good American, but it is as yet only colloquial English. At the moment, it is out of place in the written language; but it may establish itself later beside such expressions as "before you could say Jack Robinson/say a word/look round".

> (v) . . . shows that the lesson which Lord Ammon sought to impart has at last sunk home.

"Sunk *in*" but "struck *home*".

> (vi) . . . a scheme which stands to bring considerable benefits to the people of these countries.

The meaning is not clear; but the intended idiom is probably "which *bids fair* or *promises* to bring". At any rate, "*stands* to bring" is not a recognised English expression. Perhaps there is some confusion with "stand to reason", "stand to order".

(vii) . . . an account of the Morant affair which caused Sadler's resignation from the Board of Education and cast a tragic element into his career.

"*Introduce* a tragic element *into*", "*cast* a shadow *over*".

(viii) The wealth of circumstantial detail, of extracts from correspondence, and of what the author calls 'sidelights', though often interesting, equally often proves repetitive and blurs the focus.

"*Throw* something *out of* focus", "*blur* the picture". The fastidious writer (or reader) would consider whether *wealth* was a quite 'dead' metaphor (see page 169); and, if it is not, would omit it, amending the sentence like this "The circumstantial detail, the extracts . . ., the 'sidelight' . . . prove . . .".

Clichés

Idioms and, indeed, other expressions (especially familiar quotations) sometimes die of overwork. They were once fresh and living, but after constant and familiar use wither away and die—or rather, do not die, but linger on, in a kind of living death, in speech and writing. Some years ago *Punch* had a picture of a man "exploring every avenue" and another of a man "leaving no stone unturned". These, and many other expressions like them, have outlived their usefulness. They are often called *clichés*, from a printer's term in French meaning 'a stereotyped block'. *Stereotyped, unoriginal, stale*—these are the epithets that might be, and indeed often are, applied to them. Even so, many people use them still for the very reason that they are "stereotyped blocks"—something ready-made, and therefore saving the speaker or the writer the trouble of creative effort. We have, in fact, already met a few in the paragraph on journalese; here are half-a-dozen others, all mentioned in Fowler: "the irony of fate", "a work of supererogation" (see page 149), "was the order of the day", "to be made the recipient of" (=to be given), "the defects of his qualities", "to the tender mercies of".

It is natural, but a pity, that the great phrases coined by poets and writers should be particularly liable to become *clichés*. A snatch of Wodehousian dialogue will illustrate the point. "It is," said Jeeves once, "a consummation devoutly to be wished, sir." Bertie Wooster, who was himself no great Shakespearian scholar, was quite startled. "That's rather well put, Jeeves," he said. "Your own?" "No, sir," said Jeeves, "the Swan of Avon." There is in that piece of foolery something to remember, especially when these and other quotations rise to the lips, or threaten to flow from the pen: "They also serve who only stand and wait", "Some have greatness thrust upon 'em", "the cup that cheers", "far from the madding crowd", "the first fine careless rapture", "one far-off divine event", "too deep for tears".

Not that these and many other familiar quotations like them are never apt or permissible. They are; but we have to be discriminating in their use. Charles Lamb once called certain classical books "Great Nature's stereotypes"; and the term might be applied to those expressions that, created once for all by genius, remain to enrich the language. But they are, after all, stereotypes—in the literal sense *clichés*—as we use them afterwards. That is true also of proverbial expressions, which have their origin in the ordinary traffic of language, especially speech. At some time or other, in the distant past, "a rolling stone gathers no moss", "a stitch in time saves nine" and "birds of a feather flock together" were fresh and vivid expressions. Somebody coined them; but now, to continue the metaphor, they have become so worn in use as almost to be taken out of currency.

Metaphor

Idiom is often closely associated with metaphor—the figure in which "a name or descriptive term is transferred to some object to which it is not properly applicable" (*S.O.E.D.*). Much of our language is almost unconsciously metaphorical, as when we talk of life as a *pilgrimage*, or use

such phrases as a "*fiery* temper", "*piercing* eyes", "a *gust*
of anger", "His face *lit up*", "Time simply *crawled*".
Indeed, so much is this kind of transference a part of language that many words, originally with 'transferred'
application, have become what Fowler calls 'dead' metaphors: that is to say, in using them we are no longer conscious of the transference or 'change' (the word *metaphor*
means literally 'carry across'). Many Latin derivatives
are, for example, originally metaphorical but have no
metaphorical sense—especially to the non-Latinist—in
English. Thus *eradicate* (Latin *ex*, out + *radix*, a root) is
not a live metaphor, whereas the English equivalent 'root
out' or *uproot* is; *grade* (Latin *gradus*, step) is dead, but
English *step* is at any rate half alive. The 'dead' metaphor
gives us no trouble; the living or even half-dead metaphor
often does, for we forget, or find it difficult, once having
ventured on a particular figure, to be consistent and sustain
it to the end.

If we are writing or speaking in conscious metaphor,
we are apt to mix our images, as Shakespeare did when he
makes Hamlet say "Or to *take arms* against a *sea* of
troubles"; if we are writing or speaking in unconscious
metaphor we often treat the metaphor as dead, follow it
up with language incongruous to the original (possibly
rather faint) image, and so achieve what is either a mild
mixed metaphor or a false mingling of the metaphorical
and the literal. All this is best made clear by illustration.
Here, to begin with, is a somewhat ornate metaphor in
which the imagery is cleverly sustained:

> The steep steps cut in the congealing ice a week ago to let
> the pound climb down from its chilly and unprofitable
> eminence loosed off an avalanche, and it is still too soon to
> say how much of the fallen débris lies in the path of the
> pound's own descent.

The only word open to criticism here is *unprofitable*, which
in this context is a literal, not a metaphorical, epithet;
"and unprofitable" should be omitted. The metaphor is

then sound. But here are two sentences in which the metaphors have become more than usually mixed:[1]

> "We shall overcome the adverse current", he said; "it will serve as a spring-board for the future. It was no Waterloo".—Quoted in *Punch*.

> Since then the snowball of knowledge has swept relentlessly on, stamping with each year another rivet of reliability and craftsmanship into the name of . . .

Such confusion of images is beyond most ordinary people; it has about it the magnificence of the incredible. The less daring writer is tempted into a less obvious but equally culpable mixture, of which the following are examples:

> No poet's position is likely to be finally stabilised except by his posterity, and even the game of literary fashion will toss it high and low.

The writer, having begun with a non-metaphorical statement, then introduces an incongruous metaphor in which a game tosses high and low an already stabilised position.

> A local civilisation flourished intact until the two world wars began to shake its close texture.

"Shake the foundations", perhaps; it is difficult to see how it could shake a texture. But it may be argued that *texture* has become such a vogue-word with reviewers

---

[1] A mixed metaphor is one in which incongruous images are incorporated in a single basic figure. It is not to be confused with a succession of separate metaphors in one sentence or unit of expression. Such metaphors may, of course, be incongruously related; but they do not, in combination, make up a mixed metaphor. Reviewers and critics are often oddly ignorant of such technical points as this. Here is an example:

> He regards it as the principle of order, the mother of repose, the child of habit, the guardian of values, and the calm mediator between the extremes of Right and Left. It is only fair to Mr. Viereck to state that his own metaphors are not so mixed.

There are no mixed metaphors in the first sentence—indeed, it is doubtful whether there are any metaphors at all.

(who apply it particularly to the prose of the latest Book of the Week) that it has lost all its metaphorical and nearly all its literal meaning.

> Thanks to Reith's handling of wireless facilities in that crisis, the disaster gave England a flying start in an unexplored field.

> No one would maintain that we have as yet surveyed the seas of potential ability.

> The author is intent to explore the conflict of reality and ideology to its depths.

These three sentences are taken together because the idea of exploration is common to them all; but surely one is given a flying start in a race, not in "an unexplored field"; one surveys the land rather than the seas; and one plumbs, not explores, to the depths. The metaphors are not mixed crudely and obviously, but they are nevertheless mixed.

> The anomaly of the nation solemnly punishing itself must become commoner with every sweep of the socialising tentacles.

> They have a keen sense of place, and of the roots that tie us to places.

Both might conceivably pass: but do tentacles, whether socialising or nor, make a *sweep*, and do roots *tie*? The writer should have sought for less metaphorical words (e.g. *movement, hold*) which were more congruous to his main images. For the other fault in the first sentence ("of the nation punishing") see page 53.

> Poetry has rejected the aesthetic atmosphere, the stained-glass silence out of which a kind of inspiration fertilised itself.

What a "stained-glass silence" is only the writer knows; and how inspiration can fertilise itself out of it is one of the sex problems that must for ever remain unsolved.

That same technique, the science outpost, has been developed into the four corner-stones of Unesco's scientific work.

The development of four corner-stones out of an outpost seems nothing short of a miracle, especially in this modern world, where building of any kind is usually so difficult.

The mood and point of view are the same as in his great Autobiography, which still flares across our literary sky with its sunset fires.

A queer, and totally unnecessary, mixture of sunset and meteorite. It is the one word *across* that betrays the muddleheadedness of the writer. If he had written *in* for *across* his metaphor would have been sound.

But what threatens his freedom today is not the angry roar of his constituents, but the quiet pressure of a Party machine, without whose endorsement as a candidate he has little chance of success.

A machine that presses quietly and afterwards endorses must be a queer engine. The metaphor is almost, but not quite, mixed; probably the writer was hovering all the time between the literal and the metaphorical.

A Cabinet Minister in a recent speech allowed another machine to get sadly out of control:

Let the extravagant Tory machine and the vested interests think again instead of losing their heads and going off the deep end.

And an eloquent shop steward introduced a remarkable red herring:

We will not be swerved from our purpose by the red herring with which Sir Patrick Dollan is trying to cloud the issue.

As if this was not enough, he mixed his idiom: we will not *be turned* / will not *swerve*.

Pearsall Smith did a small thing perfectly; but with the perfectionist every blemish is fatal and all success limited; the virtues of the enthusiast can be infinite and his vices swallowed and disinfected in the noble flood.

This noble flood is a mysterious one. That it should swallow the perfectionist's vices is not altogether surprising; that having swallowed them it should disinfect them is difficult to believe.

The home counties are drenched in it. As we proceed towards the Midlands we find that Reading has completely succumbed. Oxford—the city, not the university, which may be suspected of acting as a secret agent to draw the city within the iron curtain—holds out boldly, but how long can she endure and what will happen if that dam bursts?

A good (or bad) example of the kind of English written by the elephantine humorist. The *it* of the first sentence, by the way, is the cockney accent. We begin with a metaphorical verb *drenched*, which suggests seas or rivers or rainstorms; but this is forgotten in the next sentence, and Reading unmetaphorically or, at best, half-metaphorically, *succumbs*. To what? Then the University of Oxford is likened to a secret agent drawing the City of Oxford "within the iron curtain". It is difficult to determine the significance of this ludicrous image; but not so difficult as to explain why, just as the City seems to be putting up a fight, it (and we) should be confronted with a bursting dam.

And here are a few examples, not of mixed, but of unsustained or inconsistent metaphor:

The standard of literary expression normally shown by far too many children leaving the schools is already causing grave concern.

This is an example of mild confusion of 'half-dead' metaphor; a standard is *reached* or *attained*, *ability in* or *aptitude for* is shown. It may be objected that this is a pedantic comment; but the sentence quoted occurred in a rather acid article called *Bad English*.

> If in the others there is the clean cutting edge of mania or mission, in Leskov there is a weed-like diffusion of the impressionist, the non-stop sketchiness of personal kindness, sanity and experience.

The sentence has no intelligible meaning; but a razor blade, weeds, and a train seem to be the basic images in an odd riot of metaphor.

> In the Russian novel of the nineteenth century we are hypnotised by the great peaks, the riotous and the serene, the prophetic and the sickly crests. We do not notice the foothills from which they rise. We suppose anything below the snowline to be choked by the vegetation of provinciality, regionalism, folklore, and the merely typical.

On the whole, the writer has managed his mountain scenery fairly well; but in the epithets *riotous, serene, prophetic* and *sickly* (and especially the last two) he descends—to borrow the figure—to the literal: that is, these epithets apply to the novels as novels, not as peaks.

> The result is a maze, delightful to wander in, but a nightmare to the systematic reader and the reference-hunter.

A venial fault, perhaps: but there is, after all, something queer about a maze that suddenly becomes a nightmare, even though the phrase "a nightmare to" has by now lost nearly all its metaphorical meaning, and simply means 'difficult'.

> When the vestiges of village custom and festival are examined, they are nearly always discovered to be fragmentary and attenuated versions, artificially revived or detached from their context, of far richer sources that were once pregnant with meaning.

This confused sentence has some kind of meaning; but vestiges become versions of sources, versions are fragmentary, attenuated, artificially revived and detached, and sources were once pregnant, in a disconcerting and incongruous progression of images.

> It is, however, the faith of this pamphlet that spiritual
> convictions are the vital element in the democratic way of
> life, the handful of yeast, the grain of mustard seed, the
> candle set on a candlestick.

This writer remembers his Bible in a vague, woolly fashion, and takes from it three metaphors. But unfortunately only one, the first, has any relation to "vital element"; (Luke xiii. 21); the grain of mustard seed (Luke xiii. 19) and the candle set on a candlestick (Mark iv. 21) have a different significance altogether.

> It is easy to find scapegoats. The Ministry is the obvious
> target for the public and possibly there are times when the
> local authorities feel themselves to be the predestined
> recipients of Ministerial slings and arrows.

The reader is left to study at leisure this remarkable hotch-potch of the Bible, *Hamlet*, target-imagery and jargon. There is, perhaps, a disturbing moral in the fact that the sentence is taken from a leading article in a leading educational journal.

These examples illustrate, well enough, the chief perils of metaphorical language. They are not intended to be a hint to the reader not to write in metaphor at all; they are quoted as a reminder to him that all metaphor, however mild, requires careful and consistent thought. Other examples will be found in the various passages and sentences quoted in the Second Interlude.

Other Figures

One or two other figures may be, like the metaphor, not only an extraneous ornament but also an integral part of the vocabulary and language generally. There is hyperbole, or exaggeration, as when we say, "I've been waiting ages", "He is as old as the hills", "I was so thirsty that I drank gallons of water". As a definite figure of speech hyperbole has a honourable history; it is, for example, a favourite with Shakespeare:

> Hold off the earth awhile,
> Till I have caught her once more in mine arms.
> Now pile your dust upon the quick and dead,
> Till of this flat a mountain you have made
> To o'er-top old Pelion or the skyish head
> Of blue Olympus.[1]

Purists, however, are apt to frown upon its more colloquial manifestations, and lament the downfall of the words *awful*, *excruciatingly*, *terrible* in such expressions as "He is an *awful* bore", "The play was *excruciatingly* funny", "She had a *terrible* hat on". But the fact is that those words, and others like them, can still hold their own in an appropriate context. We may write of "an *awful* doom", an *excruciating* pain", "a *terrible* disaster", and the words are not spoilt for us by their colloquial use. The purist argument, therefore, falls to the ground. It is, in any case, vain, since it runs counter to the genius of the language. Indeed, in modern times hyperbole has revealed itself in other usages: a dispute becomes a war, an incident becomes a crisis, a mishap becomes a disaster. True, the use of hyperbole can go too far; but hyperbole is a living and lively element in the language, and indiscriminate condemnation may be rather worse than indiscriminate use of it. *Awfully*, *excruciatingly* and the like, with their hyperbolical meaning, are indeed better kept to colloquial English; but beyond that, good sense and discretion have to decide.

It is interesting to see how our hesitation to mention directly and bluntly unpleasant or embarrassing matters is reflected in language. The Victorian even went so far as to call *trousers* 'unmentionables'. We are not so mealy-mouthed to-day, but propriety still prompts us to say, when we do not exactly mean, *lavatory*; commiseration to say

[1] See also a curious and interesting example in John xxi. 25.

that a man has 'passed away' when we mean he has died; and politeness to say that a man is putting on weight when we mean he is getting fat.[1] In colloquial language this wrapping up of things either in a roundabout phrase or in a single substitute word is very common. Euphemism, as it is called, is a legitimate and important element in modern usage because our present custom of communication demands it. Not that the spoken language, especially among some (not always the lowest) classes, is noticeably refined; it is, perhaps more than ever, full of strange oaths—and worse. But it is at this point—the point of blunt directness about what are commonly the 'taboos' of life—that the written language differs most from the spoken. In another age (for example, Shakespeare's or the early eighteenth century) the written language was blunter—and we are apt to call it coarse. To-day the modern novelist and the playwright are attempting to return to 'plain' writing, especially in matters of sex. They are, in their own sniggering way, fighting euphemism; but, like the spelling reformers and the self-appointed arbiters of vocabulary, they have but very little real effect on usage. Every now and then, however, one scores a hit. Bernard Shaw's "Not bloody likely" in *Pygmalion* was something more than a theatrical triumph; it was a triumphant blow in the battle of euphemism. But it took one no less doughty than Shaw to deliver it; the murky novelists, strange as it may seem, merely beat the air.[2]

It is a pleasant trick of language by which we are enabled

[1] H. G. Wells based an amusing short story, *The Truth About Pyecraft*, on this very euphemism, but unfortunately called it *euphuism*—which is, in fact, the affected manner of writing, common in Shakespeare's day, imitating John Lyly's romance *Euphues*.

[2] Euphemism is an important element in service slang; but the subject is outside the scope of this book, and has been fully treated by other writers, especially Mr. Eric Partridge. In war-time, whether among service men or civilians, euphemistic expressions were helpful in sustaining courage and hope. It was not for nothing that the explosion of a bomb was called an 'incident', or that flying bombs were playfully called 'doodlebugs'.

to call a thing or a person by the name of something associated with it or him—to call, for example, clergymen 'the pulpit' and the people who sit under them 'the pew'; to call the English Government 'Downing Street' and the American Government 'Washington'; to call the King 'the Crown' and the Lord Chancellor 'the Woolsack'. Those who rejoice in technical terms will be glad to know that this figure is called *metonymy* and is not to be confused with *synecdoche*, in which the part represents the whole, as when a worker is called 'a hand', and fifty cows are called 'fifty *head* of cattle'. Both figures are established in modern usage, though their use is limited.

Personification, by which we represent a thing (especially an abstraction) as a person, and simile, which is a likeness, are in the main purely literary figures. They belong to the poet and the orator. One curious piece of colloquial personification, however, is that in which we playfully or affectionately personify a thing by using a personal pronoun (usually the feminine) when referring to it—a railway engine, a motor-car, a ship are all *she* to those who drive or control them. Again, the usage is an illustration of the sensitiveness of language to life.

A simile, when it is not a poetical or rhetorical ornament, often elaborated (as in Milton) for its own sake, should be a visual and explanatory image—brief, apt, and to the point. When P. G. Wodehouse says of a cat lapping that "its tongue went in and out *like a piston*", he uses an excellent simile because the picture suggested is apt and relevant. The following simile (from C. E. Montague's *A Writer's Notes on His Trade*) fails, on the other hand, because it is pretentiously allusive without being relevant, or even correct in its application: "We cannot fancy him [Shakespeare] vowing he never, never would let some darling child of his invention be cut (i.e. abridged), *like the fond mother in the law-suit heard by Solomon*". Our best similes, perhaps, are those which we use in desperation or exasperation—to bring something home to a bewildered or obtuse mind. "He is like . . .", or "It was like . . .", we say, without overmuch thought or pondering on an exact (as distinct from a relevant) image. "He ran like hell" is a simile that defies analysis; but there can be no question about its aptness or vividness.

The Right Word in the Right Place

The difficulties and problems in the specialised use of words—that is, their use in figurative senses, mainly metaphorical, and in those expressions or *idioms* that are individual or peculiar to the language—have been treated, quite deliberately, before the difficulties and problems of their general use. And for this reason. The choice of the precise word that will alone express the intended meaning in its context, and the correct use of the word syntactically or idiomatically, are the two basic elements that go to the making of prose style. Of that much could be written, but it is beyond the scope and intention of this book. There are, however, in the use of words, certain fundamental principles which belong as much to the everyday 'good' English of the ordinary writer as to the prose of the great.[1] These principles are outlined below under four separate headings. The first is of general importance and interest; the others give specific 'bread-and-butter' hints for the proper use of words in both speech and writing.

Synonyms and Antonyms

No two words are identical in meaning and use; or, to put it another way, no two words are real synonyms. This is not an exaggeration. Five or six 'synonyms' may correspond almost exactly, but there is always some little shade of meaning or detail of use that separates them; so that in a given context only one of them is the 'right' word. It is because we forget this so often that our writing becomes 'woolly' and our speech full of halting substitutes or long circumlocutions.

[1] The conditions are somewhat different in verse and are not discussed here.

There is a time (to adapt the words of Ecclesiastes, or The Preacher) to use *easy*, and a time to use *facile*; a time to write *felicitous*, and a time to write *happy*; a time to speak of an *edifice*, and a time to speak of a *building*; a time to call a thing *earthly*, and a time to call it *terrestrial*. The context, the occasion, the type of vocabulary appropriate to the theme, the very sound of the words when spoken— all these things, and some others, are factors in the choice. It is for this reason, as explained on page 147, that so much of the agitation for 'plain' English is wrong-headed and even fatuous. In one context "I gave him ten bob" is plain English; in another "I sent him half a sovereign as a gift"; and in another "I remitted him ten shillings as a donation".

The choice of words, then, is the responsibility of the speaker or writer. If the choice is careless or thoughtless, he fails to express exactly what he intends to say. The word he uses will be, as it were, just a little off the mark. It will not be the inevitable word—the right word in the right place. Even in factual, everyday English—the English of the home and shop and market-place—this 'rightness' of words to express the meaning of the user is important. Technical terms and words peculiar to a particular trade or profession must be used with accuracy and precision—if not, they easily become part of the language of jargon (see page 152).

A light-hearted or indiscriminate variation of words in the same sentence or passage for the mere sake of variation should be avoided, if only because it may deny the principle of 'synonyms' already stated in this note. This type of variation, which is not by any means always to be condemned, since it is designed to avoid awkward repetition, is represented at its simplest when, having mentioned a *cricket bat*, we afterwards refer to it as a *willow*, or when *doctor* progresses, in the course of a few lines, first to *physician* and then to *medical officer*. But all this is so obvious as not to be serious. In the following sentence, however, the variation of words has tended to obscure what little sense there is:

A life's endeavour to teach nations through their literatures to know and respect each other and so rise to higher
levels of culture is a thought which may be eternally
applied, and Professor Strich is exceptionally endowed to
trace the origins of this all-embracing concept.

Endeavour mysteriously becomes *thought*, and then for the
sake of "elegant variation" (see page 146) *thought* becomes
concept. The equation (see page 38) *endeavour*=*thought*
makes no, or at any rate little, sense; and "thought which
may be eternally applied" sounds more like a poultice than
a concept.

It is impossible to teach the way of choosing the right
word; the writer is simply warned that choice is necessary
for the writing of what, in the best sense, is 'plain English';
—that, in short, the first word that leaps to the mind will
not necessarily be the right one. However, there is some
fun and benefit to be had in trespassing on other men's
preserves, or, to drop the metaphor, of inserting the 'right'
word in the context of other writers. So here, as a matter
of interest, are three passages in which certain key words
have been omitted; the reader is asked to choose and fill
the blanks. The first passage is from Doctor Johnson's
Lives of the Poets; the second from a modern Science Note
(Penguin—*Science News* V); and the third from Trevelyan's
England of Queen Anne. The reader is reminded that his
chosen words should be appropriate not only to the sense
but also to the style of the original writer, whose own
choice is given on pages 244–5.

(a) In the midst of his power and his politics (1710–13) he
    kept a — of his visits, his walks, his — with ministers,
    and quarrels with his servant, and — it to Mrs. John-
    son and Mrs. Dingley, to whom he knew that what-
    ever — him was interesting, and no accounts could be
    too — . Whether these — trifles were properly ex-
    posed to eyes which had never — any pleasure from
    the presence of the Dean may be — doubted; they

have, however, some odd attraction; the reader, finding — mention of names which he has been used to
consider as important, goes on in — of information;
and as there is nothing to fatigue attention, if he is
disappointed he can hardly — . It is easy to perceive from every page that though ambition pressed
Swift into a life of bustle, the wish for a life of — was
always returning.

(b) Epoch-making has become quite a — in modern
engineering. It cannot be — that another epoch
was opened when for the first time radar came in —
with the Moon. — that echoes might be obtained
from the moon were never taken — until Sir Edward
Appleton — stated that it was possible. Less than a
year later his prophecy was — by the United States
Signal Corps. Wireless — assert that the conditions
were of the utmost — . The equipment was an
ordinary and old-fashioned Army Signal — of such
size that it could not be lifted. Therefore the — had
to be performed when the moon had just risen and
was standing on the — . That meant that the
atmosphere did its worst to — the signals. But
nothing of all this — a full success, and on January
10, 1946, at 11.58 a.m., contact — the moon was — .

(c) In one — the progress of science and scepticism had
already won an important — for humanity. The
— of supposed witches had reached its — under the
Puritan Commonwealth. It had since been — ,
most — among the educated class. The reign of
Anne — the real end of witch trials. Judges and
country magistrates refused to — old women of —
with the Devil, on the evidence of their neighbours'
— imaginings, or even of their own frantic — . This
marked a great — of common kindliness and good
sense over — cruelty and superstition. It was a
victory of — imposed by an educated aristocracy — a
rural population that still — its old belief in witches,
but was in no position to — it against the will of its
'betters'.

It follows that since the meaning or significance of a word varies according to the context, any one word may have more than one *antonym* or opposite. Thus the opposite of a *slender* cane would be a *thick* cane, of a *slender* man would be a *fat* man, of a *slender* chance would be a *good* chance. Few, if any, words have one function or meaning only; few, if any, words therefore have only one antonym. But, indeed, except for spelling, pronunciation and possibly inflection, there is no purpose or reason in isolating words; they are only 'living' when they are at work, and it is only then that synonyms and antonyms can be determined. To sum up, an isolated word can have half-a-dozen 'synonyms' and two or three 'antonyms' (*slender—thick, fat, good*); but a word correctly used in its context can have no 'synonyms' at all, and only one antonym.

Homophones

The vagaries of English spelling (Chapter VI) and the varied derivation of our vocabulary have left us with several pairs or groups of 'homophones'—words with the same sound but different spelling and different meaning or function. *To—too—two, their—there, in—inn, ring—wring, write—right—rite, gauge—gage* are simple examples. These have, for the most part, to be learnt by rote. It is a good idea to look them up in a dictionary and find, above all, their derivation, which will usually shed light on both their spelling and their meaning. There are one or two useful aids to memory: *there*, for example, may be associated with *where*; the *w* in *two*, the numeral, is obvious in the associated words *twice* and *twenty*; *inn* and *too* belong to a little group of words which have doubled their final letter when they are no longer prepositions leaning on the following word. Such aids, and others like them, should be intelligently used. They will at least save the writer from a choice that depends, it may be literally, on the toss of a coin. The speaker, of course, is relieved of the difficulty.

One or two pairs are particularly troublesome, and deserve somewhat more detailed treatment:

(a) *principal—principle*. The root of both is the Latin *princeps*, 'chief'. *Principal* is normally an adjective (for *-al* as a typical adjective ending, see the next section, page 187)—'*principal* street', '*principal* argument of a speech', '*principal* point to be considered'. But like most adjectives it can, in the usual economy of language, become a noun; so the principal master of a college or school, the principal clerk or secretary in a department of the Civil Service, the principal sum of money invested (as distinct from *interest*), and the principal actor or singer in a performance are all designated *principal*, the simple word, now a noun, doing duty for the descriptive phrase. *Principle* is normally a noun, meaning 'a fundamental quality or attribute', 'a general law of nature, art, or morals'; so we say "A serious *principle* is involved", "a man of high *principle*", "the *principle* of the internal combustion engine", "stick to one's *principles*". It is interesting to note that *-al* for *-le* is not nearly so common as *-le* for *-al*, which crops up in the most unexpected places. Some time ago I found "*principle* sources of income" (or a similar phrase) in a Government document, and a Principal of a Training College tells me he is quite often addressed as *Principle* in communications from the Ministry of Education itself.

(b) *practice—practise*. This pair gives considerable trouble, and rather unnecessarily, since parallel pairs *advice—advise*, *prophecy—prophesy*, *device—devise*, which are not homophones, establish in their very pronunciation the simple rule "*c* in the noun and *s* in the verb". It is, however, necessary to remember the noun turned adjective: "*practice* pitch", "*practice* shot", "*practice* sum"; and that participles, though adjectives, are parts of verbs:

"*practising* dentist", "a *practised* performance". It is perhaps charitable to the author, if uncharitable to the printer, to suspect a misprint in the following sentence[1] from a leading article:

> But though her taste for earthly music may not have developed until she had practiced the celestial mode, she has proved a most worthy patroness of and successor to the Muse.

(c) *stationary—stationery*. The first is normally an adjective, 'standing still'—a *stationary* car, engine; the second is a term for the wares of a man who was not a wandering pedlar, a *stationer*, one who sold from a station or 'standing place'. The common agent suffix *-er* (*baker, butcher, draper*, etc.) affords a clue to the distinction.

There are many others, but few give quite so much cause for hesitation and error as these three. *Dependent—dependant* might act as first reserve; the first is normally an adjective ("a dependent relative") and the second a noun ("a poor dependant"), but the distinction is not yet final. On the whole, however, it is not wise to think too consciously about homophones. To classify them mentally in pairs or groups as is done in this paragraph is sometimes to make artificial difficulties; and the writer is reduced to the state of the golfer who cannot hit the ball because he knows so many rules for hitting it, or the famous centipede which

> was happy quite
> Until the Toad in fun
> Said "Pray, which leg goes after which?"
> And worked her mind to such a pitch
> She lay distracted in the ditch
> Considering how to run.

The real secret is in the use of the dictionary, as the doubt or difficulty arises; and the note given here, with specific examples, is intended to be a guide to such use.

[1] Nevertheless, the passage in which it occurs has so many errors of English that it qualified for a place in the interlude (page 135).

Homonyms, words which are identical in form (i.e. spelling) but of different meanings are even more suitable for dictionary study, if only because they occur together, usually on the same page, in the dictionary itself. Thus in *Chambers's*, p. 714, are to be found these entries:

> *port* (*etym. dub.*) the left side of a ship;
> *port* (Latin *portare*, through French) bearing, demeanour;
> *port* (Latin *portus*) a harbour;
> *port* (Latin *porta*) a gate, an opening in a ship;
> *port* (*Oporto*, a Portuguese town) a wine.

There is usually no difficulty about homonyms in writing or speech. They are interesting mainly as studies in etymology.

The Influence of Prefix and Suffix

Words are built or constructed on one of the following patterns:

(a) simple root (*house, soldier, potato*)
(b) prefix+simple root (*un-tie, trans-late, mono-tone*)
(c) simple root+suffix (*truth-ful, hope-less, rest-ive*)
(d) prefix+simple root+suffix (*un-like-ly, dis-appoint-ment*)

This is, perhaps, an over-simplification. There may be, for example, two or even more suffixes, as in *rest-less-ness*; a Latin prefix or suffix may be hidden in what is here called the simple root (as in *appoint*, originally Latin *ad-+punctam*); and the simple root may itself be, not a recognisable word, but a Latin or French root, like *-fact-*, *-scrib-*, *-sens-*. But the generalisation will serve. It follows that prefixes and suffixes influence the meaning of the root—that if I add the prefixes *e(x)-*, *de-*, *in-*, *sub-* in turn to the root *scrib(e)*, I get four words with easily distinguishable meanings: *escribe, describe, inscribe,* and *subscribe*. But sometimes the prefixes or suffixes themselves have a certain 'synonymity' that renders the complete words either difficult to distinguish or, if they are in fact quite different in meaning, liable to be confused. The most troublesome pair of suffixes is -*ous* and -*al*, and the most puzzling pairs of words in which they occur are set out in the table below:

Root	ous	al	Remarks
continue	continu-ous	continu-al	In general, *continuous* applies to something continuing in an unbroken line or sequence (a *continuous* narrative); *continual* applies to something which keeps recurring at intervals or goes on for a very long time ("the continual barking of a dog", "a continual anxiety"). But it is difficult to tell where one ends and the other begins, or whether, indeed, in modern English there is any real or vital distinction at all.
judici-	judici-ous	judici-al	*Judicious* is general: 'with judgment', used of things (a *judicious* criticism) or persons (a *judicious* critic); *judicial* is legal (the *judicial* bench, a *judicial* decree).
offici-	offici-ous	offici-al	*Officious* is used in a bad sense, 'fussy', 'pettifogging'; *official* (adject.) means 'from the office', that is with the stamp of authority (*official* news).
industri-	industri-ous	industri-al	The first is connected with *industry* in its general sense (=work, labour) and means 'working earnestly' (an *industrious* farmer); the second is connected with *industry* in its narrowed modern sense (=the making or manufacture of articles), and is not applied to persons (the *industrial* revolution, an *industrial* district). An *industrious* town would be one where everybody worked hard; an *industrial* town one full of factory chimneys.

Root	ous	al	Remarks
virtue	virtu-ous	virtu-al	*Virtue* means (*a*) goodness or (*b*) by derivation and in certain special usages, strength or power. *Virtuous* belongs to (*a*) and means simply 'good'; *virtual* belongs to (*b*) and means 'having a certain effect of power without the actuality' (a *virtual* triumph, promise, confession).
sensu-	sensu-ous	sensu-al	*Sensu-ous*, aware of or appealing to the senses, in a good sense—an epithet often applied to poetry and poets; *sensual*, aware of or appealing to the senses, in a bad (especially sexual) sense. *Sensual* originally had both meanings; the distinction was made by Milton.

These half-dozen pairs are treated in some detail in order to suggest a way of approach. Other groups will give rise to similar difficulties. Here are a few. The prefixes or suffixes are italicised: cred*ible*, credul*ous*; express*ive*, express*ible*; sensi*tive*, sens*ible*; value*less*, *in*valu*able*; respect*able*, respect*ful*, respect*ive*; *dis*qualified, *un*qualified; *dis*interested, *un*interested; benefi*cial*, benefi*cent*; observ*ation*, observ*ance*; histori*c*, histori*cal*; econo*mic*, economi*cal*; *for*go, *fore*go. All these, and others as they arise in reading, can be the starting point for some profitable and interesting research in the dictionary.

Some words are more difficult than others and therefore are more badly treated by careless writers. Few people would confuse *respectable* and *respectful*, though "Yours respectably" has been known to occur at the end of a letter; but *respective(ly)* has its own perils. It is a word that, used properly, enables the writer to take a short cut. Thus, with the help of *respectively* I can express this sentence "The History course will be held at Oxford and the

Geography course at Cambridge" like this: "The History and Geography courses will be held at Oxford and Cambridge, respectively". The construction is:

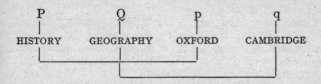

and it is obvious that the correspondence must be correct—P:p, Q:q. There must not be, for example, P, Q, R in the first part of the sentence and only p, q in the second. This correspondence may sometimes be implied, not stated, especially with the adjective *respective*. Thus *respective* is justifiably used in the sentence, "Boys and girls will now go to their *respective* rooms", which means "Boys will now go to the boys[1] room, and the girls to the girls[1] room" (P:p, Q:q). Similarly, *respectively* is justified in the following sentence from a Board of Education pamphlet (The Hadow Report): We consider it important that, wherever possible, separate new post-primary schools should be provided for boys and girls *respectively* that is, some for boys, some for girls—not 'mixed'.

But in the following sentence from a letter in a periodical the writer has come to grief with his *or* for *and* at the end:

> For the policy will result in a further widening of the gap in educational opportunity of the bright boys whose fathers are respectively a lavatory attendant and a peer or brewer (or both)

This incredible sentence raises some curious questions: Are there two boys—A, whose father is a lavatory attendant, and B, whose father is a peer-brewer? or three—A (f=lavatory attendant), B (f=peer) and C (f=brewer)? or

_____
[1] See page 126.

four—the first three as already specified, and the fourth, D, whose father is a peer-brewer (both)?

All this is intended to be a warning not to use *respective(ly)* unless it is absolutely necessary; and if it is, to take care of the *p*'s and *q*'s.

Dean Inge once said, "Don't fancy yourself disinterested when you are only uninterested". The sentence neatly distinguished the two words: *disinterested* means "without ulterior motive", "with no axe to grind"; *uninterested* simply "not interested". It is important to note that *disinterested* is an 'absolute' word—that is, it is never part of a prepositional phrase "disinterested *in* or *by*". But the writers of the following sentences forgot all this; and their lapses, though regrettable, are useful warnings:

> Not many people *disinterested* in party strife will regret the passing of the displaced Middlesex plan for secondary education.

> And for those who are *disinterested* in the particular personalities but interested in human nature in general it provides a rich source of speculation.

> No one could say Mrs. Hilton was on her game against the all-round power of stroke produced by her adversary, who herself seemed a little *disinterested*.

> Life moved ponderously, the Harmsworths hadn't yet begun their work, and the grander commonplaces still seemed soundly *disinterested*.

The first three certainly meant *uninterested*; what the fourth writer meant is known only to himself, but "disinterested commonplaces" is arrant nonsense.

The words *mutual* and *reciprocal*, though not differentiated by affixes, may conveniently be treated here. They both have the sense of 'each-otherness', but in certain respects *reciprocal* differs in use from *mutual*. We can express the fact that A and B respect each other in the sentence "A and B have a mutual (or reciprocal) respect".

Mutual "regards the relation from both sides at once" (Fowler); so also may *reciprocal*. But *reciprocal* "can [also] be applied to the second party's share alone" (Fowler). We may say (if B respects A) that A had a *reciprocal* (but not a *mutual*) respect for B. It is important, by the way, to remember that *mutual* and *reciprocal* are superfluous when "each other" is used.

Mutual is often loosely used for *common*, especially in the phrase (popularised by Dickens) "a mutual friend"—a friend, that is, *common* to two people. This use, as Fowler remarks, has now become so familiar that it is generally accepted, at any rate in speech.

The normal uses of *mutual*, *reciprocal* and *common* can best be summarised diagrammatically:

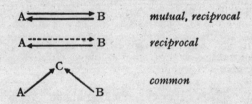

These examples will be sufficient to warn the writer that the prefix and the suffix (or both) are to be carefully looked to, especially when apparently they are similar in effect. A quick mental analysis of the difficult words often sheds light on the problem: *in-valu-able* resolves itself into 'not able to be valued', that is, 'beyond price', whereas *valueless* is simply 'without value'. The suffixes *-ive* and *-ible* are now and then confusing; but for the most part, *-ible* is the equivalent of 'able'; so *expressible* means 'able to be expressed' and *expressive* (as in 'an *expressive* face') means 'with striking expression'. This is not quite true of *sensitive* and *sensible*, but the distinction here is not difficult: *sensitive* (*to*), 'with delicate feeling', 'thin-skinned'

('sensitive to criticism'), and *sensible*,[1] 'with sense' or 'possessed of the senses', that is, *conscious* ("a *sensible* decision, person"; "the patient, though badly hurt, was *sensible*"). *Senseless* is the antonym of *sensible* in its first meaning, and *senseless* or *insensible* in its second. In one pair, *practical* and *practicable*, the force of *-al* and *-able* is difficult to define; but in general, *practical* is the opposite of *theoretical*, while *practicable* means 'able to be put into practice", and is an epithet suitable to words like *scheme* and *plan*. The negative form of *practical* is *unpractical* and of *practicable* is *impracticable*. In the following sentence from an evening paper the writer probably meant *impracticable*, but achieved only a verbal monstrosity: "Mr. Wilson considered such schemes impractical."

Finally, to round off this medley of troublesome root-affix words, here without comment (which might do more harm than good) are four examples to pin down four of the most difficult of all: *effective* speech, action; *efficient* worker, machine; *effectual prayer* (James v. 16); *efficacious* medicine, drug.

Malapropisms

The confusion of words which have only superficial likeness (in spelling or sound) is not as common as playwrights and comedians would have us imagine. Shakespeare was fond of it in a crude, artless way (Launcelot Gobbo's *reproach* for *approach*, Dogberry's *dissembly* for *assembly* and Bottom's *obscenely* for *seemly* or *obscurely* are examples). Sheridan brought it to a fine art in the speeches of Mrs. Malaprop (*The Rivals*). It also pops up

[1] These words have considerable historical interest. Milton and other early poets use *expressive* for *expressible*: "the *inexpressive* nuptial song"—that is, "beyond expression", *inexpressible*. *Sensible*, in Shakespeare, is the equivalent of *sensitive*. He speaks (*Julius Caesar*) of a man's hand "insensible of fire", where modern English would have "insensitive to fire". In its original meaning (given first in *S.O.E.D.*), "perceptible by the senses", *sensible* is not now in common use; but reviewers love to use it so: "Such a reader opens the book with a *sensible* reluctance". In normal English "perceptible reluctance".

sometimes in B.B.C. variety. Here, by way of warning, are a few examples from the main literary source (Sheridan), and a few from actual speech or writing, vouched for by readers of *John o' London's Weekly* some years ago:

(i) Sheridan (Mrs. Malaprop—*The Rivals*):
progeny—prodigy, supercilious—superficial, contagious—contiguous, geometry—geography, superstitious—superfluous, illegible—eligible, orthodoxy—orthography, reprehend—apprehend, malevolence—benevolence, accommodation—recommendation, conjunction—injunction, preposition—proposition, persisted—desisted, 'derangement of epitaphs'—'arrangement of epithets'.

These are the most important and suggestive. Mrs. Malaprop's "the very pineapple of politeness" is in the same class as our modern "casting nasturtiums" for "casting aspersions".

(ii) From *John o' London's Weekly*[1]
(The reader is invited to make the necessary corrections)

. . . the germ was so small you couldn't see it, even if you looked for it with a *microbe*.

. . . could not *emasculate* their food properly.

Have you heard of young Dr. — ? He has been so hard up he has had to pawn his *biceps*.

The owner of the property says if we damage her hedge, she will give us an *injection*.

. . . a young lady who had become *intimidated* with a certain young man.

She simply *analysed* that boy.

The head brewer said he was going to mix two vats of beer until they were thoroughly *inebriated* together.

[1] By kind permission of the Editor.

I never want to travel on the sea, I much prefer *terra-cotta*.

The birth of the Prince of Wales was a *suspicious* event.

. . . suffering from a *chronicle abyss*.

. . . can't clean the floor today. I have to *consecrate* on Mr. So-and-so's room.

One part of the road is to be kept for motors, one part for cyclists, and another for *presbyterians*.

. . . bathing near some rocks when she was seized by an *optimist*.

The air in Edinburgh is very *embracing*.

A *convenience* was waiting at the station.

Apprehensive policies.

There is a nurse in attendance and she thinks the doctor really ought to come and *subscribe* for the old lady. Of course, the nurse herself *subscribes* as well as she can, but she can't tell whether the trouble is outside or *eternal*.

And here is a letter, contributed to the same paper, containing some ingenious and deliberate malapropisms, which also the reader is invited to detect:

It has been brought to my intention that some of your ineffectual readers have been deriving me. Since my stage débacle some hundreds of years ago I have had to put up with much insolvence from the public, and you might think I am now manured to it. But I am not, sir. I do my best with what everyone emits are difficult words, and though I may occasionally get their meanings diffused, I never misspell—my orthopaedics are sound. I know the principals of your paper, and when I appeal to your inert sense of justice, I know my words will not be intellectual. My convention is that a good word is good whenever it is used, and the more cylinders a word has, in my opinion, the better that word is. Meanings, of course, are important; but the pleasure I take in words comes as much from the sound as the sense. When a fine rare word like 'hypercritical' occurs to me, I do not rush for a dictionary. That would be a waste of time. I know appropriately what it means, and I find a use for it quickly. I may be precipitous in this, but at least, Sir, there is madness in my method. May I add that my niece, Lydia Languish, has been in journalese all her life, and for years distributed to your paper?

The malapropist is, at worst, an ostentatious fellow who loves to parade a vocabulary he has never mastered, or, at best, is a lover of what Mr. Polly called 'verboojuice'. But, of whichever type, he offends against good and plain English; and malapropisms are not justified on the score of their being funny.

Some Awkward Words

Here, with comments, are a few miscellaneous sentences in which single words are misused in one way or another:

> On these three their voices are, with the rarest exceptions, unanimous.

Unanimous is one of those superlative or 'absolute' words (*unique* is another) which cannot be modified. "Almost unique" and "unanimous with the rarest exceptions" have in them a kind of self-contradiction. To be of one mind (Latin *unus*, one+ *animus*, mind) with the rarest exceptions is surely beyond the power even of an educational conference. And as if that were not enough, the writer has fallen into the half-dead metaphor trap (see page 169); *unanimous* still retains enough of its Latin origin to make "unanimous voices" an oddity; and if it is argued that *voices*=*votes*, then the phrase should be "unanimous vote" (not *votes*).

> There is some talk of the *nearby* monastery being 'took over' by the government.

Little Gaddesden can have changed little since the legions of Imperial Rome by-passed it on their way to found Verulamium, *nearby*.

Nearby is, as yet, an unlawful union, but common usage is tending to legitimise it. *Chambers's* (1943) gives *nearby* as the adjective form; *S.O.E.D.* gives *near by* (separate words) for both adjective and adverb. But many people, like the writers of the above sentences, anticipate the marriage and write *nearby* for both. Another unlawful union is *alright* for *all right*, and *forever* for *for ever*; the second of these, like *nearby*, is now in common use. It is important to remember that *altogether* (normally an adverb) and *all together* (pronoun+adverb) are different things: "He is *altogether* wrong", "We were *all together* in the drawing room".

These dreary gods, these meticulous rules, impose a welcome pattern on the lives of the order-loving Londoners, though probably few are aware of it.

Certain words, in every age and especially in our own, come under the ban of the pedant or the crank. *Meticulous* is one of them. In one of his less happy articles Fowler inveighs against this "wicked word irresistible to the British journalist". He goes back to Latin, derives it from *metus*, 'fear', and says therefore that it means 'frightened', and can be used in only certain limited, but by no means clearly defined, contexts. One might as well argue that it is wrong to talk of a *candidate* (Latin *candidus*, white) for an examination if he does not actually appear in white robes. *Meticulous*, like many another English word, has simply by usage (of the British journalist, perhaps) extended its meaning and use. In the phrase "meticulous rule" the word *meticulous* simply reflects the 'fear' of the framer of the rule that he may not have made it 'watertight' or foolproof. Words often make a 'jump' in meaning like that. For example, from the legal sense '*execute* judgment or the sentence upon' *execute* has come to mean the actual process of judicial hanging, and we *execute* a criminal. Even *aggravate* in the sense 'tease' ("aggravate a person", "an aggravating boy") derives naturally from its original and proper sense 'make heavier, greater' ("aggravate the symptoms, an evil"). True, in this sense it has not yet properly established itself in usage; but it probably will, in spite of Fowler and the rest. A reviewer in *The Times Literary Supplement* is not afraid to use it so:

> At times he looks at his subject with the steely gaze of the psycho-analyst; this leads him to such aggravating conclusions as the suggestion that there was something 'inordinate' in Lewis Carroll's fancy for little girls.

The popularity of word-baiting and word-banning is indeed remarkable, seeing how vain and foolish it is to fight against the moving, vital element in the living language.

> Charles Williams is a writer so out of the way that he might easily be forgotten in an age uniquely concerned with itself and as nearly as possible quite contemporary. It is timely, therefore, that a standard edition of his novels should be appearing now.

It is to be hoped, and presumed, that the reviewer meant something; but what it is is difficult to arrive at. "An age *uniquely* concerned with itself"? "Peculiarly concerned" perhaps; or "concerned only with itself"; but "*uniquely* concerned" is as great a puzzle as "as nearly as possible quite contemporary". Not quite, however, since this astonishing phrase is beyond all comprehension. There still remains *timely*, and here the reviewer reveals a subtler confusion that betrays the muddled mind. *Timely* means 'appropriate or suitable at this particular time'; so it needs no adverb of time like *now* or *then* to go with it. The reviewer should have written either "It is appropriate, therefore, that a standard edition of his novels should be appearing now" or "The appearance of a standard edition of his novels is timely".

. . . the Anglo-American oil interests in Austria would be left with a wasting asset.

The word is *assets*, which is a 'false' plural, derived from French *assez* (=enough, sufficient). Purists, including Fowler, condemn the new singular formation *asset*; but usage is against them. Such expressions as "His voice was a real asset" are by now too well established to be summarily dismissed. Besides, the formation is a natural one; original forms and meanings cannot trammel the living language. No one objects to the singular formation *pea* from *pease* (as in "pease pudding"), the Old English *pise*; and to frown on *asset* is mere pedantry.

In the last two decades farming has become a much more integrated industry though its units have stayed small.

Most of these essays do succeed in showing the integration of priest and poet.

The piece straggles loosely and some characters are scarcely integrated with the main idea.

Joint Commonwealth defence, integrated at certain vital points with the American defence system is ceasing to be just a blueprint.

Integrate is the latest reviewers' word. It sounds well and can be made to mean almost anything within reason. Basically, it means 'complete by addition of parts', 'combine (parts) into a whole' (*C.O.D.*). Whether it will ever fill a want as a word meaning something more (or less) than *organised* (sentence 1), *unifying* (sentence 2), *associated* (sentence 3 and 4) it is too early yet to say. Meanwhile, like *awareness*, *evoke* and one or two others it belongs to the precious language of those who write for the literary weeklies. (So, by the way, does the metaphorical *blueprint* for *plan* in the last sentence.) By a queer freak, its negative *disintegrate*, 'fall to pieces', is far more familiar to the common man.

And here, to end this section, are a few miscellaneous questions on words. The reader is invited to answer them for himself, before he turns to page 245.

1. Is the word *continuous* (see page 187) used correctly in both, or either, of the following sentences?

   (a) Direct broadcasting is supplemented by a *continuous* stream of over 100,000 records a year distributed to overseas broadcasting organisations.

   (b) And underlying a book which is both suggestive and filled with instruction, there is the warm, *continuous* implicit plea for a complete inner life.

2. Comment on the use of:
   (i) *virtually* in the following sentence: "Ruskin was *virtually* burned out when he was sixty".
   (ii) *literally* in this sentence: "He *literally* glued his ears to the ground".

3. What is the meaning, if any, of the word *inquisitive* in the following sentence?

   Such is the argument of Mr. Duffin's inspiring essay. It is written in a prose that is as imaginative as it is *inquisitive*.

4. Do you object to the word *paged* in the following sentence from a publisher's advertisement? If so, why? What, in your opinion, does it mean?

   The book is selling fast for a happy Christmas. More than forty contributors from early Waugh to late Kavanagh are *paged*.

5. Comment on the words italicised in the following sentences and phrases, which are all taken from the periodicals and newspapers mentioned in the Preface:

   (a) His castle *disponges* rheums and catarrhs.

   (b) I had forgotten to tell you about the husband, *incidentally*.

   (c) Terror is apt to be suspended in a *voluptitude* of laughs.

199

(d) . . . the fairness and *correctitude* of the law.

(e) He appears to blame the Jacobean Bible, indeed, for the fact that Shakespeare is 'such a mass of obsolete words'. But surely the *obsolescence* of many of the words in Shakespeare is due to the fact . . .

(f) The Christmas shopper with the real Christmas spirit should always contrive his purchases so that the gifts and cards sent to others *nicely* exceed in gross number and value those he receives.

(g) I can easily imagine the admirable advice that Dr. Joad, *philosophing* in a Sunday paper, would offer . . .

(h) . . . there was no taint of that meretricious reporting which these episodes of history so often *evoke*.

(i) For Mr. Foster, unlike his party chief, is no *epicure*. He neither drinks nor smokes.

(j) Instead of that I found myself surprisingly *assisting* at a serious film about the American negro problem.
[Note: This is written by a film critic, not by a producer or actor.]

(k) In a book which is marked by an astonishing *cumulative* weight and vividness of characterisation, the character of Sheila Knight stands out because of the *menacing* demand which it makes upon our *apprehension* and sympathy.

(l) . . . the paper would be recognisable inside as well as *externally*.

6. Write an answer to each of the following letters:

SIR, Mr. Archibald Lee states that the use of technical terms denotes an inability to think clearly, and goes on to suggest that the words deflation and disinflation are synonymous.

I would like to point out that the economist

uses these terms precisely, the former to mean a fall in prices accompanied by depression, and the latter to mean a beneficial price fall.

Every science uses precise terms in order to gain economy of language. The economist is aware that his is not an exact science, but attempts to differentiate between one situation and another as accurately as possible. Should he, therefore, be accused of possessing a "shallow and sluggish mind"?

Yours faithfully,

GRAHAM J. EDWARDS.

SIR, We invariably read that people have been "conscripted". The verb is *to conscribe;* the nouns, *conscription* and *conscript*. A doctor prescribes, or gives a prescription. Likewise *describe, inscribe,* &c.—

Yours faithfully,

E. E. ALLENDER

SECOND INTERLUDE FOR ENTERTAINMENT

In the following pages are brought together some miscellaneous examples of literary journalism and re-viewers' English which illustrate many of the points made in the preceding chapter, together with a few others as they arise. No attempt has been made to deal with the modern Americanised style of popular journalism. That is a subject in itself, outside the scope of this book; for this style may be a preliminary symptom of a revolutionary change in the idiom and even the syntax of the language. The sentences printed here illustrate rather the slipshod English to which even literary writers sometimes descend, and which is all the more dangerous since we are apt to read it uncritically and accept it without question. The italics throughout are mine, not the writers', and they indicate the particular word or phrase under fire.

1. The first example consists of a few brief extracts from an article in a Sunday newspaper on a Rugby Football match. The italicised passages state, in various ways, that a goal was not kicked or a try was not converted:

Montgomery dropped a goal, *but the ball didn't feel like work.*

Crossley scored again, *and again the kicker couldn't do it.*

Cormack cut clean away to score perhaps the best try of the match. *The sullen ball again resisted conversion.*

This is the old "odd goal in three" type of jargon (see page 153) developed here by the modern 'literary' sports writer, and used even more queerly, in another sphere, by the wireless commentator. It is, though alas! it is not meant to be, laughable; but the reader with an acute sense of the ridiculous might well consider how the writer could have made his variations on a mainly lugubrious theme in plain rather than facetiously elegant English, or whether, indeed, it was necessary to make them at all. It is a big question, which deserves some anxious thought.

2. (a) In return for the trust invested in him the critic must subdue his personal tastes and preferences as much as possible, although he is foolish, I believe, *to abjure the perpendicular pronoun altogether.*

(b) The point of *Pinky* is that the heroine really looks pink (or white, to use the official description) in a Southern community *in which the pigmentation is predominantly sable.*

Elegant variation with a vengeance. In plain English, "to refuse to write in the first person", "which is predominantly black". Only rarely does the type of facetious pomposity illustrated in these two sentences become effective. It does when Dickens says of Squeers that he had only one eye, *though popular prejudice ran in favour of two*, because Dickens really meant this, and not simply "though most people have two eyes". It does not in the above sentences, or in this, from Professor Green's *The Mind of Proust*: "a rising young physician but in all else the type of imbecile designated in English by the second and sixth letters of our alphabet". Perhaps, however, a sense of propriety inspired this remarkable euphemism.

3. (a) She is always aware of her environment, north, south, east and west; and for that vigil she has eyes in the back of her head, and can see, like the fly, a hundred things at once. And those things include the intangibles, the subjectives, that furnish the human mind, the house of our imaginations, fears, passions and hallucinations.

(b) I admire her work, both in prose and verse because it is a garment worn with courage by a tragic spirit.

(c) If Ophelia, instead of committing suicide, had committed pen to paper, she might have written a novel in this manner. For here is a prose style that has daisies in its hair, and comes to the reader with mutterings of privacy, its fingers plaiting straws and counting dandelion silks.

This is the blurred, cloudy English of the gushing writer. Passage (a) suggests certain questions—Why all the points of the compass? What vigil? Which nouns are in apposition to which in the second sentence? Do intangibles differ from subjectives, or are they one and the same thing? Passage (b) calls up the ludicrous image of the tragic spirit, or ghost, of a lady novelist, walking about courageously clad only in the pages of her prose and poetry. Passage (c)

opens with a childish play on words[1] and then endows a
prose style with hair, legs (since it "comes to the reader"),
lips (that give utterance to "mutterings of privacy", whatever that may mean) and fingers. Such uncontrolled
vocabulary and muddled imagery makes clearness and
precision of prose style impossible.

4. (a) At home, his mentors are constantly reminding
       him, he must forget his insularity and be friendly
       and frank and heartily welcoming to the foreign
       visitors who wander in increasing numbers amid
       our alien corn.

   (b) How, in the theatre, does time gallop withal?
       Here is an opinion from *Old Vic Saga* (Winchester
       Books, 12s. 6d.), another history of that well-
       publicised temple of the Muse.

   (c) Shakespeare observed in "Hamlet" that "every-
       man hath business and desire," and on Wednesday
       I had certainly a busy and desireful day, having
       spent three hours aboard *A Streetcar Named
       Desire* (Aldwych) in the afternoon and proceeding
       to Rossetti (New Chepstow) in the evening.

Apt quotation is an ornament of prose; inapt and ostentatious quotation a blot upon it. The older writers, like
Lamb and Hazlitt, quoted frankly, if sometimes incorrectly. They usually marked time, as it were, on the page,
set the quotation by itself, and then went on again. We
prefer to insinuate the quotation into our own sentence,
not even troubling to acknowledge it with quotation
marks.[2] I have done so myself once or twice in the text of

---

[1] The revival of punning or word-play is one of the more dis-
tressing phenomena of modern literary journalism, especially in the
weeklies. True, a good pun is not to be despised; and now and then,
it must be admitted, a good pun does appear in a wilderness of
verbal quirks and smirks. However, the subject is too big to be
treated here; it requires, indeed, a whole book to itself.

[2] The one use for which quotation marks might usefully be
retained (see page 114).

this book. The first quoter above remembers the alien corn of the *Ode to a Nightingale* and triumphantly and incongruously rounds off his sentence with it. Yet nothing could be more inapt than that particular quotation in that particular context. What, after all, are London, Brighton and Blackpool doing for our foreign visitors? The second quoter, in deliberately garbling his quotation (Shakespeare wrote "Who does Time gallop withal?") writes nonsense; *withal* in Shakespeare means simply *with*, in Modern English *also*. So in neither Shakespearian nor Modern English does the garbled quotation mean anything. After that it is not altogether surprising to find the Old Vic called "that well-publicised temple of the Muse". The third quoter carelessly misquotes—Shakespeare wrote *every man*, a very different thing from *everyman*—and his quotation is used only to give point to a mild word-play on *desire*.

5. A few selected journalistic metaphors:

    (a) Picking over the fragments which remain after so many political explosions, we can at least reassemble some serviceable crockery.

A storm in a teacup is familiar enough, but an explosion?

    (b) Though his brush firmly delineates, in the first part, the influence of foreign literatures on Goethe, and in the second, the poet's effect on the writers of his time and after, there is wealth of detail around the central theme and the pulse of small events proclaims the presence of a new life-blood injected by Goethe into the arteries of literature.

    (c) They are repositories of thought, self-communications, meditations, and into them was poured for forty years the life-blood of an enquiring spirit.

Blood transfusion indeed!

(d) It is not hard to accept the committee's criti-
cisms of the tangle of unrelated courses which
have come by a process of accretion to fill the gap
today. Through this the committee seeks to
drive several main highways.

To drive several main highways through a tangle filling a
gap is certainly a feat worth recording.

(e) Miss Wynyard has kindled the Queen's flame
before the Court. In the last sadness she is hard
to hear: her voice has glimmered to a spark.

(f) There is all the difference in the world between
the infant monopoly of 1927, even the lusty
adolescent of 1936, and the immensely powerful
machine of 1949, still constantly seeking new
avenues of expansion, both at home and abroad.

The machine metaphor seems peculiarly liable to break
down. See page 172.

(g) With reasonable luck the slings and arrows of
outrageous fortune will cease to find their mark on
Middlesex officials, and, with a clear run in front
of them, confidence in planning can be restored.

Slings and arrows again (see also page 175); but where they
will arrive after their "clear run" is a mystery. However,
the Middlesex officials are mercifully out of danger.

· 6. And here, with comments, are a few passages to
illustrate generally some miscellaneous faults of
that 'literary' English which so often deceives
us into thinking it good because at first sight it
seems clever.

(i) First, two examples of verbal pomposity and
circumlocution. Where possible, a translation
into normal English is given under each passage:

(a) The dull are likely to have a limited conceptual
grasp and possibly, though this is by no means
certain, a qualitative difference in intellectual
functioning.

The first half of this sentence means that the dull are unlikely to grasp things easily; what the second half means is beyond my conceptual grasp.

> (b) In a quite exceptional degree he possesses the capacity to translate visual sensations into literate verbal equivalents, and to refer them to general aesthetic principles; and his humane attitude to landscape as an art 'concerned with our whole being—our knowledge, our memories, our associations', will render his lectures of value to an infinitely wider public than that for which they were originally designed.

He is exceptional in being able to translate visual sensations into words ("literate verbal equivalents"); "to refer them to general aesthetic principles" presumably means something—at any rate, it cannot be rendered into simple English. What a *humane* attitude to landscape as an art is would puzzle most readers, as it does me; but, whatever it is, it will make his lectures valuable to many more people ("an infinitely wider public") than those for whom they were originally designed.

> (ii) And now the empty rhetoric of the confirmed 'evoker'. It is possible to make a little anthology of reviewers' favourite words and phrases from this single passage: 'current idiom' (reasonable here, but used by reviewers of almost every human activity under the sun), 'unifying vision', *intimately*, *evoke*, *sensitive* (not quite so common nowadays as *sensible*, *sensibly*—see page 192), *response*, 'supple craftsmanship' (of prose, or idiom, or even syntax). True, the meaning is tolerably clear: it is, in brief, that since Miss Sitwell is a writer given to symbolism and imagery we cannot interpret her writing literally:

We do not go to Miss Sitwell for the literally rendered scene, the character sketch, the social vignette, the echo of current idiom. Criticism that carps at the absence of these in her heraldic world, her world of heroic emblems, is at once obtuse and petty. What she does offer us is a unifying vision, intimately bound to the anxieties of our time, and likely to evoke, in any sensitive reader, a strong, simple, and positive response. Very few poets of our time have such true eloquence, such supple craftsmanship, or such inner fire.

(iii) And here is an example of 'woolly' English:

> On the whole food front one may say that we can enjoy Christmas cheer in the consciousness that though some things are dear, the basic foods are better in quality and still blessedly low in price. When you come to clothes and toys the situation is very much the same. Small toys have multiplied out of all memory and some are not dear. Big toys are expensive; imported French dolls may be three pounds each and an unfurnished doll's house may cost five pounds. The good mechanical toys, the trains and boats, not to speak of the children's tricycles, are all available again; but their price, I'm told, is double or sometimes treble what it was in pre-war days.

To begin with, "On the whole food front one may say" is utterly superfluous and meaningless in this context. It is a parrot-like repetition of what the last writer would call "current idiom". Recast, then: "We can enjoy Christmas cheer knowing that though some things are dear, the basic foods are better in quality and still blessedly cheap" (*knowing* for "in the consciousness", and *cheap* for "low in price" to preserve balance *dear—cheap*). No comment is necessary on the next remarkable sentence except that it can be briefly and simply rendered thus: "So, for the most part, are clothes and toys". The remainder of the sentence is better, but idiom twice falters. First, "out of all memory" is a valiant attempt to adapt an existing idiom "out of all knowledge" to another idea: "We cannot remember when there were so many small toys"—but idiom, as has been pointed out on page 8, will not be subject to such cavalier treatment. Second, "not to speak of" in the last sentence is quite purposeless; if this odd phrase is to be used at all, it should have some contrasting effect, not be a mere elaborate synonym for *and*.

> (iv) His definition of reality has first to be made coincident with the point of view of the individual conception adopted by the poet whom he is discussing. And it is not a simple matter. No analysis of Mr. de la Mare's work is simple, for its marked idiosyncrasy can be a disguise, just as we can all be disguised by our personal habits—wrapped, as it were, in our own limelight.

It certainly is not a simple matter. I am so puzzled that I can only express my bewilderment in questions: How can a definition be "made coincident with" a point of view? Can a point of view belong to a conception, and can a conception be adopted by a poet? The last sentence runs off the rails after the word *disguise*. It should continue: "like the disguise of our own personal habits". The last ludicrous image "wrapped, as it were, in our own limelight" is quite meaningless.

> (v) The poor, innocently reactionary, swindling policeman with his naïve justice, slowly goes mad as he tries vainly to turn himself into an agent of the secret police, looking for socialists in "Greek hats" and their women "like frogs in dark glasses". He is Shakespeare's Bottom with the ass head of politics on his shoulders. The body farce, the walloping, the cynicism, the poetry of Russian humour is in this story which is also tender and moving and has a tight-coiled spring of indignation in it.

First, this sentence has two errors in punctuation and one in syntax. The comma after *justice* separates verb from subject (see page 106), and should be taken out; and since the last relative clause, "which is also...", is almost certainly intended to be non-defining (see page 85) there should be a comma after *story*. Four separate elements are enumerated as being in this story; so the verb should be plural (*are*, not *is*). But the passage is notable mainly for two arbitrary and undeveloped figures—the simile of Shakespeare's Bottom, which is as unintelligible to those who know *A Midsummer Night's Dream* as to those who do not, and the sudden unrelated metaphor of the tight-coiled spring, which could be effective only if the idea of tenderness were also associated with a metaphorical image.

(vi) So that in spite of a rather *voulu* flirtation with an obvious kind of romanticism of subject-matter rather than of feeling, the main trend of English poetry to-day is still uninflated and realistic, though often descriptive rather than satirical. The critical residue that dominates contemporary taste, however, is nearer to taking a common-sense view of life than an aesthetic one.

Except that the writer indulges in the peculiar gallicism *voulu* (what a "*voulu* flirtation" is remains a puzzle), his first sentence up to the word *feeling* will pass muster. But after that difficulties arise. What is an *uninflated* trend? and, if a trend could be uninflated and realistic why could it not also be descriptive rather than satirical? In point of fact, a trend could be none of these things; the epithets are probably intended for *English poetry*. Even then, what is uninflated poetry? The imagery of the bicycle tyre and the balloon seems oddly incongruous. It is impossible to find any meaning at all in the second sentence. A critical residue that dominates tastes and takes a common-sense view of life is a personified monstrosity.

(vii) The Bermondsey novel was never written; the interesting thing about that note is its intimate, factual accuracy, the lack of any spoiling suggestion from a view of art that would be hostile to it. But seeing these few Bermondsey pages among the innumerable comments on travel in the East, in Russia and America, among the sea of faces which Mr. Maugham has put down, it is hard to see how they could have stood their ground among the distractions of civility. Mainly Mr. Maugham has been drawn to the romantic disappointment, and not to the tragedy where no illusion or expectation lay in the first place.

The first sentence is merely hazy. What is a "spoiling suggestion from a view of art", and to what would this be hostile? The second sentence has neither meaning nor form. To begin with, the participle phrase "seeing that . . ." has nothing to qualify but the impersonal *it*. Then the Bermondsey pages are apparently to be found among (i) innumerable comments, (ii) a sea of faces; and both these comments and this sea have been "put down" by Mr. Maugham. The odd juxtaposition "seeing . . . it is hard to see" and the faulty idiom "among a sea" are characteristic of the processes of thought from which this incredible sentence was evolved. The last sentence will pass syntactically; but there seems to be no reason why the adverb *mainly* should be so far out of its normal place, and it is left to the reader to interpret the vague antithesis "romantic disappointment—tragedy".

(viii) For the deciphering of the originality of this style it is not only interesting but necessary for poetry to be subjected to the new critical viewpoint that each generation comes to possess. This viewpoint seeks to appropriate, when it is not intent on destruction, that part of a poet's work which is most relevant to its own needs; and at certain historical or literary periods a way of writing reaches a saturation point, the dead-end of a tradition, which can only be revived by an apparently brutal discarding of indulged manners. Thus poets, and none more so than Byron, vacillate between being ignored and being re-discovered, to the degree in which their idiom, or a facet of it, grows over-familiar.

This passage, like Satan, rises to a bad eminence. It can be dealt with only in a series of (mainly unanswerable) questions: How is originality of style *deciphered*? It may be *necessary* but can it also be *interesting for* poetry to be subjected—that is, can *for* be common to both words? Can poetry, or indeed anything else, be subjected to a viewpoint? If so, can this viewpoint (i) seek to appropriate, (ii) be not intent on destruction? To whose own needs is "that part of a poet's work" relevant? A way of writing may reach a dead-end, but can it also reach a "kind of saturation point", and can either the dead-end or the saturation point be revived? What exactly are "indulged manners"? How do poets vacillate to a degree? When are these poets ignored, and when are they re-discovered? What is a facet of an idiom?

And here are a few sentences taken from various newspapers and magazines, for the reader to criticise. The 'answers' are given on page 248.

1. Apart from my favourite demand that the Government should undertake a radical overhaul of its whole form-filling system, there must be many little ways in which they could set a good example.

2. Nevertheless, both as a personal record and a social document, the book is of great value.

3. It is not merely that the writer is still too near the experience to recollect the emotion in tranquillity, but something more subtle.

4. One reason I am so anxious now to read the predecessors of *The Young May Moon* is to find out whether this complete authority over his material is something he has gradually achieved or whether his is one of those rare talents that seem to have been born mature.

5. As the shop—like almost all hairdressers in the West—was facing bankruptcy, her job would fold up any day now.

6. He takes the simplest things; a suburban street, a bakehouse, a woman's clothes and, with no pressing of the pedal, makes them poetic.

7. Neither the United States nor Marshall Aid are mentioned in the document; and the word "dollar" occurs only once in a passage justifying the continuance of controls.

8. Listening quietly at home, and discussing it afterwards in the pub, the voter can feel that he is really making up his own mind instead of being got at or browbeaten into a decision.

9. It would be perfectly possible to liken Mr. Woodruff's imaginary island of Cgamba as a happy introvert precipitated into temporary insanity by the rude intrusion of the outside world.

10. . . . but he keeps, as it were, a willed sanity and sense of proportion.

11. It is one of the charms of planning that its effects are felt long after the situation, for which it is designed, has disappeared.

12. But these opportunities for the widest education which cannot be offered so fully by day schools do not combine the disadvantages of most boarding schools where the boy is cut off from his home for long periods of time.

13. The teaching is carried out by the housemaster and by another teacher who is also in charge of the farm.

14. Mr. Morrison was, therefore, on strong ground in rebuking Lord Simon for his utterance on the question of election expenses which, as Lord Simon of course admits, can only be decided by the courts.

15. This throws a great responsibility on the wireless which, if the old ways are to be lost, will become greater.

16. His boyhood in France and especially his life in a French farming family where he was left for a time by his widower father, clearly formed his inclination to the formal, Latin authority.

17. The performance of the leading parts is wholly successful, to my mind, only in the case of Greer Garson's Irene.

18. One room of the house, separated from the rest and approached by its own stairway, is set aside in case of sickness.

19. Coming fresh to his work, two things struck me.

20. Confining the perspective of voters at the coming elections to men, of whom there are many still active, in their early eighties, a significant canvas may be covered with scenes of political change.

21. Since none of us can completely know ourselves, public confession, for those who are not saints, too easily becomes exhibitionism.

22. Since none of us is likely to be strong-willed enough to deny ourselves sugar, there seems to be no redress unless we follow the example of a friend who insists on proof of net weight.

23. Here a boy learns the virtue of single mindedness, holding his tongue and getting on with the game, and learns to co-operate with others by playing his part.

24. What happens to the fruit when it is gathered is, of course, another matter. Those whose faith in the remedies of nature has not been undermined by the national health service may use them for curing scalds or banishing warts.

25. Their joint reply was delivered by the Egyptian delegate and certainly does not represent the real feelings of Jordan, and possibly also of Iraq.

26. The ribald are tempted to remark, when the field workers return with their harvest of figures, we could have told you that before you started.

27. The right age for children to enter grammar schools in order to give them the best chance of passing higher examinations later on was discussed last week by the education committee of Berkshire County Council, meeting at Reading.

28. From the point of view of industry the important thing is not that they should have a knowledge of Greek art or be Shakespearians, pursuits which may be just as narrowing as any technology, but that they should have inquiring minds capable of following up new matters which affect their lives, the condition of a sound judgment.

29. Mackail regarded his Socialism as a deplorable aberration, and even in my presence was unable to quite conceal his opinion of me as Morris's most undesirable associate.

30. It is often wise to build on what already exists, but this should not be erected into a policy unfriendly to occasional fresh starts.

CHAPTER V

ON WRITING A LETTER

> " 'Except of me Mary my dear as your valentine and think over
> what I've said.—My Dear Mary I will now conclude'.
> That's all," said Sam.
>> "That's rather a sudden pull up, ain't it, Sammy?"
> inquired Mr. Weller.
>> "Not a bit on it," said Sam; "she'll wish there was more,
> and that's the great art o' letter writin'."
>
> CHARLES DICKENS: *Pickwick Papers*.

Throughout this book certain principles of expression
have been defined and explained—the meaning and function of words, the construction of sentences, the use of
idiom and imagery—and they have, for the most part, been
illustrated with excerpts from good journalism, the work,
that is, of practised writers in English as it is to-day, or
(in Fowler's phrase) "modern English usage". These
illustrations have, in fact, shown how many traps there are
in English even for those who are accustomed to writing
it, and how often the writers fall into them. Many of the
difficulties and errors in the passages quoted are subtle;
it is only when we look carefully at them that we recognise
them at all. But the very exercise of recognising them is of
value. It gives us a deeper knowledge of and a keener
sensitiveness to language; so that in our own more humble,
more ordinary writing, we may steer clear of the more
elementary errors because we have learnt to recognise
the subtler ones in the writing of other people.

We come back to the fundamental fact that language
both spoken and written is, after all, only a way of com-
municating or expressing thought. But thought itself is a
marvellously quick, wayward and complicated thing; and
the translation of thought into language is never an easy
process. True, in speech we can often use gestures and

facial expressions to help when language fails us; indeed, a frown, the raising of an eyebrow, a wave of the hand are really units, or 'words', in the spoken language. But in writing, as has been pointed out several times in this book, we have to search for the *exact* word, phrase, idiom, turn of expression that will represent our thought. To see how hard this is even to the great writers—the novelist, the critic and the poet—we have only to study the manuscript of a great work in the British (or any other) Museum; it is, usually, full of alterations, crossings out, additions, loops, arrows, blots. And what is hard to them is also hard to us in our more humble ways. English (or any other language, for that matter) is only 'bad' in so far as it does not express accurately, according to the appropriate usage,[1] the thought intended.

If we mean by 'thought' that single unit of thought which is represented in language by the simple sentence, the difficulty is not great. But thoughts do not remain isolated; they mingle together, they combine, they form themselves into patterns, they have a certain relationship one to the other. In Chapter II we see how this is true within the framework of the sentence. Thus the diagram on page 42 shows 'thoughts', or parts of thoughts (clauses and phrases) fitting into one another like the pieces of a jig-saw puzzle to make up a unit (sentence) which is no longer simple but complex. But in any sustained piece of writing (for example, a letter) we have to go further than that. We set in order our sentences inside a bigger thought-unit, the paragraph; and, in turn, the paragraphs themselves as parts of a whole.

For ordinary purposes there are three main relationships —*narrative*, in which, for the most part, thought-units (sentences, paragraphs) record events chronologically; *logical*, in which they record reasoned argument, on the pattern of cause and effect; *descriptive*, in which they picture qualities, as they suggest themselves one by one, of

[1] That is, the usage appropriate to the context; for an illustration see page 180.

the object described. They are not, of course, quite so clear-cut as that; but any single piece of writing will have, in the main, the characteristics of one of them. Thus a brief biography of a man or woman would be a simple example of the narrative, or chronological, order: birth—childhood—schooldays—young manhood—middle age—old age—death. The geometry proposition would be an example of the logical: given certain facts, it is required to prove that a certain proposition made about them is true, which we do by a series of related steps, introduced by such words as *if, then, therefore*. When we describe things, we follow normally the suggestion of the eye; we put the details in order as we naturally see them. There is an example in the letter on page 222: (i) the cover, the most obvious part of the umbrella; (ii) something closely associated with it, the ribs; (iii) the handle; and finally, (iv) the gold band. Of course, that is not a fixed order; other people might *see* the umbrella differently. It is merely given to show how suggestion by the eye usually determines the arrangement of thoughts in a descriptive passage.

Everyday writing (as distinct, that is, from journalism and literature) is restricted in scope: it is, in fact, confined—if we except filling up forms, the chief pastime of the Welfare State—to letter writing and, less commonly, making reports. The letters we write fall into two types—those addressed to relatives, friends and acquaintances ('private' letters) and those written on official business. Of private letters there is little to be said here. They are informal communications, and no rules can be made for them beyond those already outlined in this book, which belong to current usage. Indeed, sometimes even these go by the board, and friend speaks with friend by letter in an idiom and even in a spelling that is shared by themselves alone.

But the business of official letters is in another category. Here, to begin with, the writer has to observe certain conventions. He will write his own address on the top right-hand side of his sheet of paper. This may involve some minor problems of punctuation. Some people advocate peppering the address with commas, like this:

                8, Headfort Place,
                        London, S.W.1.

Others prefer no commas at all, like this:

                8 Headfort Place
                        London S.W.1.

The writer may, for once, take his choice. Under his address he will write the date, in one or other of the conventional ways—16 (or 16th) January 1950, or January 16 (or 16th) 1950, or 16/1/50. He may put a comma before the number of the year in the first two forms if he wishes. The top left side of the paper will contain his telephone number, if he has one, and his correspondent's reference marks, if he is answering a particular letter.

The formal opening of a letter is "Dear Sir" or "Dear Madam", if the letter is written, as it usually is, to the representative (Secretary, Manager, Director) of a firm or corporation, or to the Editor of a newspaper. In very formal official language the opening is "Gentlemen", when no individual representative is specified. The salutation is followed by a comma, and the letter itself begins on the next line, inset from the margin, as is usual with the beginning of a paragraph.

The simplest ending to a business letter is "Yours faithfully", or (less commonly, nowadays) "Yours truly", followed by a comma and, on the next line, the signature of the writer. "Yours sincerely" is too personal, and "Yours respectfully" has gone somewhat out of fashion. A rather more formal ending is "I am" (or "I remain") "Yours faithfully". This formula must be used if the previous sentence begins with a present participle and ends with the writer's name ("Trusting you will consider this suggestion favourably, I am . . ."). At the bottom left side of the paper should be written the name, or far more commonly, the official title of the person to whom the letter is written, with his official address.

Here are three examples.   Between them they illustrate the conventions, with the alternatives mentioned above.

(i) A letter in answer to the following advertisement :

> A Young Man wanted as assistant manager of a thriving hardware business in a Midland town.   Write giving age, particulars of education and experience, and any other relevant information to the Proprietor, Smith's Stores, 12 Low Street, Hanbury, Staffs.

11 North Road
Southtown
Surrey

17 January 1950

Dear Sir,
    I wish to be considered for the post of assistant manager as advertised in the current issue of the *Westown Echo*. My age is twenty-five.   I was educated at Southtown Grammar School, where I took the School Certificate Examination with 'credits' in English and Mathematics. Since leaving the Army, in which I served from 1942 to 1945, I have been employed in the hardware department of a large store in South London.   My employers, Messrs Jones and Co. Ltd., are willing to give you any information you require concerning my character and competence.
    I am a single man, and should not, therefore, be unduly troubled by problems of accommodation.

Yours faithfully,
Edward Brown.

The Proprietor
Messrs Smith's Stores
12 Low Street
Hanbury
Staffs.

The language is formal.   The applicant gives the information required and, quite wisely, one or two other details which he thinks would count in his favour.   In this letter, the order of sentences is determined largely by the layout of the advertisement. Note the convention "Messrs Smith's Stores", not "Smith's Stores", in the address.

It is permissible, and may be desirable, to tabulate or 'display' the factual information in a letter of application. Thus the above letter might be set out like this:

11 North Road
Southtown
Surrey

17 January 1950

Dear Sir,

I wish to be considered for the post of assistant manager as advertised in the current issue of the *Westown Echo*. The following is a brief statement of personal particulars and qualifications:

Age and Date of Birth
25; Born 12 December 1924.

Education
Southtown Grammar School, 1935-1940;
School Certificate, with credits in English and Mathematics, 1940.

War Service
King's Royal Rifle Corps 1942-1945; Rifleman, promoted to Sergeant 1943. Service in Italy, France and Germany.

Previous Employment
Salesman, Messrs Jones & Co. Ltd. (Hardware Dept.) Sydenham S.E.26, 1945 to present time.

My employers, Messrs Jones & Co. Ltd., are willing to give you any information you require concerning my character and competence.

I am a single man, and should not, therefore, be unduly troubled by problems of accommodation.

Yours faithfully,
Edward Brown.

The Proprietor
Messrs Smith's Stores
12 Low Street
Hanbury, Staffs.

Note that the punctuation in such a tabulated statement is at the writer's discretion—for example, the full stop at the end of the various items may be omitted. Date forms throughout the letters should be consistent. Period dates may be written in two ways: 1935–1940 or 1935–40. In the formula "Messrs Jones & Co. Ltd.", note that *Messrs* is spelt without a period (.) indicating a contraction, and that the ampersand (*&*) may be written before *Co.* Normally, *and* should be written in full.

(ii) A report to a Railway Lost Property Office of the loss of an umbrella.

11, North Road
Southtown
Surrey
January 17th 1950

Dear Sir,

Yesterday, January 16th, 1950, I left my umbrella in a compartment towards the rear of the 9.6 a.m. train from East Croydon to London Bridge. It was a man's black-covered umbrella, with one rib badly bent, and had a brown curved handle with a silver band near the top.

Will you be good enough to let me know if such an umbrella has been returned to your office? I enclose a stamped postcard for your reply.

Yours faithfully,
Edward Brown.

The Controller
Lost Property Office
Southern Railway
London Bridge Station
S.E.1.

This letter is given as an example of one in which precise statements have to be made, without any ornament or unnecessary description. In actual practice, the particulars would probably be given on a form supplied by the office. Indeed, the use of the printed form in all departments of life is tending to reduce official letter writing to the following formula:

I should be glad if you would send me the necessary, appropriate form for . . . , for which I enclose a stamped envelope.

However, the ordering of facts (see page 218) has still to be done in letters, and more often in formal reports.

(iii) Two letters to the Editor of an (imaginary) magazine. They refer to the letters printed on page 200–201.

(a)

11 North Road
Southtown
Surrey

17/1/50.

Dear Sir,

I am in complete agreement with your correspondent Mr. Graham J. Edwards in his reply to Mr. Archibald Lee concerning the use of technical terms. Every profession and trade has its own vocabulary in which certain words have their own precise and particular meaning. Many of these words are, as it were, the monopoly of the profession or trade concerned, and their use and meaning are known only to the initiated. But many others are taken into the general vocabulary, and are used far less precisely, and sometimes ignorantly, by the layman. It is, in fact, the layman who should be accused of possessing a "shallow and sluggish mind", since he often ventures on technical language of which he does not properly know the meaning. It seems unreasonable to blame the expert for the shortcomings of the inexpert. And, after all, this traffic between technical language and general language is not altogether a bad thing. On the whole, the advantages outweigh the disadvantages.

Yours faithfully,
Edward Brown.

The Editor
Science Magazine
Fleet Street E.C.4.

(b)

11 North Road
Southtown
Surrey

17/1/50.

Dear Sir,

Like most sticklers for and writers on 'good' English, your correspondent E. Allender tries to force the language into a preconceived pattern of his own. No doubt it would be tidier and more consistent if we used the verb *conscribe* as a parallel to *subscribe*, *describe* and the rest. But we don't; we say *conscript*—a back-formation, perhaps, from the noun *conscription*. That is modern usage, and it is usage that prevails.

Yours faithfully,
Edward Brown.

The Editor
The Weekly Examiner
Fleet Street E.C.4.

The language in all three letters is direct but not abrupt. In each, the writer has something to say and says it in a manner that, without wasting words, is courteous and clear. Relevance—keeping to the matter in hand— comes first; and that in itself involves ordered thought, a proper choice of vocabulary, and an economy in words.

Much has been written of what is called 'business English' or, more frequently, 'business jargon': "We acknowledge the favour of yours of the 28th ultimo". But quite unnecessarily. Business English is the legitimate jargon of business houses; they understand both how to write and how to interpret it. It is as unreasonable to attack it as it is to attack, for example, the language of the law or of golf, or the slang of the public schools. Like all English, in any context, and all recognisable jargon, it is only truly bad when its meaning is not clear *in its own idiom*.

Only the general and elementary points in letter writing are dealt with in this chapter. It is important to remember that different professions, firms and offices have their own rules and conventions, especially for typists. More detailed treatment is given in various manuals written specifically on the subject.

Charles Lamb, in one of his own letters, pictured himself as going through the various stages from plain Mr. Lamb to Viscount Lamb and on (as he puts it) to King Lamb and Pope Lamb. No instructions are given in this book on the modes of address for members of the nobility. In the unlikely event of the reader's having to write personally to a Baron or an Archbishop he should consult a book of etiquette.

And here, as an appendix to the chapter, are three dozen sentences written (not necessarily in letters) by men and women unpractised in writing anything but everyday 'utility' English. They will help to point a moral. The errors they contain are noted on page 250 ff.

1. We pondered deeply as to the best course of action to be taken.

2. Naturally I was, at first, rather ignorant and impervious to the important significance of that daily scene.

3. The more fortunate who lie still abed turn fretfully, resenting this insistent moaning which disturbs them from their sweet oblivion.

4. As for me, I am happy; you see, I escaped before I was hammered into that rut.

5. Today we turn round yet another milestone in life's journey.

6. The mills of God having ground exceeding small the last seconds of 1949, we turn to face the year which heralds the passing of half a century.

7. Each one of us is far too concerned with our own self importance.

8. The dyeroom was a noisome place.

9. The flicker of light from the gas lamps indicated that the night was barely passed.

10. On the eve of the New Year one is reminded more than at any other time of the ephemeral nature of human life.

11. We have thought of the challenges ahead, both to us as a nation and as persons.

12. The long road had been travelled many times before it was decided to pay close attention to one of the many hives of industry that had their permanent place at its side.

13. Here was centred a very important industry indeed, namely, the repairing of ships, one of the essential works as far as this port was concerned and without which it could hardly hope to survive.

14. On reaching the end of the year, events appertaining to the political world afford considerable and weighty thought to each one of us.

15. There is the question of whether you feel that the Government is justified in spending fantastic sums of money on such a scheme.

16. On the other hand you may feel that the Government has carried out a difficult and onerous task, and that given a further term in which to carry forward their ideas they will make their policies pay.

17. *Wuthering Heights* is centred round the place of that name on the wind swept moors of Yorkshire.

18. The homely wisdom of Mrs. Dean and the sanctimonious hypocrisy of old Joseph are amongst the minor characters who together succeed in bringing the story to life.

19. The rain seems to glide across the mountain in a driving curtain which gives the effect of the mountain hurrying away as the moon seems to hurry from the clouds.

20. Even Winston Churchill couldn't bring his eloquence to very much avail on phrases like these.

21. . . . although in many cases the churches and schools have become derelict, and appear as the last remains of a bygone age.

22. And the sound of tug-boats' whistles are endless.

23. Looking back on 1949, there are many significant happenings that spring to mind.

24. The river looked even more impressive due to the bright sunshine.

25. The men returning from their night's toil, and who soon will be having a well deserved rest, give a cheery greeting to the new shift and relief.

26. Long before dawn in every mining village, there is to be seen lights in nearly every home.

27. What better time than the New Year for an examination of your past record and a judicial amount of self-criticism.

28. Unlike most boys' books, these characters are credible.

29. The atom bomb looms over us.

30. Readers will once more be humoured by the satire of that irate pamphleteer, Dean Swift, whom we are told is once more back in Ireland.

31. Each of us is to be asked to solemnly decide in which of the two main streams of political thought our country is to go forward. If any one of us votes on this issue any less responsibly than we would if our vote alone were to decide it, we will have failed our generation.

32. The shapes of these buildings are very square and tall.

33. Not being a market day, the square was utilised for the parking of several cars.

34. The village could only boast two streets of any importance.

35. Rain or fine, the scene remained the same, and to the eyes of the solitary watcher always had and always would.

36. The colours of the fields, truly golden, are uncomparable in any other part of the British Isles.

CHAPTER VI

THE BUGBEAR OF SPELLING

> But above all, Sir Anthony, she should be mistress of orthodoxy,
> that she might not misspell.
>
> R. B. SHERIDAN: *The Rivals*

The difficulties of English spelling, which are nearly
always exaggerated, arise mainly from the fact that one
symbol (that is, letter or combination of letters) can represent more than one sound, and one sound can be represented by more than one symbol. Thus the symbol *s*
represents different sounds in the following words: *sing, his,
sugar*, and no sound at all in *isle, aisle*; and the sound most
conveniently written *ee* (*reed, seen, speech, beech*) may also
be written *ea* (*read, speak, beach, dream*), *ie* (*believe, achieve,
siege*), *ei* (*receive, deceive, seize*), *eo* (*people*), *i* (*machine,
intrigue*), *e* (*scene, precede*).

There are other peculiarities, as for example the retention
of a symbol for a sound that does not exist: *s* in *isle* (above),
p in *psalm, psychology*, *g* in *gnaw, gnarled, design*, *k* in *know,
knuckle*, *b* in *comb, dumb*, *w* in *sword*, *h* in *hour, honour,
heir*, *l* in *calm, half*, the first *m* in *mnemonic*, *n* in *solemn,
hymn*, *gh* in *dough, bough, fight, daughter*.

Most of the apparent aberrations arise because, in the
main, words are spelt in modern English etymologically—
that is, according to their historical shape or form—not—
phonetically—that is, according to their sound. It was
not always so. Chaucer, Shakespeare, and Milton all spelt
sensibly; they let the shape of the word, the symbols in
which it was written, represent the sound as far as it was
possible. The sentimental people who oppose spelling
reform always forget this; just as Wordsworth falsely
imagined that "we speak the tongue that Shakespeare
spoke", so they wrongly assume that we write the language

that Shakespeare (or Milton) wrote. As a matter of fact, the general pattern of modern spelling was determined as late as the eighteenth century by such pedants as Doctor Johnson, who himself, for example, in his Dictionary spelt the old English verb *ake* with a *ch* for the *k* (*ache*), as if it were derived from Greek (see below). But one thing is certain: if English is to become an international language, a reasonable reform in spelling is of far more importance than, for example, an artificial simplification of vocabulary, as in 'Basic' English.

However, we have to take our spelling as we find it. There is no obvious law controlling the odd contradictions of pattern and sound, the apparent arbitrariness and inconsistency of symbols. We learn the form of common words by the mere process of seeing them. And it so happens that many of the words in which sound and symbol are at variance are the oldest and most familiar—those, that is, which belong to the native language, Old English, or (as it is sometimes called) Anglo-Saxon.

A few further examples are tabulated below, rather for general interest than as a help to the speller:

Symbols Concerned	Examples	Notes
k ck c ch qu	kill, strike kick, stick cat, cucumber, coal fantastic, elastic chaos, character, distich psychology, school, echo picturesque, mosque	At the end of words the hard *k* sound is represented not by simple *k* but by *ck* or *c* (except in one or two foreign borrowings like *yak*). The *c* is hard as a final consonant and before the vowels *a, o, u,* soft (see below) before *e* and *i*; *ch* is hard in words derived from Greek, which are often technical or scientific terms, but soft in ordinary familiar words (*chatter, cheerful, chime*); *qu* is French, and occurs chiefly in the combination -*sque* at the end of words. At the beginning of words *qu* (*question, quit*) is the equivalent of *kw*.

Symbols Concerned	Examples	Notes
s ss c sc	sing, sit, settle	
	less, grass, blessing	
	certain, cell, civil, ceiling	*c* soft before *e* and *i* (see above).
	scissors, science, descend, acquiesce, effervesce, nascent, miscellaneous	*sc* from Latin verbs, especially *scando* ('climb'), *scio* ('know') and those ending in *-sco* (e.g. *quiesco*, *nasco*).
	at the end, for example, of plural nouns and the third person singular of verbs (*dogs*, *windows*, *tries*, *runs*).	The *s* is voiced (—*s*) after certain consonants. For the endings *-ise* and *-ize* see the note on page 242.
sh s sc t c	shall, shake, ash, fisher	
	sugar, sure	
	conscious	
	patient, nation	*sc*, *c*, *t* in combination with a following *i*.
	gracious	
f ff ph gh	fall, fire, if, draft	Note that in the word *of* the single *f* has the sound of *v*
	chaff, off, stiff	
	philosophy, phial, photography	*ph* in words derived from Greek.
	cough, rough, laugh, draught, enough	The *gh* represents the Old English guttural sound, which no longer exists. In those words where the symbol remains we either do not sound it at all (see page 228) or sound it as an *f*.

Symbols Concerned	Examples	Notes
g gu gh	garden, game, gauge, goal, gutter	*g* (like *c*) is hard before *a, o, u,* soft before *e, i.* The chief exception is in the word *give*.
	guardian, guile, guest, guarantee, league, tongue	Note *gauge* (above) not *guage*.
	ghost, ghoul	The two most familiar words beginning with *gh*; *ghetto* and *gherkin* are two less familiar ones.

These are all consonant variations. Variations in vowels and vowel combinations (like those illustrated on page 228) are so common, and so much an integral part of English spelling, that they cannot be systematically tabulated. They have to be visualised and learnt; there is no other way.

But though there are no fixed laws or rules for spelling, there are certain helpful, if not altogether reliable, guides. The chief of these are set out here:

1. It is a great help to recognise the basic pattern of words as outlined on page 188, and mentally build up words from their component parts (e.g. prefix— root—suffix) rather than spell them as whole units. Thus if we add the familiar Latin prefix *dis-* to the following root words,[1] *appear, appoint, satisfied, solve, similar,* we get *disappear, disappoint, dissatisfied, dissolve, dissimilar*; there would be no risk, that is, of writing *dissappear, dissapoint*, of spelling the other three with one *s*. Similarly, if we add the Latin prefix *inter-* to the Latin roots *-rupt-* and *-rogat-*, we get *interrupt* and *interrogate*; if we

[1] Some of these 'root' words themselves are, in fact, made up of prefix and root. See under 2.

add the adverb suffix *-ly* to an adjective that already ends in *l* (like *occasional, literal, joyful*), we are bound to get two *l*'s—*occasionally, literally, joyfully*; and if we add the suffix *-ness to green, thin,* we get two *n*'s *greenness, thinness.* It is important to remember, by the way, that if we add *-ly* to a word ending in *-ll,* we get two, not three, *l*'s—*fully.*

Sometimes certain changes occur at the point where the prefix or suffix is added. They may be briefly classified like this:

(a) *assimilation.* This is the term applied to the process by which the last consonant of a prefix is 'made like' the first consonant of the root word. Thus, the word *assimilation* itself is made up of the prefix *ad-*+the Latin root *similis* (like); the *d* of *ad-* has been 'made like' (assimilated to) the *s* of *similis.* Here are a few more representative examples. Root forms (usually Latin) which are not actually English words are printed in small capitals:

Prefix	Root	
in-	regular	*irregular*
	mortal	*immortal*
	mobile	*immobile*
	legal	*illegal*
	legible	*illegible*
	NOCENS	*innocent*
com-	NECT-	*connect*
(form of Lat. *cum*=with)	LABOR-	*collaborate*
	LAPS-	*collapse*
	LECT-	*collect*
	RUPT-	*corrupt*
	RECT-	*correct*
	RUGAT-	*corrugate*
	MEMOR-	*commemorate*

Prefix	Root	
ad-	LITERAT-	*alliterate*
	CUMULUS ('heap')	*accumulate*
	FECT-	*affect*
	FILIUS ('son')	*affiliate*
	GRESS-	*aggression*
	NIHIL ('nothing')	*annihilate*
	NEX-	*annex*
	PEND-	*append*
	PLAUD-	*applaud*
	ROG-	*arrogant*
	SENT-	*assent*
	SEVER-	*asseverate*
	SOCI-	*associate*
dis-	FER-	*differ*
	FID-	*diffident*
sub-	FER-	*suffer*
	GEST-	*suggest*
ob-	PORTUS ('harbour')	*opportune*
	POSIT-	*opposite*

Assimilation had usually already taken place in Latin, before the words found their way into English; and it appears equally when a word comes into English by way of French, as *arrive*, *appoint*. But the important thing to remember is that usually the result of assimilation is a double consonant. Not quite always, however: when, for example, *ad-* is prefixed to the roots *quaint*, *quit*, *quiescence* we get *acq-* not *aqq-*; and where *dis-* is prefixed to a root beginning with soft *c* no assimilation takes place: *discern*.

233

(b) *adding a suffix beginning with a vowel:*

    (i)   to a word of one syllable ending with single vowel+single consonant—the consonant doubles: *sad—sadder, dig—digging, sun—sunny.*

    (ii)   to a word of more than one syllable ending in single vowel+single consonant—the consonant doubles only if the last syllable of the word is stressed: *begin—beginning, prefer—preferred, submit—submitted.*

The best way, perhaps to prove (and properly understand) this useful but not altogether safe guide is to find the exceptions among the following: *preference, traveller, flannelette, civility, galloping, biased, occurrence, gossiping, devilish, buses, befitting, benefiting, wedding, forgetting, gases, unparalleled, dactylic.* Why are the following not exceptions?—*sober, reader, deciding, gracious, precarious, uses.*[1]

It is useful, at any rate, to remember that double consonants may, and often do, occur at the junction of prefix or suffix and the root word. To know this is to be alert to the possible difficulties; and the exceptions are better seen against the background of the general rule.

The following words illustrate some representative difficulties in connection with double consonants, mainly in the actual roots. Latin and other origins are given where they throw some light on and give a clue to the modern English spelling.

abbot: Not *-tt*, but note *abbess.*

aberration: *ab* + Latin *erro*, 'wander'. Compare *errand* and *erratic.*

accommodate: *-cc-* by assimilation: the root word is Latin *commodus*, as also in *commodity, commodious.*

---

[1] Answers on page 252.

addition: From *add*, which is itself formed by assimilation from Latin *ad*+*dare*, 'give'.

agree: Note one *g*. Contrast with *aggressive*, where the double *g* is by assimilation.

asinine: One *s*: from Latin '*asinus*'. Our simple word *ass* is the Old English *assa*, which is cognate with the Latin word.

assassin: -*ss*- twice over.

barrel: -*rr*-, and single *l*.

barricade:
barrier: Note -*rr*-.

battalion: -*tt*-, single *l*. The simple word *battle* gives a clue to the spelling.

biennial: Double *n*. The ultimate root is Latin *annus*, 'year'. So *annual*, *perennial*.

constellation: Latin *stella*, 'star'. So the adjective *stellar*.

consummation: The Latin root is *summus*. So *summary*, *summarise*. Contrast with *consume*.

desiccated: Not -*ssic*-. The Latin is *siccus*, 'dry'.

embarrass: -*rr*- and -*ss*.

exaggerate: Note -*gg*- not -*rr*-. Root is Latin *agger*, 'heap'. *Exaggerate* means, therefore, 'heap-up', or in modern idiom, 'pile it on'.

harass: One *r* and double *s*. Contrast *embarrass*, above.

massacre: Note the -*ss*-. *Massacre* is one of several words (like *fibre*, *centre*, *calibre*, *theatre*) that have the characteristic French ending -*re*, pronounced in English as if spelt -*er*, and so spelt in American.

mattress: Note the -*tt*-.

medallion: One *d*. The simple *medal* gives the clue to the spelling. Compare *metal*, from which root the word *medal* itself is derived; and remember *mettle* ('on your mettle') and *meddle*.

millennium: Double *l* and double *n*. Latin *mille,* 'thousand'+ultimate root *annus,* 'year'. See *biennial,* page 235.

necessary: *c* and *ss*. The word contains two spellings of the same sound. So, of course, *necessity* and *necessitate.*

oppress: *-pp-* by assimilation. It is important to remember the *ss* when a suffix is added: *oppression, oppressive.* So, *success, succession, successive.*

paraffin: One *r*. The prefix *par* means 'little'. The word *affinity* gives the clue to the double *f*. *Paraffin* means 'having little affinity with (an alkali)'.

parallel: The prefix is the Greek *para-* (as in other English words, *paragraph, parasite*). Hence not *-rr-*. Note *unparalleled* and *parallelogram.*

possess: Double *s* twice over.

predecessor: Two spellings (*c* and *ss*) of the same sound, as in *necessary.* So *intercessor.*

proffer: The clue is *offer.*

quarrel: *-rr-* but single *-l*.

resort: One *s*. The construction is prefix *re-* +
resource: *sort, source.*

satellite: Not *-tt-*.

syllable: *-ll-*. Note derivatives: The adjective is *syllabic,* which is often compounded with Greek numeral prefixes, especially *mono-* ('one'), *di-* ('two'), *deca-* ('ten'), giving *monosyllabic, dissyllabic,* and *decasyllabic.* The double *s* in *dissyllabic* is obviously wrong, according to derivation; Fowler and the *Shorter Oxford Dictionary* advocate *disyllabic,* but usage is against them.

tyranny: -*nn*- not -*rr*-; *tyrant* gives the clue. The adjective is *tyrannical*.

vacillate: Not -*cc*-.

vaccinate: Not -*nn*-.

  (c) adding a suffix to word ending with mute (or silent) *e*:

     (i) if the suffix begins with a consonant the mute *e* remains: *safety, immediately, sameness, wideness* (but *width*, whose pronunciation, however, is a guide), *baneful, awesome* (but *awful*, an important exception), *judgement, acknowledgement* (or *judgment, acknowledgment*, "according to the taste and fancy of the speller").

    (ii) if the suffix begins with a vowel the mute *e* is dropped: *bake—baking, sane—sanity, decide—deciding, monotone—monotonous*. It remains, however, after *c* and *g* if it is necessary to keep them 'soft' before *a, o, u* (see page 231): *outrage—outrageous, service, serviceable, change—changeable*.

To both parts of the rule there are minor exceptions: we write *duly* and *truly* instead of *duely* and *truely*, *singeing* (from verb to *singe*) instead of *singing*, *wholly* instead of *wholely*; we hesitate between *blueish* and *bluish*, *moveable* and *movable*, *likeable* and *likable*, *mileage* and *milage*, *lineage* and *linage* with a preference for the first out of each of the last two pairs. But the rule's the thing. The exceptions only keep us in a pleasant state of suspense.

  (d) *y* and *i*

    The final *y* of a word is only an *i* with a tail added to it in recognition of its strategic rearguard position. When a suffix is added to such a word the tail is usually cut off, and the *y* becomes a simple *i* again. But, unfortunately, there is no very safe rule. A few guiding suggestions are given below:

(i) *y* becomes *i* in words ending in consonant +*y* before any suffix except one beginning with *i*: *ally—allied, happy—happiness, beauty—beautiful, spy—spied, try—trial, sixty—sixtieth, marry—marriage, carry—carriage, pity—pitiable, lonely—lonelily, dry—drily, pity—pitying.* Note as exceptions: *beauteous, plenteous, piteous, shyly, shyness, dryness, slyly, slyness.* The *y*>*e* in the first three because *ti* would give the *sh* sound (see page 230).

(ii) *y* remains in words ending in vowel +*y* before a suffix beginning with vowel: *boyish, conveyance, annoyance, delayed, stayed, volleyed, player, enjoyed, joyous.* (But note: *lay—laid, say—said* and *pay—paid*). Before a suffix beginning with a consonant there is some hesitation. The following are worth remembering: *gaiety, daily, gaily, joyful, playful, says, enjoys.*

(e) The rule for making the plural of nouns in English is: add *s* to the singular form. What exceptions there are are mere survivors of the older language (like *men, children*) or borrowings from other languages (like *termini, bureaux*) and they offer no real difficulty.[1] But the *a* of the plural, like any other suffix, may have repercussions on spelling. Thus:

[1] That is, if the dictionary is used intelligently. There is a tendency for words of this kind which are in very common use to go over to the normal English plural in -*s*. Or we sometimes get two different plurals, one native and one English, with different meanings or uses: *formulae* (Latin) in scientific and *formulas* in common use. Similarly, *indices* (Latin) in mathematics but *indexes* of a book, and *genii* (Latin), 'spirits', but *geniuses* 'men possessed with a spirit'.

(i) in nouns ending in consonant+*y*, the *y* changes to *i* and *-es* (not simple *s*) is added: *lady—ladies, baby—babies, territory—territories*; but nouns ending in vowel+*y* follow the rule: *donkey—donkeys, boy—boys, play—plays*.

(ii) nouns ending in a sibilant (i.e. hissing sound, *s, ss, sh, ch*) add *-es*: *gas—gases, lass—lasses, ash—ashes, church—churches*.

(iii) nouns ending in consonant+*f* hesitate. Some follow the rule, some turn the *f* into *v* and add *-es*, and others allow us to use our discretion. Fowler gives the following preferences for the chief doubtful ones: *hoofs, scarfs, turfs, wharfs*.

(iv) Most familiar nouns ending in *-o* add *-es* for the plural: *hero—heroes, potato—potatoes, tomato—tomatoes*. Nouns borrowed from other languages, and less familiar words generally, follow the normal rule, and add *-s*: *folio—folios, ghetto—ghettos, solo—solos* (but in the technical terminology of music, the Italian *soli*) *arpeggios*. However, the matter is not very serious. Even the experts are divided. Fowler, for example, says that the plural of *manifesto* is *manifestos*; but the *Shorter Oxford Dictionary* says *manifestoes*, which is certainly the popular, and therefore the correct, form in Modern English.

2. One cause of difficulty in spelling is the neutral unstressed vowel, especially in suffixes, which may be represented by different letters or combinations of letters. This sound is often shown in phonetic script as an *e* upside down (ə). It is most troublesome in:

(a)   agent nouns, where the spelling may be *e*, *o*, or *a*: *baker*, *builder*, *diver*, *propeller*, *actor*, *author*, *beggar*;

(b)   words with suffix *-ance*, *-ant*, *-ence*, *-ent*: *obser*vant, *persever*ance, *preponder*ance, *repent*ant, *interfer*ence, *potent*, *resplend*ent, *sentence*;

(c)   words with suffix *-able*, *-ible*: *compar*able, *lik(e)*able, *lov*able, *reason*able, *compat*ible, *cred*ible, *defens*ible, *feas*ible, *sens*ible;

(d)   words ending in *-ary*, *-ery*, *-ory*: *ordin*ary, *prelimin*ary, *probation*ary, *salut*ary, *cemet*ery, *monast*ery, *mem*ory, *transit*ory;

(e)   words ending in *-or*, *-our*: *govern*or and other agent nouns (see above), *horr*or, *stup*or, *terr*or, *behavi*our, *hon*our, *hum*our, *savi*our, *val*our. These all originally had the *u* in English— for example, *governour* in the Prayer Book, *horrour* in Johnson and other eighteenth-century writers. But in some it has dropped out, and in others remained. It is a great pity that in this matter English does not conform to American usage, and spell all these words *-or*. This would immediately solve the more serious problem which arises when a suffix is added to a word *-our*. As it is, the *u* is sometimes dropped and sometimes retained. Thus we have *honourable*, *honoured* but *honorary*; *humouring* but *humorous* and *humorist*; *coloured* but *discolorated*; *evaporate* and *vaporise* from *vapour*; *invigorate* and *vigorous* from *vigour*. If the original ending were always *-or*, there would be no doubt about these derivatives.

Sometimes a neutral vowel is dropped before a suffix beginning with a vowel, except the normal participle endings (*-ing* and *-ed*). Thus we have *enter*, *entering*, *entered* but *entry, entrance; remember, remembering, remembered* but *remembrance. Deliver,* however, makes *deliverance, delivery.* Other forms worth noting are: *actor—actress, conductor—conductress, executor—executrix, tiger—tigress, winter—wintry* (but *summer—summery*). *Lighten* (verb) has present participle *lightening,* but the noun is *lightning*: "It is lightening vividly", "a vivid flash of lightning".

No attempt is made to give exhaustive lists of words containing neutral vowels. These notes will merely help the reader to classify them mentally, and therefore to be on the alert when he is faced with the difficulty of spelling them.

3. The vagaries of the consonant *l* are worth a special note. Simple monosyllabic words ending in *-ll* sometimes, but not always, lose one *l* when they are compounded with another word. Thus:

all   *almost, alone* (='all one'), *always.* For 'all right', 'all together' and *altogether* see page 196.

full   One *l* is always dropped when *full* becomes an adjectival suffix—*beautiful, hopeful, joyful.* Note also *fulfil, fulsome.*

still   *distil, instil*

till   *until*

well   *welcome* but *farewell*

4. The familiar rule "*i* before *e* except after *c*" is valid only when the *ie* or *ei* is pronounced *ee.* There are only two exceptions—*weird* and *seize.* Such words as *leisure, their, counterfeit, forfeit, heir,* in which the *ei* is not pronounced *ee,* do not come under the rule. It is worth while remembering that in all of them the *e* precedes the *i.*

5. Pedants and printers keep alive a distinction between
   -ise and *-ize* as verb endings. No one knows why.
   The ordinary man does not care a brass farthing, and
   uses *-ise* for them all. If those who write for
   publication would only stick to their guns and defy
   the tyranny of the influential Printing Houses,
   they would soon bring about a minor but useful
   spelling reform. An artificial distinction based on an
   etymological subtlety that cannot be known to the
   ordinary man is an unnecessary archaism, and ought
   to be abolished forthwith in the interests of everybody—including printers.

We have touched only the fringe of the matter. There
are hundreds of words with basic difficulties that give us
pause. But this does not profess to be a spelling book, and
no long lists are given to tease the reader or lure him into a
false security. The bad speller is advised to go to the
dictionary whenever he is in doubt about the individual
word. His very effort in doing so will help to fix the spelling in his memory. Meanwhile if he wants to test his
powers of observation—by what is called among young
children the 'look and see' way—he could not do better
than try his eye on some of Swift's inventions in *Gulliver's
Travels*, especially *Brobdingnag* and *Houyhnhnm*.

But in spelling both eye and ear often fail, and then there
must be a real effort of mind and memory. Reform will
have to come gradually, possibly somewhat on the lines
hinted at or suggested in this section. In general, we might
well follow enlightened American usage. The subject was
discussed in Parliament as recently as 1948, on a Private
Member's motion, and several specimens of reformed
spelling startled the readers of newspapers and magazines.

But the real way, strange as it may seem, may be back
to the spontaneous, phonetic spelling used by Chaucer,
Spenser, Shakespeare and Milton, before (in the words
of Bernard Shaw) we became "entangled in the absurd
etymological bad spelling" of Doctor Johnson. Then,

provided we make our symbols represent the sound, we shall be at liberty to spell as we please: *receive, recieve, receave* and *receeve* will all be equally correct. We shall have the noble freedom of the men of old—a freedom that was lost for English by the lexicographers of nearly two centuries ago.

ANSWERS TO QUESTIONS

I. Pages 181–182

(a) In the midst of his power and his politics (1710–13) he kept a *journal* of his visits, his walks, his *interviews* with ministers, and quarrels with his servant, and *transmitted* it to Mrs Johnson and Mrs Dingley, to whom he knew that whatever *befel* him was interesting, and no accounts could be too *minute*. Whether these *diurnal* trifles were properly exposed to eyes which had never *received* any pleasure from the presence of the Dean may be *reasonably* doubted; they have, however, some odd attraction; the reader, finding *frequent* mention of names which he has been used to consider as important, goes on in *hope* of information; and, as there is nothing to fatigue attention, if he is disappointed he can hardly *complain*. It is easy to perceive from every page that though ambition pressed Swift into a life of bustle, the wish for a life of *ease* was always returning.

(b) Epoch-making has become quite a *phrase* in modern engineering. It cannot be *denied* that another epoch was opened when for the first time radar came in *contact* with the moon. *Assumptions* that echoes might be obtained from the moon were never taken seriously until Sir Edward Appleton *categorically* stated that it was possible. Less than a year later his prophecy was *fulfilled* by the United States Signal Corps. Wireless *experts* assert that the conditions were of the utmost *unsuitability*. The equipment was an ordinary and old-fashioned Army Signal *apparatus* of such size that it could not be lifted. Therefore the *experiments* had to be performed when the moon had just risen and was standing on the *horizon*. That meant that the atmosphere did its worst to *attenuate* the signals. But nothing of all this *prevented* a full success, and on January 10, 1946, at 11.58 a.m., contact *with* the moon was *achieved*.

(c) In one *respect* the progress of science and scepticism had already won an important *battle* for humanity. The *persecution* of supposed witches had reached its *height* under the Puritan Commonwealth. It had since been *declining*, most *rapidly* among the educated class. The reign of Anne *saw* the real end of witch trials. Judges and country magistrates refused to *convict* old women of *compacts* with the Devil, on the evidence of their neighbours' *prejudiced* imaginings, or even of their own frantic *confessions*. This marked a great *advance* of common kindliness and good sense over *primeval* cruelty and superstition. It was a victory of *reason* imposed by an educated aristocracy *on* a rural population that still *retained* its old belief in witches, but was in no position to *assert* it against the will of its 'betters'.

II. Pages 199–201

1. (a) Yes; correct as an epithet for *stream*.

   (b) No; a *continual* plea, that is, a plea that occurs from time to time throughout the book.

2. (a) Correct; *virtually* is here an antonym to *actually*.

   (b) If a man took a glue-pot and a brush and, by some acrobatic contortions, with the glue fastened himself to the ground by the ears, *literally* would be correctly used in this sentence. I *literally* fly to a man's help only if I go by aeroplane from where I am to where he is. To use *literally* with a metaphor is, obviously, to confuse the literal and the metaphorical. (See page 169). But the usage is very common; *literally*, in fact, loses its own literal meaning, and becomes an intensive or emphasising adverb in a kind of hyperbole. (See page 176).

3. Only the reviewer knows. A writer may be inquisitive, and he may, conceivably, write a kind of prose that is the result of his inquisitiveness; but the prose itself will not therefore be inquisitive.

4. This raises an old question. The English language has a genius for making verbs out of nouns: *pen* (a letter), *table* (a motion), *sky* (a cricket ball), *bell* (the cat), *paper* (a room),

book (a date); and this process, like the established use of nouns as adjectives makes possible considerable economies in language; that is, each verb so made and used represents in itself a phrase ("to hang a bell round the cat's neck"="to bell the cat"). But where do we draw the line? If the writer of the blurb meant simply 'represented', then *paged* is both unnecessary and meaningless. If he meant something more ("represented by their writings on the printed page"), then *paged* may be justified. It is, however, probable that the word has the sense given to it in hotel parlance—'called upon' (by the pageboy). But the word is an odd one in this context; and since its meaning and use are doubtful it should be objected to here.

5. (a) In Service slang, we haven't a clue. The word does not appear in the *Concise Oxford Dictionary*. Can it mean 'dispenses'? or is there some hidden connection with *sponge*?

   (b) Passable. The adjective *incidental* means 'casual, not essential', as in "An incidental result of the Act was the development of a new interest in Technical Education". But the adverb *incidentally* has become, in its most popular use, a synonym for 'by the way'. It generally stands at the beginning of the sentence, not, as here, at the end.

   (c) and (d) Two inventions. *Voluptuousness* and *correctness* are recognised nouns; but these writers, fascinated by nouns ending in -*itude* (*multitude, fortitude* and the like), coined similar formations. Probably the second writer had *rectitude* at the back of his mind. It must be admitted that "a voluptitude of laughs" has an air about it. The word might, indeed, be added as a modern invention to the curious nouns of assembly that survive from mediaeval English—"a *pride* of lions", "a *gaggle* of geese", and the rest.

   (e) *Obsolescence* means 'the process of becoming obsolete'. But the writer obviously does not mean this; he should have used *obsoleteness*.

   (f) The adjective *nice* suffered long ago a deterioration of meaning, and became a mere colourless epithet (a fact which Jane Austen noted in *Northanger Abbey*). The adverb *nicely* followed suit. But *nice* meant originally 'fastidious', 'precise', 'scrupulous', as in the surviving phrase "a nice distinction". This writer has used the adverb *nicely* with its archaic meaning. He can be accused of nothing worse than a precious affectation.

(g) This was, perhaps, a mere misprint for *philosophising*; more probably it is a facetious formation.

(h) Modern reviewers can rarely resist *evoke*; but "evoke a taint" is, as Polonius would say, "a vile phrase".

(i) The implication is that an epicure is one who drinks and smokes, a kind of anti-teetotaller. Cassius, who "once held Epicurus strong" and Chaucer's Franklin, who was "Epicurus owen sone", would have considered this a quite inadequate definition.

(j) The writer means 'viewing' or 'looking at', but cannot resist a precious and misleading gallicism: '*assister à*' in French means 'to attend', 'to be present at'; but the English '*assist* (at)' means quite a different thing.

(k) *cumulative*: If the writer means that the weight and vividness of characterisation is x on the first page of a book of n pages and that it increases by y on each page, so that the weight and vividness on the last page is

$$nx + \frac{(n-1)}{2}\left\{ y + (n-1)y \right\},$$ then, and only then, *cumulative* is correct.

menacing: a striking example of fatuous hyperbole.

apprehension: The meaning is obscure; *apprehension* usually means 'fear' in modern usage. Possibly (especially after *menacing*) that is the intended meaning here. But "make a demand upon our fear" is difficult to understand. Is *comprehension* the word intended?

(l) The writer sacrifices balance to elegant variation. (See page 146). Why not "as well as outside" or even "as well as out"?

6. Suggested answers to these letters are given in Chapter V. (See page 223).

III. Pages 212–215

1. 'Apart from . . .'. (See page 94).

2. 'both . . . and'. Faulty bracketing. (See page 62.)

3. Faulty balance. The writer began with a not *merely* (=*only*) construction, and failed to finish it properly. Probably the best amendment is to put a semicolon after *tranquillity* and continue: 'it is something more subtle than that'.

4. *Reason* again. (See page 161). 'One reason is . . . that I want to find out'. If the infinitive of purpose is used, *reason* is superfluous. Amend: 'I am anxious . . . in order to find out'. The repetition of *whether* (See page 63), in this sentence is difficult to avoid.

5. If the noun *hairdressers*='hairdressers' shops' (as it may do in English idiom), the construction is sound. See also page 126. The idiom 'would fold up' is modern—and very expressive.

6. Colon, or, better still, a dash instead of a semicolon after *things*. The metaphor 'with no pressing of the pedal' seems to have no relevance here.

7. '*Neither* . . . *nor*'. (See page 24).

8. This sentence is perfectly sound in construction. It is included merely because it contains the once-vulgar contraction *pub*, now, by a kind of inverted snobbery, a favourite with reviewers, to whom anything said, or argued, or read in a pub is automatically better than anything said, or argued, or read anywhere else.

9. Confusion of construction '*liken* . . . *to*', '*regard* . . . *as*'.

10. This sentence is included because of the queer, affected use of *willed*. As for a '*willed* sanity', it baffles comprehension.

11–16. These sentences all illustrate confusion of defining and non-defining clauses. (See page 85). Correction is merely the addition or deletion of a comma in the appropriate places. In sentence 16 the single comma after *father* separates subject and verb. (See page 106).

17, 18.   *case*. (See page 142). Sentence 18 should end 'for sick patients'. The phrase 'in case of sickness' should normally begin a sentence, and be related to a person, thus: 'In case of sickness, students should report to the matron'.

19, 20.   False relationship of adjective (participle) phrase. (See page 54).

21, 22.   The problem of *none* (see page 16): 'know *ourselves* or *himself*?' 'deny *ourselves* or *himself*'?

23.   The construction is apparently 'Here a boy learns the virtue of (a), (b) and (c); but the writer throws in a superfluous *learns* before (c), and omits a desirable though not absolutely necessary *of* after *virtue* in the last two phrases. Read: 'of holding his tongue . . . and of co-operating . . .'.

24.   *fruit* collective and singular at the beginning, and plural ('may use *them*') at the end. (See page 15).

25.   Ambiguous. If the feelings of Jordan and Iraq are identical the sentence is correct; if not, the last phrase should read 'and possibly not those of Iraq'.

26.   An odd mixture of direct and indirect speech. (See page 119).

27.   A subtle but rather common confusion of two constructions: 'The right age for children to enter grammar schools if they are to have the chance . . .' and 'The right age for parents to enter children in the grammar schools in order to give them . . .'.

28.   False apposition (see page 96): neither a knowledge of Greek art nor being Shakespearian is a *pursuit*. It is impossible to discover what the last tacked-on phrase 'the condition of a sound judgment' means.

29.   Is this split infinitive justifiable? (See page 71).

30.   The demonstrative *this* has no recognisable antecedent (See page 78). From his use of the verb *erected* the writer seems to have a vague idea that *this* relates to

a building. But it is difficult to see how a building can be "erected into a policy". Since he seems intent on a 'building' metaphor, he might have written his sentence thus: "It is often a wise policy to build on what already exists, but this should not develop into a policy unfriendly to the laying of new foundations".

IV. Pages 225–227

1. ponder *on*, not *as to*. (See page 156).

2. ignorant *of* and impervious *to*. False economy. (See page 156).

3, 4, 5. Mixed idiom (See page 160):
    wake them from their sweet oblivion ⎫
    disturb their sweet oblivion   ⎭

    before I got into that rut   ⎫
    before I was hammered into that shape ⎭

    turn another corner   ⎫
    reach another milestone ⎭

Either will do, but not a mixture of both.

6. In the proverb, the mills of God certainly grind slowly, but what they grind is not specified; or, to put it in grammatical terms, *grind* is intransitive. To make it transitive (as here) is to misuse the quotation.

7. (See page 75).

8. The point is that *noisome* is not another form of *noisy*. Either word may be intended here, though the two are far apart in meaning. See dictionary.

9. Or *past*? Past is the adjective form, and is preferable here; *passed* is the spelling when there is any verbal force implied: 'The night had *passed*', not *past*.

10. (See page 143). Say, 'that human life is ephemeral' or 'of the transience of human life'. The noun *ephemerality* is uncommon; the more familiar *transience* or *brevity* is better here.

11. (See page 62).

12. Passive for active. (See page 70). Verbose at the end. Say: 'to look carefully at the factories beside it'.

13. 'and-whichery'. (See page 89).

14. For the relationship of the opening phrase see page 52. The sentence should continue: 'we are all compelled to give serious thought to political events'. The idiom with *afford* is 'afford us an opportunity of thinking' ⎫
                                      'for thought' ⎭

15. 'question of whether'. (See page 158).

16. (a) comma after *hand*
    (b) number of collective noun (*Government*). (See page 15).
    (c) mixed idiom (see page 160):
       (i) carry out an order ⎫
           perform a task   ⎭
      (ii) carry forward an amount, a sum ⎫
           forward a scheme or plan   ⎬
           put into practice an idea   ⎭

17. Centred *on* (see page 164);
wind-swept, with hyphen.

18. (See page 94). Amend: 'Mrs. Dean, with her homely wisdom, and old Joseph, with his sanctimonious hypocrisy, are amongst . . .'

19. Metaphor mixed (a *gliding* curtain). For the gerund question in 'effect of the mountain hurrying' see page 53.

20. Mixed idiom (see page 160);
'bring his eloquence to bear'
'Winston Churchill's eloquence could not avail . . .' ⎫

21. *case* (see page 412): 'appear to be' rather than 'appear as'.

22. Number. (See page 17).

23. Relationship of participle phrase. (See page 54).

24. *due*. (See page 58).

25. *and*+relative pronoun. (See page 89).

26. Number: *there* + singular verb + plural subject. (See page 23).

27. *judicial or judicious*?

28. (See page 95).

29. Mixed idiom (see page 160);
    (a) looms large
    (b) cast its shadow over us }

30. (See page 82).

31. (a) *each, any one—we.* (See pages 16, 75).
    (b) metaphor mixed ('go forward in a stream')
    (c) confusion of *shall* and *will* } (See page 27).
        should   would

32. The *buildings* (not the *shapes*) are . . .

33. Participle phrase. (See page 50).

34. Position of *only*. Is it justifiable? (See page 50).

35. Is the economy here justified? ('it always had and
    always would'='it always had *remained* and always
    would *remain*').

36. (a) *in*comparable
    (b) but even *incomparable* should be *unmatched*.

V. Page 234

The exceptions are *traveller, buses, gases.*

The words given are not exceptions to the rule for the
following reasons:

sober:	a 'root' word. No suffix is added.
reader:	Root word (*read*) ends in two vowels + consonant.
deciding:	Root word (*decide*) does not end in single vowel + consonant. (See under mute *e*, page 237).
gracious:	as *deciding*. The root word is *grace*.
precarious:	derived direct from Latin *precarius*. No addition of a suffix to a root ending in a single consonant.
uses:	The root is *use*. See *deciding* and *gracious* above.

INDEX

The frequent references in the text to the following works are not indexed: the Authorised Version of the Bible, the Plays of Shakespeare, *Modern English Usage* (Fowler), Cobbett's *Grammar of the English Language*, various dictionaries, especially the *Shorter* and the *Concise Oxford*, and *Rules for Compositors and Readers at the Oxford Press*.

₁ Called 'parentheses' by the printer, who reserves the term 'brackets' for what we ordinarily call square brackets—[ ].